Winfield & Rebecca Massie
Waverly. Virginia 1972

INTERNATIONAL SERIES OF MONOGRAPHS IN
PURE AND APPLIED BIOLOGY

Division: **ZOOLOGY**

GENERAL EDITOR: G. A. KERKUT

VOLUME 45

GENETICS FOR CAT BREEDERS

GENETICS FOR CAT BREEDERS

BY

ROY ROBINSON, M.I.Biol.

PERGAMON PRESS

Oxford · New York · Toronto
Sydney · Braunschweig

Pergamon Press Ltd., Headington Hill Hall, Oxford
Pergamon Press Inc., Maxwell House, Fairview Park, Elmsford, New York 10523
Pergamon of Canada Ltd., 207 Queen's Quay West, Toronto 1
Pergamon Press (Aust.) Pty. Ltd., 19a Boundary Street,
Rushcutters Bay, N.S.W. 2011, Australia
Vieweg & Sohn GmbH, Burgplatz 1, Braunschweig

First edition 1971

Library of Congress Catalog Card No. 77-120591

PRINTED IN HUNGARY

08 015647 9

CONTENTS

	Preface	vii
I	Introduction	1
II	Reproduction and Development	12
III	Principles of Heredity	26
IV	Breeding Practice	69
V	Colour and Coat Inheritance	105
VI	Genetics of Colour Variation and Breeds	131
VII	Abnormalities	153
VIII	Record Keeping	177
IX	Further Reading	183
	Index	187
	Other Titles	191

PREFACE

THE writing of this book springs from the belief that the continued advancement of cat breeding relies upon an acknowledgement of modern trends in animal breeding. It should be recognized that the world of small animal breeding is discarding "rule of thumb" methods for a more balanced programme of scientific method and skilful breeding. The science of genetics has much to offer both to the theory and the practice of cat breeding. The thoughtful breeder should ponder on the fact that once his cats are provided with a good home, properly fed and receiving expert veterinary care, the sole hope of producing the superlative animal lies in the art of breeding.

In the preliminary chapters an endeavour is made to outline the elementary principles of heredity. The theory has been subdued to a large extent in deference to the more practical considerations. Quite considerable advances have been achieved in the practical application of genetics to the larger, economically regarded, livestock and these techniques may, with profit, be adapted to cat breeding. The cat may be thought of as "different", especially in its psychological make-up, but its heredity differs little from other animals.

An account of proven heredity of the cat is of considerable interest in itself, and of immense value for the complete understanding of the animal. A fair amount of information on the genetics of the cat has been published, in the main, in relatively inaccessible scientific journals. A simplified summary of this work is given with special regard to the constitution of breeds which, so far as the author is aware, has not previously been attempted in a comprehensive manner. Research into feline genetics has been carried out in many different countries, for the cat is truly cosmopolitan, and the benefits to be derived are similarly universal. It is hoped that this book will be of service to breeders wheresoever in the world they may reside.

A special chapter is given on those abnormalities which are either suspected or known to be genetically determined. Some abnormalities are due entirely to genetic causes and some result from a genetically determined constitution interacting with a dietary deficiency or developmental defect which would not necessarily upset a normal cat. It is hoped that this chapter will be of service to veterinary surgeons in the pursuit of their profession.

I am indebted to the many breeders who have discussed various problems with me and for their interest. Discussions with Alison Ashford, Peter Dyte, Roy and Maureen Silson and Patricia Turner, knowledgeable breeders all, have been particularly valuable. My thanks are due to Animal Photography Ltd., Anne Cumbers, Cat Information Centre, Will Green and Hugh Smith for permission to reproduce photographs.

ROY ROBINSON

I. INTRODUCTION

A FEW words may not be out of place on the sort of information a cat breeder might be expected to obtain from genetics. Three aspects will probably be of special interest. Firstly, there is genetics itself, especially that part of it which is concerned with coat colour in mammals. No breeder should confine himself to cats alone in his reading. Studies on variation in other species of animals could give valuable insight into similar variation in cats. This is an aspect which makes Searle's (1968) interesting book on colour variation so useful, dealing as it does with the whole spectrum of mammalian species.

Secondly, a detailed account of the known genetics of the cat. The various mutant genes which have been reported and the effects they produce. The variation of colour and coat types which result from combinations of the genes. How these have been seized upon by breeders and skilfully woven into established breeds. An account of variation both within and outside the breeds which is of intrinsic interest and which might be useful for creating new breeds. All of these aspects will be discussed in succeeding sections. Some can be covered in depth but others can only be lightly touched upon because of sketchy information or lack of reliable knowledge.

Finally, there are the methods of animal improvement which could be used in cat breeding. What constitutes inbreeding and if or when to employ it. What is selection, when to apply it and which traits should be concentrated upon. A discussion of these problems is undoubtedly called for and should be satisfied. In dealing with methods of animal improvement, it is rarely possible to go beyond a general discussion because only the breeder has the data from which to make correct judgements. In a sense, animal improvement at an elementary level remains an art rather than an exact science. It is a question of gauging the worth of the individual by inspection, rather than by measurement, and of making decisions based on shrewd judgement, rather than on a set number of matings or on the passage of a certain number of generations.

When all has been said and done, the occasion may arise when certain observations appear "odd" and do not fit into the scheme of things. One possibility which should be looked into at the onset is that a mistake has not been made. A mistaken identification, an error in the breeding records or an accidental mis-mating. Only saints are perfect—the rest of us make all sorts of errors. If mistakes can be ruled out, then it may be that the genetic explanation is not as accurate or as complete as it could be. Alternatively, something new has been discovered, such as the discovery of two genes for rex coat of some years back or the folded eared mutant of recent years. In this event, it is wise to seek competent advice. Whenever unexpected results occur, it is always advisable to consult other people. The chances of discovering something novel are slim but the possibility is always there.

Mendelism and Genetics

The first accurate description of the principles of heredity was enunciated in 1866 by Gregor Mendel. Alas for the inspired reasoning of this remarkable man, the scientific climate was not ripe for ready acceptance of his simple, almost blunt, account and Mendel's discovery languished until 1900. Round about this time, the prevailing ideas on heredity and evolution were being critically appraised by inquiring minds and, in particular, biology was beginning to emerge as an experimental, as opposed to an observational, science. About 1900, Mendel's work was acclaimed by three biologists, independently and more or less simultaneously. This fact should demonstrate perhaps more than any other how biological thought had changed in the intervening 34 years.

It is common knowledge that Mendel carried out his experiments with the ordinary garden pea. Once the basic principles were grasped, there were many people who were eager to discover if his ideas applied to other plants and to animals. It was soon found that they did, in most cases with astonishing similarity and, in others, with subtle variations which served to strengthen and to extend the principles he had formulated.

Mendel's laws of heredity, as his principles are known, stood up to the test of repeatable experiment. Their generality for all species of plants and animals implied that they were fundamental. In the early days, the study of heredity was known as "Mendelism" until W. Bateson in 1906 coined the word "genetics" for the new biological discipline. Thus, heredity became a science, with principles which can be checked and with laws of real predictive value. From the humble beginning of a man pottering around in a spare corner of his garden, genetics has grown to such an extent that research establishments are devoted to the subject and no corner of biology or medicine can escape its impact. For those who find pleasure in learning a subject by reading of its historical development, Dunn's (1965) book is recommended.

There is no grand design in science. This means that the growth of fundamental ideas and their application can be very uneven. In some respects, genetics has had more than its fair share of opposition from established practice. Possibly this is understandable since heredity has often been thought of as something intangible and difficult to pin down. Thus, it became shrouded in mystery and bedeviled with mystical ideas. Unfortunately, animal breeding has a very rich quota of legend based on all sorts of queer prejudices. This has delayed the practical application of genetics to some forms of animal breeding; particularly, it would seem, in those branches less exposed to economic pressures. However, there are encouraging signs of increasing awareness that genetics has something worthwhile to offer the person who is willing to make the effort.

It required several decades for the foundations of genetics to be laid. In the meantime, animal breeding carried on more or less as usual. There was indeed more emphasis placed on selection but this was merely an intensification of current practice. That selection was the key to animal breeding had been known since Darwin focused attention upon how effective the process can be. On the other hand, a rational genetic theory of animal improvement had to wait upon an understanding of the effects of inbreeding, cross-breeding and the relative effectiveness of various methods of selection. The work of Lush (1945) is monumental in this respect. There is now a very considerable and impressive amount of theoretical and experience on the genetic aspects of animal improvement.

Once the mechanism of heredity had been satisfactorily settled, it became obvious that concepts based on the "percentage of blood" and the overestimated influence of remote ancestors had to be revised. Even the use of pedigrees in breeding became suspect unless one is very familiar with the ancestors listed and could recall their apparent worth. A tabulation of names, devoid of accurate description, is scarcely any value at all except for intimating that the individual is derived from a well-known stock. If the ancestors have high-sounding names, but are unknown: how can the worth of the animal or its potential breeding be assessed?

Nomenclature

The domestic cat is often referred to as *Felis domesticus*. The word *Felis* indicating that the animal belongs to the main genus of cats and the word *domesticus* indicating that it is a domesticated form. This is fair enough. However, Carl Linne, the founder of scientific classification, named the domestic cat as *Felis catus*. This designation is also often employed. Everything would still be straightforward but for the fact that Linne singled out the blotched type of tabby as *catus*, apparently neglectful or oblivious to the equally common mackerel type. In some people's eyes, this omission needed rectifying, so the mackerel has come to receive the designation of *torquata*.

The name of *domesticus* is seemingly the most appropriate even if, in strict nomenclative terms, it is not correct. As a designation, it certainly describes the present status of the cat. It is unfortunate that the origin of the cat is so obscure, for the animal must obviously be a domesticated form of a wild species. If the wild ancestor was definitely known, the use of the species may seem preferable, even if *domesticus* is added. However, at present, the presumptive wild ancestor is not known with certainty although there seems to be excellent grounds for suggesting that it belongs to the *silvestris–lybica* species complex. The typical tabby pattern of these species is the mackerel type. For this reason it is customary to refer to the mackerel form as the "wild type", from which the blotched sprang as a mutant.

Origin and Species Hybridity

Few writers on the domestic cat can resist speculation on the origin of the animal. It is well known that the ancient Egyptians revered the cat and worshipped a cat-goddess. Egypt is commonly regarded as being a major centre of origin but whether it is the only centre is perhaps open to question. There is nothing to prevent anyone attempting to domesticate the cat anywhere and at different times. Certain Asiatic peoples may have had a hand in the domestication. It is doubtful if the problem will ever be definitely solved. Like the dog, cats of wild origin but of slightly less fearful disposition than the average, may have acted as food stealers or scavengers and eventually may have been accepted or, at least, tolerated. The animal's adeptness in keeping down rats and mice may have been appreciated, who knows?

Presumably, the acceptance of the cat would occur at the hutment or village level. Also, there must have been sufficient genetic variation for docility of tameness within the species for the cat to become trusting of men and to breed either close to or within the village. Barter of animals probably occurred and cats may have become part of the paraphernalia of traders. In this manner, cats would have reached the towns and cities and probably would have acquired status as exotic pets (witness the Ocelot of today). There would be selection against the wilder individuals and possibly in favour of colour variation. Once accepted, the spread of the cat is more or less assured. Though not a prolific breeder, the animal is a persistent producer of litters and has a long span of reproductive life.

Zeuner (1963) appears to provide a good general account of the domestication of the cat. Some of the very early finds (molars and jaw fragments) could be those of a domestic cat although it seems more likely that they are from the wild cat. It seems possible, as is claimed by some archaeologists, that the cat was domesticated by the Egyptians as early as 3000 B.C., but Zeuner considers that the evidence is ambiguous. Yet, by 1900 B.C., it is possible that the cat was in the process of semi-domestication. The swamp scenes of this period could depict a wild cat just as well as a domestic. However, by 1600 B.C., the cat was clearly domesticated and was regarded as a sacred animal. Outside Egypt, for instance in Greece and Palestine, the cat was known but was relatively uncommon because the Egyptians did not allow them to be taken from the country. The Egyptians were also apparently not adverse to carrying off every cat they saw to Egypt. This could be a factor in the belief that Egypt is the centre of origin.

The rise of Christianity caused the cat to lose its sacred position. The Romans carried the cat back to their home-land and throughout their empire. It was soon to be found in central Europe and even in Britain. The remains of several cats have been discovered in a Roman villa at Silchester and thought to be domestics. The cat also travelled eastward, probably via Babylonia, into India where it is known to have been domesticated for some 2000 years.

On the assumption that the Egyptians domesticated the cat, the problem becomes: from which wild species did the animal descend? The Egyptians apparently kept a number of cats, among which the Jungle cat *(Felis chaus)* and the African wild cat *(Felis lybica)* may be mentioned. Morrison-Scott (1952), in his study of Egyptian mummified cats, suggests that *chaus* may not have been domesticated in any true sense of the word since these are poorly represented. The majority of skulls which he examined belonged to a form smaller than *chaus*, yet larger than *lybica* or the present-day domestic cat. This form is named *Felis lybica bubastis* and is thought to be derived from, or to be a race of, the widely distributed African wild cat *lybica*. Apart from size, the skulls of mummified cats and of *lybica* were closely similar. Curiously, there does not seem to be any existing known wild form which matches *bubastis* exactly. On present showing, the above is likely to be the extent of direct evidence for the origin of the cat.

However, another approach may be made and this is by a consideration of the number and distribution of wild species. The two most likely ancestral forms are *Felis silvestris* and *F. lybica*, the European and African wild cats, respectively, on account of their size, characteristics and coloration. The former occurs in Britain, throughout Europe (except for Scandinavia), South-West Russia, Caucasia and Asia Minor. The latter occurs in most of the larger Mediterranean Islands, much of Africa, Arabia, Turkestan and northern India. It is of interest that while most taxonomists are prepared to accept *silvestris* and *lybica* as two distinct species, each one is divided into a large number of geographical subspecies and races, based mainly on differences of background colour; intensity and distribution of striping; whether or not the striping is breaking up into spots; and the evanescence of the striping or spotting.

Thus, there is the diversity to be expected of a widely distributed species. In general, there is a north to south gradation of coat thickness, intensity of ground colour and amount of tabby markings. Of the two, *lybica* displays the greater variation. If one examines these species complexes as a whole, it does not seem incongruous to merge *silvestris* and *lybica* into one species, with geographical groups. A recent study by Weigel (1961) has done this, giving *silvestris* as the embracive species name. That indefatigable student of the Felidae, R. I. Pocock, is on record as stating that the two species possess a similar tabby pattern which is not possessed by any other of the felids.

The results of inter-species hybridization affords another approach and, from a genetic viewpoint, the most interesting. Much of the literature on hybridization is very old and, unless a critical stance is taken, it is easy to believe that the domestic cat will produce hybrids with practically any wild species (e.g. Hamilton, 1896). This could be so but too many of the early claims are based on breeders' reminiscences and travellers' observations to be reliable. On the other hand, of course, if two species so different as the lion and tiger can be crossed reciprocally—tigron from the union of a male tiger and lioness and liger from a male lion and a tigress—then it is conceivable that a large number of the smaller cats might be capable of producing hybrids. The above cross is fairly easily obtained, but the disparity between the two species is revealed by partial sterility. The male hybrids are thought to be completely infertile while the female hybrids are only partially fertile. These facts reveal the genetic remoteness of the lion and tiger.

Several sources of error have to be heeded if claims of hybridity are to be taken seriously. Simple observation is not sufficient. Feral domestic cats abound in many parts of the world and many resemble wild species in colour and temperament. The domestic cat is a variable creature and no variation of colour or bodily proportions should be construed as positive evidence of alleged current or past hybridity. Only if a person has intimate knowledge of the animals concerned can a claim be entertained; yet this is not conclusive. To be conclusive, it is necessary for the parents to be confined and the matings controlled. This can be managed by zoos and a certain amount of information is available from this source.

Authentic hybrids between the domestic cat and various races (Scottish and European) of *silvestris* have been obtained on several occasions. In the majority of cases, the offspring are mackerel tabby in colour and wild in temperament. In one instance, however, a male hybrid was observed to be "as tame as a fire-side cat, so that after a while he was allowed out of his cage to wander about" (Gillespie, 1954). This is interesting because it denotes genetic variation for "tameness", one of the prerequisites for domestication. The hybrids seem to be regularly fertile. This could be significant since it is usually indicative of not too distant genetic relationship. Several of the domestic females carried mutant genes and these can be expressed by the hybrid genotype. Self black (the wild male was evidently a heterozygote!), piebald with white spotting and Manx taillessness have been transmitted (the last two genes being dominant). Though the transmission and expression of mutant genes (the numbers were too few and the variation of expression was not closely studied), are not of great weight, again there is indication of some degree of genetic identicalness. Most of the hybrids possessed the bushy tail of *silvestris*, but this was not always the case, and, in one instance, the second generation showed variation in the amount of hair on the tail.

Alleged hybrids between the domestic cat and various races of *lybica* (both African and Indian) are claimed on several occasions in the older literature. More recently, fertile hybrids have been obtained between the domestic cat and the Steppe cat *(lybica caudata)* under controlled conditions. Furthermore, Pocock (1907) was able to produce hybrids between *silvestris* and an African race of *lybica*. These were typical mackerel tabby, similar to the parents. Two were eaten by the *lybica* mother shortly after birth while the surviving kitten at nine weeks was showing signs of having the well-covered hairy tail of *silvestris*. Thus, there is direct, as well as circumstantial, evidence that hybrids can be secured with *lybica*. In this respect, the early claims are upheld. If credence is given to these early accounts, there may be found stories of fertility and variable degrees of tameness for the hybrids.

Hybrids between the domestic cat and the Jungle Cat *(Felis chaus)* have been obtained. The hybrids are tabby in colour and with somewhat more tabby striping than is apparent in *chaus*. Morphologically, the resemblance is closer to *chaus*, for the hybrid is larger, longer legged and shorter tailed than the domestic. The hybrid is apparently fertile, for daughter hybrids have been mated back to the *chaus* father and have reared litters. The hybrids appear to be well cared for and are said to be tame. Piebald white spotting, introduced by the domestic cat, showed the usual dominant expression on the hybrids (Jackson and Jackson, 1967).

Two further crosses may be noted because of the implication that they can be productive of hybrids. The crosses were between the domestic cat and the bobcat *(Lynx rufus)* and Oncilla or Little Spotted Cat *(Felis tigrina);* two species from the new world. In both instances, the hybrids tend to resemble the wild species, rather than the cat and were of wild disposition. Nothing is known whether or not the hybrids were fertile. The intriguing aspect is that hybrids could be produced at all since the point of departure for the old and new world species must have been a vast number of years ago. Yet, despite this, the three forms can come together to produce viable offspring. The implication is that the production of offspring, *per se*, from the domestic cat and either *silvestris* or *lybica* loses some of its significance. Only the probability, if not certainty, that these offspring are fertile may turn out to be important for demonstrating genetic kinship.

No matter how much time is spent on detailed systematic examination of species appearance or how supposedly diagnostic features are compared, the crucial test of genetic relationship is that of crosses. The fact that the wild species and the hybrids are fearful and barely manageable is an unfortunate complication but one which can possibly be overcome. Already, certain European zoos are making determined attempts to breed and rear *silvestris* in captivity. The lack of kinship between the domestic cat and a wild species may show itself in one of two ways. Firstly, there is the obvious one that the animals may copulate but no viable young are forthcoming. Or, secondly, young may be born but these are sterile either in one or both sexes. These various possibilities are sometimes taken to represent different degrees of relationship. The former implying a most distant relationship than the latter.

However, the important item is that the putative wild ancestor of the domestic cat should be capable of producing fertile hybrids. Perhaps a clearcut answer may not emerge; for it is possible that the ancestral species may have become extinct or that the cat may be capable of producing fertile hybrids with more than one wild species. The latter seems possible because of the apparently fertile hybrids with *chaus* in addition to *silvestris* and *lybica*. This need not necessarily indicate that the cat descended from initial crosses between more than one wild species. In this context, *silvestris* and *lybica* are not to be regarded as true species, but rather as geographical races, since they will produce young when paired together. Whether or not these offspring are fertile is something which deserves to be further studied.

Suppose that the Egyptians did confine more than one wild species together and that hybrids did occur under these artificial conditions. Subsequent events would be determined by the degree of control exercised by the Egyptians, and the viability and fertility of the hybrids. It would be doubtful if any real control was exercised or, if so, it would be largely that of allowing the best and more vigorous cats to reproduce. The outcome could be that a genetic constitution will emerge which rapidly shed itself of any weaknesses, which, in general, would be the hybrid genotype. There will in fact be a selective return to the species genotype. It should not be imagined that this process would not occur. Hybrid animals are often exceptionally hardy and vigorous, but these features often fail to recur in subsequent generations (indeed there can be a decline) and the species combinations of genes finally reappear as the best means of breeding the animals with a semblance of normal health. In other words, a viable type could be evolved which had incorporated the best features of more than one species but, nevertheless, the likely to resemble one species more than the other. Phenotypically, this seems to be the *silvestris–lybica* complex.

There seems little doubt that the present-day cat population of the world is a single genetic entity. By that, it is meant that cats brought together from the remotest localities will inter-breed and produce fertile young. Even cats brought from Asiatic countries are fertile with European cats, in spite of the possibility that these have been separated since the early days of domestication. One final point will be made: no matter how diverse the modern cat may be in coat colour or body conformity, all of the variability can be interpreted in terms of gene mutation and recombination which has occurred after domestication.

Discredited Beliefs

Several discarded ideas will now be briefly discussed. One or two have some inherent interest but they are essentially false trails despite the fact that they were widely accepted by breeders prior to the turn of the 19th century or even more recently. Their unfounded speciousness is exposed by failure to pass the tested of repeatable experiment.

Telegony is the alleged influence of one sire upon the offspring of another when mated to the same female. In its most common form, the fear is expressed that a pedigree queen, accidentally mated by a mongrel cat, will now be useless for pedigree breeding because all of the subsequent kittens will be mongrels however she is mated. This fear is groundless. The use of one male has no means of influencing the young of another. Telegony also fails in another respect. If true, a mating with a first-class sire should guarantee the production of superior kittens however the queen is subsequently mated. Alas, this will not work, as anyone can prove to himself if he wishes to take the trouble.

Maternal impressions is another belief which would make breeding so much easier if it was true. This term is given to the alleged influence of the surroundings on the offspring while these are still in the uterus. A pregnant female kept in close proximity of outstanding animals might be induced to produce kittens of above average merit. Or, a certain colour might be induced by keeping a pregnant female in company with other cats of the desired colour. Unfortunately, neither of these artifices has any hope of success, except by chance which has no connection with the principle involved.

Acquired inheritance is a general term to denote an environmental influence which, working on the body, is able to allegedly modify the germ-cells so that the influence may be seen in subsequent generations. Now, the environment encroaches upon the development of the individual from the moment of conception. Firstly, there is the pre-natal maternal environment and, later, there is the pressures of the post-natal world. Thus, there is ample opportunity for the environment to buffer or modify the body. In fact, it does so in a myriad of ways but the contents of the germ-cells which constitute the hereditary material escape the influence. On occasion, the germ-cells can be reached but the effect is usually so damaging that procreativity is out of the question.

The cruder aspects of acquired inheritance have long been disproved (such as the breeding of tailless mice by chopping off their tails), but ever so often more subtle versions of the myth appear to gain credence. Eventually these, too, are shown to have little validity. In general, any bodily experience or mutilation is extremely unlikely to be inherited. A disease affecting the mother during pregnancy could produce diseased or deformed offspring but, even so, neither the germ-cells of the mother nor of the offspring are affected.

The only environmental factors which are known to affect the germ-cells are X-rays, atomic emanations and a variety of chemical mutagens. These agents do so by inducing chromosome aberrations and gene mutation. Furthermore, the mutation is entirely at random and occurs at a very low frequency. The possibility of increasing the mutation rate of certain kinds of mutants to bring about a desired change has been discussed among scientists, but the likelihood of this is remote.

II. REPRODUCTION AND DEVELOPMENT

REPRODUCTION in the cat is a fascinating topic in its own right and it is presumed that most breeders are familiar with the general outline, even if they have not troubled themselves overmuch with details. The majority of cats will reproduce quite happily; if in good condition and are not interfered with more than absolutely necessary. In any case, except for trivial complaints, if certain aspects are not all they should be, it is always advisable to call in a vet. His skill and experience is invariably greater than that of most breeders and this should be drawn upon without hesitation. The more valuable the animal, the greater the need for expert advice and attention.

Practical Aspects of Reproduction

This section makes no pretence at being exhaustive, but constitutes a summary of the more practical aspects of the subject. The summary will form a preamble, so to speak, to a more detailed discussion of what is actually transmitted from one generation to the next at the act of coitus.

Under optional conditions of husbandry and diet, sexual maturity or puberty in the female normally occurs between the ages of 7 to 12 months, depending on a variety of factors, such as month of birth and growth. Exceptionally, a rapidly growing female may reach puberty as early as 6 months. Size is probably the governing factor since one report gives the female as being able to commence breeding when weighing about 2·5 kg (5·5 lb). However, regardless of the actual onset of puberty, it is usually judged prudent not to breed from a queen until she is about 12 months of age.

The attainment of puberty is less obvious in the male but is usually taken to be a month or two later than in the female. A weight level of about 3·5 kg (7·7 lb) is thought to be a convenient point. Queens will continue to produce litters until they are many years of age. The actual cessation of breeding is a gradual affair, usually accompanied by a rise of sterile copulations and decline in litter size, although a figure of between 8 and 10 years has been mentioned as not untypical. It is rare for a female to reproduce beyond the age of 14 years. If males attain puberty a month or so after females, they are also capable of breeding for a number of years beyond the latest age for the female.

Oestrus or heat is the period in which the female is receptive of the attentions of the male. The duration is normally from 3 to 6 days although persisting as long as 10 days if the queen is denied access to the male. The period is marked by relatively distinctive behaviour which enables an experienced breeder to judge the most propitious time for the two animals to meet. For a day or two (the pre-oestrus stage) the female becomes very affectionate, demanding unusual attention and rubbing herself against objects and indulging in playful rolling. There is usually much howling and "calling" although there are differences between breeds in this respect.

The second stage is characterized by treading and the adoption of the coital crouch (flattening of the back and raising of the hind quarters) to gentle stroking or a nudging of the genital region or the presence of a male. The cat is now fully receptive and coitus (mating) will occur. Successful intromission is accompanied by a loud cry or growl. After the two cats have parted, the female usually engages in quite vigorous rolling, rubbing and licking which subsides into a short period of inactivity. Mating may be resumed within an interval of 15 or 30 minutes. Several matings per day for all but the last day of oestrus may occur if allowed.

Litters may be born at any time of the year although less frequently during the winter months. The typical breeding season is from January to July or even somewhat longer. The winter pause, however, can be effectively reduced by the provision of artificial illumination to counteract the lack of day-light. Two, or even three, litters are normally produced per year, the peak months being March to April and July to August. In the absence of coitus, the female usually shows recurrent oestrus at intervals of 14 days although it is reported that some animals may have irregular cycles. An infertile mating is usually followed by a pseudo-pregnancy which lasts about 30 to 40 days, whence the female comes into oestrus.

The cat is one of the few mammals in which the eggs are released by the ovary as a result of nervous stimuli provided by coitus. The gestation period is about 65 days although the extraordinary variation of between 58 and 71 days have been recorded. Some latitude must be given, however, to imprecise information on the actual day of the release of the eggs, especially for matings spread over several days. The number of eggs is probably always in excess of the number of kittens born, due to intra-uterine mortality of foetuses. Unfortunately, precise data on the extent of the mortality is lacking.

A survey to determine weaned litter size revealed that the average litter consists of 3·9 kittens, with an extreme range of 1 to 10, based upon 5073 litters (19,813 cats). Size of litter varies with weight of mother, heavier females tending to have larger litters than the lighter females. Probably as a result of this but not necessarily, because average gestation period should be taken into account, kittens born to smaller females are heavier than those born to larger mothers. The sex ratio has been found to be 104 males : 100 females, based on 16,820 kittens.

The lactation period may vary from 50 to 60 days although partial weaning may commence before this. Complete weaning leads to a rapid cessation of the milk flow. There is no oestrus immediately following parturition (post-partum oestrus) but the oestrus cycle usually recommences between 2 to 4 weeks after weaning.

The ideal litter for a queen seems to be about 4 to 5 kittens. Few females seem capable of nursing more than this number unaided if rapid growth of the kittens is to be expected. Kittens from large litters can be transferred to queens with small litters or kittens may be supplementarily fed with milk in a doll's bottle or special cat feeding bottle. It must not be overlooked, of course, that the ability to suckle a complement of four young is inherited and to assist an incapable queen is not good policy in the long-term. It is beneficial for the young, no doubt, but the young themselves could inherit the incapacity and this is something to guard against. Breeding stock should only be chosen (as far as possible, after other aspects are taken into account) from queens who have reared kittens with a good record of growth.

Stories abound of cats reaching a ripe old age, but people interested in geriatrics are loath to accept undocumented statements. A report on authenticated cases of cats living beyond 20 years brought to light a range of longevity from 19 to 27 years, with an average of 22 to 23 years. Unsubstantiated claims have gone higher, the figure of 31 years being the highest recorded. Unfortunately, the errors involved in recalling past events and establishing the age of an animal are notorious. It is of interest that aged cats reach a well-preserved senility as regards retention of teeth, condition of coat and activity. This is in contrast to dogs (a comparable domestic carnivore) where senility is said not to be so kind to the individual.

It should be appreciated that genetic factors may influence most of the features discussed above. This means that strain and breed differences may exist. The Siamese is often singled out in this respect although not always with substantiating statistics. The Manx, for instance, will usually have smaller litters than the average due to the intra-uterine mortality which is associated with the tailless condition.

TABLE 1. BASIC DATA ON REPRODUCTION AND THE LIFE CYCLE OF THE DOMESTIC CAT

Item	Average	Typical variation
Puberty, males	12 months	10–14 months
Puberty, females	9 months	7–12 months
Oestrus cycle	14 days	Irregular
Oestrus	3–6 days	3–10 days
Gestation period	65 days	58–71 days
Weaned litter size	3–9	1–10
Sex ratio	104 : 100	75–130 : 100
Breeding period	Jan.–July	Jan.–Oct.
Lactation period	50 days	48–60 days
Cessation of breeding	8–10 years	To 14 years
Longevity	22–23 years	To 27 years

Germ-cell Lineage

The cat as an entity commences life as the union of two germ-cells. This occurs in the oviduct, a thin tube of tissue which conveys the egg (female germ-cell) to the uterus upon its release by the ovary. Though the act of coitus provides the stimulus, the eggs are not liberated until many hours have elasped. The delay allows the sperms (male germ-cells), which have been deposited in the vagina, to make their way to the site of fertilization either to meet or to be on hand for the arrival of the eggs. Fertilization accomplished, the egg undergoes cleavage, passing through the morulae and early blastodermic stages. Implantation is said to occur about the 14th day. From this point onward, growth and development is rapid and the tiny blob of protoplasm becomes transformed into a recognizable foetus. After about 65 days, the cat is ejected into the world as a young kitten, not fully able to fend for itself but equipped with a suckling reflex to obtain nourishment from its mother.

Since a new individual is created by the union of germ-cells, it follows that their contents must form the material link between successive generations. The male and female germ-cells differ greatly in size and structure as befitting their different functions. The egg is relatively large and spherical, being rich in nutriment to carry it over the developmental period from fertilization to implantation. On the other hand, the sperm is a fragile thing, microscopic in size and possessive of a long tail, with just about sufficient energy for it to reach and enter the egg for fertilization. The function of the egg and sperm is to house a nucleus and to ensure that two nuclei (one from the egg and one from the sperm) can come together and fuse. Genetically, the important constituents of the two nuclei are the chromosomes. These are extremely small bodies, but visible under the microscope, and are bearers of the hereditary material. Their joining up to form a common nucleus enables the egg to commence development as an independent entity.

In biological terms, the body of an individual is known as the "soma". It consists of myriads of cells, all of which are concerned with either the structure or the innumerable physiological functions which are necessary for sustaining life. The greater bulk of the somatic cells are not involved in reproduction although some are indirectly. The reason for this is that, as the fertilized egg gradually changes into an embryo and then into a foetus, the various path-ways of development become sorted out and diverge at a progressive rate. A fundamental divergence is between those cells which are destined to produce the soma and those which are destined to form the germ-cells. Developmentally, once separation has occurred, growth can then be semiautonomous, subject only to the restriction, if growth is proceeding normally, that the various processes must not become out of step with one another.

It is possible, therefore, to postulate a continuum of cells directly concerned with reproduction: the "germ-cell lineage". The reproductive organs (testes and ovary) for the production of germ-cells are known collectively as the "gonads" and the rudiments of these are laid down at an early stage. The germ-cell lineage may be envisaged to be semi-independent of the soma and to alternate as gonads–germ-cells–gonads–germ-cells on an unbroken line, bridging generations via the germ-cells. Figure 1 is an attempt to show this concept. The germ-cell lineage is depicted as immortal while the soma is built up anew in each generation for the sole purpose of nurturing and facilitating the passage of the germ-cells. This does not mean that the germ-cell lineage is unvarying. Far from it, the genes on the chromosomes within the nucleus are subject to mutation and recombination, and the genetic constitution as a whole is responsive to the forces of artificial and natural selection.

FIG. 1. The distinction between the germ-cells and the soma or body. The former is the bridge linking generations and enabling the germ line to continue indefinitely. The germ-cells have only 19 chromosomes but, by fusion, the number is doubled to produce 38 chromosomes in the somatic cells.

Hereditary versus Environment in the Shaping of the Individual

A careful distinction should be made between the genetic endowment and subsequent development. The former is completed at fertilization and is heredity in the strict sense. In other words, this represents the extent of the parental contribution. True, development has yet to proceed and this is where the genetic inspired growth processes and the effects of environment can interact. Now, in genetics, the environment has a wider, yet more technical, meaning than just that of the surroundings. All tangible non-genetic influences constitute the environment. At first, the developing individual has to contend with the maternal environment (pre-natally, as provided by the uterus, and post-natally, as provided by the level of maternal care) and later by the impact of the physical world.

As development proceeds, it is buffered on every side by environmental influences. The picture is complicated by the fact that the various characteristics which make up the individual are affected to different degrees by the innate genetic constitution. For instance, at one extreme, it could be held that post-natal growth is largely governed by the diet. If this is inadequate, a poorly developed and stunted animal will result. The animal may even languish, become susceptible to disease and die. Somewhat similar results could follow if the individual is reared in cold, damp, surroundings. These two items are singled out because the two main environmental factors are the diet and temperature. The former is obviously of great importance since growth is dependent on nourishing food. Yet, it should not escape notice that the dietary effect is almost entirely negative. Given adequate food, the growth is then largely governed by the genetic constitution.

At the other extreme, some characteristics are scarcely affected by the environment. To cat breeders, coat colour and hair type are important attributes and these are almost completely controlled by heredity. True, the Siamese pattern is modifiable to some extent since the amount of pigment deposited in the hairs is influenced by the temperature. Yet, this is the exception which tends to emphasize the rule, for only one particular series of genes (of which Siamese is a member) is affected in this way. In general, it is next door to impossible to modify the colour by manipulation of the diet.

A third item is worth mentioning for completeness. This is developmental error and it arises from accidental quirks and irregularities of development peculiar to the individual which cannot be easily attributed either to genetic or environmental causes. This source of variation is possibly of little concern for practical cat breeding, though it is advisable to be aware of its existence. In general, variation of this nature is relatively small but the odd occasion may occur where this is not the case. A good example is provided by the variation of piebald white spotting. Though the variation can be described in broad terms, no two white marked cats are exactly alike. In part, this is due to erratic development of the white areas during embryonic growth and is a feature of the particular individual.

The Chromosomes

Since the chromosomes within the germ-cells are the hereditary material which is passed on from generation to generation, the mechanism by which this is achieved deserves to be discussed in more detail. Two sorts of cell division will be described: ordinary cell division ("mitosis") and two special divisions which lead up to the formation of the germ-cells. These divisions are known as "meiosis". The treatment will be admittedly oversimplified in order to bring out the essential similarity and to show that meiosis is a subtlety modified form of mitosis.

In ordinary mitotic cell division, which takes place during growth or to replace worn-out or damaged tissue, the membrane containing the nucleus dissolves away and the chromosomes (38 in the cat) orientate themselves so as to form an ordered line-up in a plane across the centre of the cell. This is a period of intense activity within the cell and presently it can be seen that each chromosome has given rise to a partner, alike to it in all respects, by a process of self-copying. The chromosomes lie in close proximity for a while and then commence to move away, as if by mutual repellence. Each of the 38 chromosomes behaves in the same manner and the two groups tend to move in unison and eventually huddled together at each end of the cell. A nuclear membrane forms around each group, to bring into being two nuclei, and the cell may constrict between the nuclei or simply throw up a cell wall. The nuclei are now contained in separate cells and these increase in size until they are identical to the previous single cell.

The mitotic divisions are responsible for the growth of the soma, cell by cell, until the tissues, bones and various organs are built up. They are also responsible for the formation of the gonads, these being formed at the appropriate stage of embryonic development. The fact that the gonads are formed so early in life does not mean that they are functional. This does not occur until many months later, when somatic growth is completed, or almost completed, and the animal attains puberty. It does mean, however, that the gonads are semi-independent of the soma, remaining quiescent until, under the influence of hormones, they become active and commence to produce germ-cells. It is at this stage that the mitotic divisions are transformed into the slightly more complicated meiotic.

As in mitosis, meiosis begins by dissolution of the nuclear membrane and the orderly line-up of the chromosomes. However, instead of the chromosomes behaving as separate bodies, they come together in pairs. The pairs of chromosomes do not join up but the pairing, none-the-less, is very intimate. Careful examination has revealed that the pairing is not at random but only involves those chromosomes of similar size and shape. It is clear that the 38 chromosomes are in reality 19 pairs of chromosomes (i.e., two of each kind). This explains why pairing can occur since different chromosomes as a rule behave independently of each other. Whatever is the attraction which brings the similar chromosomes together, it soon wanes, and the repellent phase sets in. The chromosomes move apart towards opposite ends of the cell and the 19 chromosomes remain bunched together while a nucleus forms around them. A cellular wall divides the cell and two new cells are engendered. This is the first meiotic division. A second follows which is essentially a mitosis. The chromosomes line up but do not pair. Instead, a partner chromosome is formed by self-copying and the chromosomes fall apart to form a separate nuclei. The appearance of a cellular wall results in two new cells. Note that this division only involves 19 chromosomes.

The important meiotic division is the first and the above account merely skims the surface of the processes involved. The important aspect is the reduction in number which takes place. There are 19 different chromosomes in the somatic cells of the cat but, since each one is present twice, this gives a total of 38. This number is known as the diploid, the reduced number of 19 being denoted as the "basic" or "haploid". The products of meiosis are transformed into germ-cells, each containing 19 chromosomes. The transformation is more or less direct for the male, the meiotic divisions leading to the production of sperms. The transformation is less direct for the female, though the end result is the same, the production of a fertilizable egg nucleus containing 19 chromosomes. The union of two germ-cells, each with 19 chromosomes, restores the diploid number of 38.

The necessity of reducing the somatic chromosome by half should now be apparent. If this did not occur, the number of chromosomes would double in each generation, which would be absurd. However, the substitution of meiotic divisions just prior to the production of the germ-cells is an elegant mechanism for maintaining the constant number of chromosomes. True, there is alternation of $38 \rightarrow 19 \rightarrow 38 \rightarrow 19 \rightarrow 38$, but this is in fact the fundamental mechanism. The arrangement of the chromosomes in pairs is also part of the mechanism. It is not sufficient that the germ-cells should receive any random collection of 19 chromosomes but the same basic 19 in every cell. The line-up ensures that this occurs by sending one of each pair to opposite ends of the cell. However, the chromosomes may be jumbled up in the cell before a division, the meiotic line-up effectively sorts out the pairs. The diploid-haploid alternation, of course, is confined to the germ-cell lineage, the soma invariably containing 38 chromosomes except for accidents of division. These accidents tend to be rare but, when they do, they can lead to abnormalities. The production of the tortoiseshell male cat, to be discussed anon, is one such instance.

The latest information on the haploid number of chromosomes for both the small and large cats is given by Table 2. It may be seen that the number of 19 for the domestic cat is by no means exceptional. Indeed, detailed studies by karyologists (people who study chromosomes) have shown that not only do the majority of felids possess a similar number but the sizes and shapes of the individual chromosomes do not differ a great deal between species. This explains why it is possible to obtain hybrids between many of the species even if the hybrid is somewhat infertile.

TABLE 2. THE NUMBER OF CHROMOSOMES FOR VARIOUS SPECIES OF THE LARGE AND SMALL CATS

Common name	Zoological name	Haploid number
Black-footed cat	*Felis nigripes*	19
Bob cat	*Lynx rufus*	19
Cheetah	*Acinonyx jabatus*	19
Domestic cat	*Felis catus*	19
Fishing cat	*Felis viverrina*	19
Geoffroy's cat	*Felis geoffroyi*	18
Jaguar	*Panthera onca*	19
Jaguarondi	*Felis yagouaroundi*	19
Leopard	*Panthera pardus*	19
Leopard cat	*Felis bengalensis*	19
Lion	*Felis leo*	19
Margay	*Felis wiedii*	18
Ocelot	*Felis pardalis*	18
Puma	*Felis concolor*	19
Serval	*Felis serval*	19
Temminck's golden cat	*Felis temmincki*	19
Tiger	*Felis tigris*	19
Tiger cat	*Felis tigrina*	18

Sex Chromosomes and Sex Determination

The normal complement of 19 pairs of chromosomes of the cat differ among themselves. Some pairs are larger than others and so forth. In general, the pairs of chromosomes are identical in size and shape.

The reason for this, of course, is that each chromosome is represented twice in the somatic cells, hence their identicalness is no cause for surprise. According to the latest examinations, there are nine pairs of large chromosomes and nine pairs of medium to small chromosomes.

What is interesting, however, is that in addition to the above, one pair of chromosomes are not identical. Their most obvious difference is in size. One is a medium sized chromosome while the other is quite small. Why should this be? A clue may be found in the fact that the unequalness is confined to the male. Observations have shown that the female has ten pairs of medium to small chromosomes while the male has nine pairs plus the unequal sized pair. It may be deduced that the latter are associated with sex. In point of fact, they are sex chromosomes. This makes the pair rather novel and to distinguish the other chromosomes from them, all of the ordinary chromosomes are called "autosomes". The sex chromosomes themselves are further distinguished by calling the medium sized chromosome the X and the smaller chromosome the Y. Since the Y chromosome is carried only by the male, it is commonly referred to as the "male" chromosome. Therefore, the male is XY and the female is XX, the symbols indicating the sex chromosome constitution of the two sexes.

A check that the unequally sized sex chromosomes are a true pair is provided by a study of meiosis in the male. In the line-up of chromosomes, the sex chromosomes can be seen to pair up and migrate to opposite ends of the cell. This means that the two cells formed by the division are not fully identical. Each cell contains a set of identical autosomes but one cell contains an X chromosome while the other has the Y. These cells are transformed into sperms and it follows that there are two sorts of sperm, those carrying an X and those carrying a Y. Furthermore, since the cell divisions are proceeding continuously, the two sorts of sperm are produced in equal numbers.

In the female, on the other hand, this differentiation of the germ-cells cannot occur since the sex chromosomes in this sex are an identical pair. At meiosis, the XX sex chromosomes come together at the line-up, and separate in the usual manner, but it does not matter which member of the pair ends up in the fertilizable egg nucleus. The result is always the same, the egg will contain one X chromosome. When the egg and sperm unite at fertilization, the sex chromosome constitute of the individual will depend upon the sperm. The egg will contribute one X but the sperm will contribute either an X or a Y. The two sorts of sperm occur in equal numbers, hence two sorts of individual are formed at fertilization. Namely, those with XX and those with XY chromosome. The former will develop into females and the latter into males. The cycle of sex chromosome reduction and reconstitution is mediated in the male. It follows, therefore, that the sex of the individual is determined by the male (Fig. 2). It is also determined at the moment of fertilization and the XY and XX chromosome constitution of the embryo will see to it that the developing sex organs will be appropriately male or female.

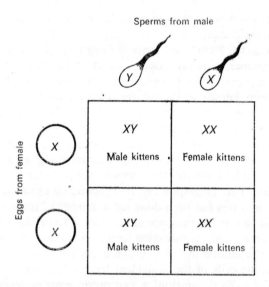

FIG. 2. Sex is determined by the X and Y chromosomes. The male is of constitution XY and the female is XX. The male produces two sets of sperms (X and Y) while the female produces only one (X). These uniting at random give an expected 1 : 1 sex ratio among the offspring.

Sex Development

Sex is initially determined by XY and XX constitution of the individual and in most instances subsequent development is perfectly normal. However, in some cases, the normal development is upset and one of a variety of anomalies may arise. Most cases of anomaly tend to be rare and this is an indication that the cause is an exceptional event.

In some instances, the abnormality will be independent of the sex chromosome constitution. It will either be due to accidents of developments or be caused by genes on the autosomes. For example, a not infrequent anomaly is unilateral or bilateral cryptorchidism. A male with one testis fully descended is usually fertile and will sire both male and female kittens, indicating that his XY constitution is unimpaired. The defect is clearly one of development. The cause of the anomaly is not known with certainty but the problem is discussed in a subsequent chapter.

On the other hand, some sex anomalies are known to be due to unusual sex chromosome constitutions. These cases are of particular genetic interest. Whereas the Y chromosome may carry very few genes, the X may carry a fair number. It is not possible to say how many because their discovery is dependent upon the rare event of mutation. Yet, one X borne mutant has been known in the cat for a very long time. This is sex-linked orange, the gene responsible for the tortoiseshell pattern. The reason why this pattern ordinarily occurs only in the female is due to sex-linkage. The genetic situation is fully discussed anon but one aspect is of relevance at this point. Tortoiseshell males occur as a rare event and one of the explanations for their appearance postulates an abnormal XY constitution. This suggestion can be checked by examination of the chromosomes and this has been done for a number of males.

The simplest case is the presence of an extra X to produce XXY. This curious and anomalous constitution could occur as mistakes during meiosis or in the mitotic divisions which occur after fertilization. Whatever the cause, the cells of the individual have gained an extra X chromosome. While a XXY constitution can produce an externally normal male, the animal is usually sterile. Other unusual constitutions which have been found are cats with mixtures of XX and XY cells, of XX and XXY cells and of XY and XXY cells.

These combinations occur because of rare mishaps of either fertilization or of cell division. In each case, the animal is a male or is predominantly male externally. Most often, they are sterile but not invariably. Some of the above combinations do not necessitate sterility and it is a fact of observation that some tortoiseshell males are known to be fertile. The conclusion to be drawn from the above is that normal sex development and fertility is dependent upon a XY constitution. Add an extra X and the individual develops into a sterile male. The implication is that the Y chromosome contains a relatively powerful male determining factor. Even an animal composed of a mixture of *XX* and *XXY* cells is morphologically male.

The tortoiseshell colour is largely incidental and occurs because one of the *X* chromosomes happen to carry the gene for orange. The presence of tortoiseshell in the male does serve, however, as an indication of something unusual. Whether all tortoiseshell males are due to anomalous chromosome constitutions has yet to be discovered. It seems likely that the majority will prove to be so. Normally coloured males with unusual chromosome constitutions will also occur infrequently but the only outward sign would be sterility. It could be worthwhile to have a chromosome examination made for most cases of inexplicable sterility in otherwise healthy male cats. With modern techniques, this should consist of the minor operation of taking a skin biopsy which would scarcely inconvenience the cat.

The *XXY* condition is often attributed to rare non-separation of the sex chromosomes during the meiotic divisions, so that a germ-cell is formed with the chromosomes *XX* or *XY*. An inference of this mechanism is that germ-cells deficient in either *X* or *Y* could be formed. Upon fertilization, animals of constitution *X*0 and *Y*0 will be produced. Individuals of this type have not been detected as yet in the cat but they have in the mouse. So far, only the *X*0 type has been identified, so it may be that the *Y*0 cannot live. In the mouse, the *X*0 form is typically female, sometimes sterile, but also fertile. Given the latter, the *X*0 animal would be indistinguishable from a normal female. In a later chapter, a possible genetic means of detecting the *X*0 female is discussed. To round off the possibilities, if a *XXY* can survive, so presumably could the *XXX*. This constitution has not been isolated in the cat at the present time but it has in man. The constitution is a female but may be associated with genital abnormalities and be sterile. On the other hand, some *XXX* females are known to be of normal appearance and to be fertile.

III. PRINCIPLES OF HEREDITY

THE basic laws of heredity are relatively simple. Indeed, stripped of all detail, these can be reduced to two: (1) the law of separation of the genes in the germ-cells and (2) the law of independent assortment of the genes in various crosses. If, to these, is added the phenomenon of linkage (which itself is a more precise definition of the second law), then much of elementary genetics is easily covered.

It may be wondered if the very simplicity of the bare bones of heredity may be a factor operating in their disfavour. Some people may feel that the notion of genes cannot explain everything in the development of a complex mammal such as the cat. This adversion is understandable but mistaken. The cat is indeed a complex organism and it must be admitted that a detailed understanding of the animal's genetics can certainly lead into deep waters. Yet, a start has to be made somewhere, and where can this be but a consideration of the basic principles no matter how divorced they may seem at first sight from the living animal?

A step-by-step approach, proceeding from the simple to the more profound, is basic for most sciences and has certainly proved itself in genetics. No matter how complex an organism may be, it can always be broken down into simple attributes for expository purposes. In genetics, these are conveniently referred to as inherited "characters" or "traits". It may be felt that this approach will introduce some degree of over-simplification, but this need not necessarily be so. As the exposition unfolds successive attributes are added until the overall concept is as complex as may be felt desirable. In this way, it is possible to gain insight into the general picture. To clothe the bare bones of heredity, so to speak.

The principles of heredity can be explained to a large extent without reference to the chromosomes, but it is doubtful if this is altogether wise. It should never be forgotten that the chromosomes constitute the material basis of heredity. However, such references as are made will be kept to a minimum. In the early days of genetics the hereditary determinants present in the cells were known as "factors". In modern terms, the factor is now the "gene". In essence, genetics is concerned with the comings and goings of the genes as these are transmitted from parent to offspring and the effects of genes on the growth and appearance of the individual. Just about everything, in fact, in the life of the cat.

Genes and Alleles

The gene may be visualized as a minute portion of a chromosome and each chromosome consists of some thousands of genes. The genes are highly complex chemical structures, each neatly dove-tailing into one another to build up the chromosome (the genetic code and its development). However, a little dated, though apt, simile of the chromosome is that of a string of beads; each bead representing a gene and, the whole string, the chromosome. At an elementary level, this concept is still useful in conjuring up a mental picture of the relationship between the gene and chromosome.

The genes multiply during cell division by a remarkable process of self-copying which is of a high order of exactitude. The duplication is so good that many hundreds of thousands of daughter genes are produced before a mistake occurs and an inexact copy is made. The creation of the inexact copy is known as mutation and, the altered gene, as a mutant. The original gene and its mutant form are referred to as "alleles". The two genes are said to be "allelic" because one has originated from the other and, therefore, must occupy the same position in the chromosome. This position is the "locus" of the gene on the chromosome. The locus concept is important in genetics because each chromosome contains some thousands of loci; especially, as it is possible to represent each locus as capable of producing a characteristic mutation or series of mutations.

The occurrence of mutation is so uncommon that, for most practical purposes, the event can be ignored. Nevertheless, all of the existing colours and coat types of the cat have come into existence as a result of mutation. It is an indication of the rarity of the event that the number of varieties are so few in spite of the millions of cats bred all over the world. Only about two dozen, or so, mutant genes are definitely known. One reason for this is that a cat displaying a new mutant may not be particularly attractive at first sight. Instead of being carefully nurtured and developed, it may be destroyed out of hand as a "freak". This sort of behaviour certainly results in a loss to science and probably to the fancy.

The inherited colours of the cat provide excellent illustrations of the principles of heredity. It should not be imagined, however, that genetics is concerned merely with colour or coat types; nothing is further from the truth. The growth of the animal, its behaviour, proneness to certain afflictions and disease, and its reproductive ability, are all controlled to a greater or lesser extent by the genetic constitution. It happens that the simpler aspects of genetics may be explained more clearly, using coat colours as examples, than if less sharply defined traits are considered.

Simple Inheritance

The wild type coloration of the cat is the ubiquitous tabby pattern and it has been established that the pattern consists of two components. These are: (1) areas in which the hair fibres are banded or ticked with yellow pigment and (2) areas in which all-black hairs predominate and the yellow ticking is reduced in amount. The former comprise the drab yellowish-brown agouti coat to be found in a wide range of animals apart from the cat. The latter represent the melanistic overlay (bars, spots, rosettes or reticulation) which is a feature of the cat family. Tabby pattern, therefore, consists of two co-existing systems of pigmentation or, seemingly more likely, a background of agouti, with a superimposed system of black pigmentation.

One of the first mutants to be found in the cat was probably that of self black. This was so long ago that it is now futile to speculate just when the event occurred. It is of greater practical importance to know how the mutant colour is inherited. This was determined about the year 1918 and this knowledge may be utilized to demonstrate the transmission of a single gene. The self black colour comes into existence by a change in one of the genes controlling the agouti background. In the black individual, none of the hairs display yellow pigment. The hair fibres are mainly black, the colour fading to a blue for the lower regions of the hair shaft.

A pure breeding strain of tabby cats will, by definition, produce only tabby kittens. Similarly, a pure strain of black cats will produce only black kittens. If now, animals of the two strains are crossed, it will be found that the offspring are all tabbies. Despite their tabby appearance, these offspring are carriers of black (as indicated by parentage) and the black colour would be expected to reappear in subsequent generations. This is so, for should the tabbies be mated among themselves, the next generation will consist of tabby and black offspring in the ratio of 3 : 1. Alternatively, the tabby offspring may be mated to the black strain, in which case, the expected ratio of tabby : black will be 1 : 1. A mating could also be made to the pure tabby strain, but little would be gained thereby (as far as appearance goes) for all of the kittens will be tabby.

For purposes of discussion, the three generations and the different matings are precisely defined. The initial generation, prior to crossing, is symbolized as P (namely, the parental), the first cross generation as F_1 (namely, the first filial generation), and the generation descended from the F_1 as F_2 (namely, the second filial generation). The two other matings are known as backcrosses (BC) and it is usual to indicate to which parent or strain the backcross is made. Of the four crosses, the F_1 and F_2 are the most informative from a genetic viewpoint although the backcross has its uses.

In a preceding chapter, it is stated that the chromosomes are represented in pairs in the somatic or body cells, but only once in the germ-cells. Since the chromosomes are composed of genes, it follows that the genes must be present twice in the individual (one gene in each chromosome), but singly in the germ cells. This fact can explain the expected ratios of tabby and black kittens. The ratios are engendered by the fusion at random of germ-cells carrying different alleles. At this stage, it is convenient to introduce symbols for the various genes, since these greatly facilitate the discussion. It is usual to choose as symbols the capital and small letters of the Latin alphabet.

The symbol adopted for agouti is A and that for black (non-agouti) is a. It is mandatory to represent genes and their mutant alleles by the same letter (one by the capital and the other by the small for a reason which will become apparent anon). As each individual contains two of each gene, the pure breeding tabby will be AA and the pure breeding black will be aa. The germ-cells contain only one gene and this will be either A or a, according to strain. The F_1 tabby offspring must be of constitution Aa since it is the outcome of fusion of A and a bearing germ-cells.

The F_1 animals of constitution Aa will produce two kinds of germ-cells, those carrying A and those carrying a. The cell divisions which lead up to the formation of germ-cells are essentially impartial and any particular germ-cell is as likely to receive gene A as to receive a. The result is that the F_1 animal will form A and a bearing germ-cells in equal numbers. When two F_1 individuals are mated together, the germ-cells will unite at random. The chances of fusion of an A sperm with an A egg (to produce an offspring of AA) is as likely as that of fusion with an a egg (to produce an offspring of Aa). Similarly, the chances of fusion of an a sperm with an A egg (to produce an offspring of Aa) is as likely as that of fusion with an a egg (to produce an offspring of aa). These four unions can be depicted by the simple diagram of Fig. 3.

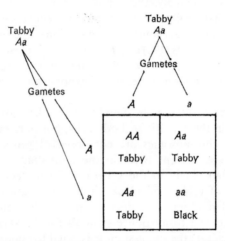

FIG. 3. The expectation from mating two F_1 heterozygous tabbies; to illustrate the 3 : 1 ratio of tabby: black for the F_2. Note that among the tabby offspring, one-third will be homozygous AA and two thirds will be heterozygous Aa.

Summing the results shows that the following offspring are produced: one AA, two Aa and one aa. The first type is a pure breeding tabby, while the second type is an impure tabby, and the last is a black. So far, so good; just one more step is required. The AA and Aa tabbies, though different in gene constitution, are of identical appearance, hence they should be grouped together. When this is done, a ratio of 3 tabbies to 1 black is obtained. This ratio, therefore, has a sound rational basis and, furthermore, has been confirmed by experimental breeding. It may indeed be verified by any breeder who is willing to make the necessary effort. The 3 : 1 ratio has been rightly described as the fundamental ratio of heredity. Other F_2 ratios occur but the 3 : 1 ratio can be discerned in each one of these.

The results so far call for the definition of several important ideas. The recovery of black individuals in the F_2 is said to be due to the "random assortment" of the genes A and a; or, rewording, to the "segregation" of gene a in the F_2. In genetics, the germ-cells are termed "gametes". The individual which results from the fusion of two gametes is termed a "zygote". Two types of zygotes exist. There is the true breeding or "homozygote" of constitution AA or aa and the impure or "heterozygote" of constitution Aa. This designation is general and is used in regard to any pair of alleles.

The fact that tabby cats homozygous or heterozygous for A, respectively, cannot be distinguished by sight, indicates that the influence of gene A predominates over a. When this occurs gene A is said to "dominant" to a or that gene a is "recessive" to A. The dominance/recessive phenomenon is indicated by the choice of symbols. When one of two alternative alleles is dominant to the other, the dominant allele is given the capital letter. In the present case, the agouti gene is symbolized by A while recessive non-agouti allele takes the symbol a. By adhering to this rule, it is easy to remember which is the dominant or recessive allele.

The phenomenon of dominance heralds an important distinction. The two tabbies AA and Aa are of identical appearance but of different genetic constitution. The outward appearance is referred to as the "phenotype" and the genetic constitution as the "genotype". Even for the simple case of homozygous versus heterozygous tabby, it will be appreciated how important is the distinction. For, although the two tabbies have a similar phenotype, their genotypes infer quite different breeding ability. The first will produce only tabby offspring while the second is capable of not only producing tabby but black kittens as well.

The backcross of the F_1 to the black parent is an interesting mating. The black parent can only produce one type of gamete, namely a, whereas the F_1 individual will produce two, namely, A and a. The offspring, therefore, will consist of tabbies (Aa) and blacks (aa) in a $1:1$ ratio. Figure 4 shows how the expectations from the backcross can be worked out. These results lead to two deductions. Firstly, the $1:1$ ratio indicates in a more direct manner than the F_2, that the F_1 is producing A and a gametes in equal numbers. Secondly, all of the BC tabbies will be carriers of black by virtue of their parentage. In this respect, they can be viewed as heterozygotes on par to the F_1 individual.

The existence of both homozygous and heterozygous tabbies in F_2

FIG. 4. The expectation from mating F_1 heterozygous tabby to a black; to illustrate the 1 : 1 ratio of tabby: black.

means that it is impossible to write down the genotype by mere inspection of the phenotype. The most that can be inferred is that the least one A gene must be present. It is customary to indicate ambiguities of this nature by inserting a dash sign (–) in the genotype. That is, to write A– to denote that the individual may be either AA or Aa. In other words, to generalize, parentage is a helpful guide to the determination of the genotype. Where one parent is of the recessive form, those offspring displaying a dominant character must be heterozygotes.

The situation is different for a recessive character. A recessive trait cannot be expressed unless the responsible gene is homozygous. The fact has two general implications: (1) that, when an individual exhibits a recessive trait, the genotype relating to it can be written down without more ado, and (2) where two such individuals are bred together, they will breed true for the character. In the present example, the black individuals produced either by the F_2 or the backcross, can only have the genotype aa. Therefore, should they be mated together, they will only produce black offspring.

The inheritance of non-agouti is quite straightforward and raises no special problems. The gene "disappeared", as it might be put, in the F_1 but reappeared in the F_2 and BC in its original form. Neither the agouti, nor the non-agouti, gene "contaminated" each other as a consequence of being in close juxtaposition in the F_1. On the contrary, the transmission was in a thoroughly wholesome manner. The various tabby or black offspring remained clearly tabby or black in appearance, displaying no evidence of a "blend" of characteristics. This aspect may be generalized to include all cases of simple gene inheritance, not only non-agouti but all those subsequently to be described in this book.

Checkerboard Diagrams

The previous section has described the inheritance of two alleles of the same locus (the agouti). In fact, the symbol A, used to represent the agouti gene, may also be used to denote the agouti locus. However, the cat has nineteen pairs of chromosomes, each one of which is composed of some thousands of gene loci. Consequently, it is important to know what will happen when animals are bred together which are heterozygous for two or more mutant genes carried by different chromosomes.

For example, one such gene could be that known as blue dilution (or dilution for short), a common mutant in the cat. The gene causes a modification of the arrangement of pigment granules in the hair fibres, with the result that the coat appears slate-grey or bluish. Dilution is inherited as a simple recessive (symbol d) to the gene producing dense pigmentation (symbol D). A black is a dense coloured animal of genotype DD and a blue is a dilute form of genotype dd. The F_1 of a cross between these is black, with the genotype Dd. In the F_2, the blue colour will recur in the ratio of 3 black and 1 blue. In other words, the mode of inheritance is similar to that of agouti versus non-agouti. This may be verified by substituting the symbols D and d for A and a, respectively, in Figs. 3 and 4, and deriving the expectations of black and blue kittens. In essence, another gene locus has been defined with the symbol D.

Since the a and d genes do not belong to the same locus, it is possible for the two genes to be present on the same individual. When this occurs, the outcome is the non-agouti blue (self blue). The animal is clearly non-agouti (because of the absence of agouti ticking) and is clearly blue (because of the colour). The genotype, therefore, is $aadd$. Now, the question to consider is what will happen when the blue is crossed with tabby having the genotype $AADD$? Since the a and d genes are independent, both will be present singly in the gametes as ad. Similarly, the gametes produced by the tabby will be AD. Note that the gametes can only transmit one of each pair of genes. The F_1 from crossing the above will have the genotype $ad + AD = AaDd$. It will be a tabby in appearance since the A and D genes are dominant to a and d, respectively. In the F_2, the genes will assort from each other and recombine at random to produce ratios of 9 tabby, 3 blue tabby, 3 black and 1 blue.

The easiest method of deriving the expectations for crosses involving two or more mutant genes is by the aid of checkerboard diagrams. The diagrams of Figs. 3 and 4 are checkerboards of a sort, but these fail to demonstrate the power of the method. Checkerboards are simple to construct and faithfully reproduce the random assortment of the genes and the complete range of expected genotypes. The rules for the construction of a checkerboard are as follows. All the possible types of gametes are written along two sides of a square; those from one parent along the top and those from the other down the left side. Vertical and horizontal lines are added to divide the square into as many columns and rows as there are different gametes. Within each cell are now written the gene symbols at the head of the column and at the side of the row in which the cell resides. To complete the diagram, it is merely necessary to examine the genotype of each cell and to write in the phenotype. Summing the various phenotypes will give the expected ratios. Checkerboards are so useful that there should be no hesitation in their use. Indeed, they provide valuable exercise in the manipulation of genes and for grasping the essence of the heredity mechanism.

There is one aspect to be carefully observed and this is that the gene content of the gametes is correct. Each gamete can carry only one of each pair of alleles. On the other hand, it must be ensured that one gene of each pair is included when the combinations are made up. An example should clarify matters. The cross of tabby ($AADD$) × blue ($aaDD$) gives the F_1 of $AaDd$; an animal doubly heterozygous for a and d. The number of different gametes produced by this genotype will be four, made up as follows: $AD + Ad + aD + ad$. It should be noted that each one contains two genes, either A or a, combined with either D or d. The essential principle is that all possible combinations of A versus a in respect to D versus d must be formed.

Once the number and composition of the gametes are found, the procedure is straightforward, as shown by Fig. 5. It remains now to establish the phenotypes and this is achieved by a consideration of the dominance relationships of the pairs of genes. Genes A and D are dominant to a and d, respectively, and produce their effects independently. This means that the genotypes $AADD$, $AaDD$, $AADd$ and $AaDd$ are tabby, that the genotypes $AAdd$ and $Aadd$ are blue tabby, that the genotypes $aaDD$ and $aaDd$ are black and the single genotype of $aadd$ is blue. The 9 : 3 : 3 : 1 ratio arises from the fact that some genotypes occur more than once. Indeed, if the frequencies of the various genotypes are examined, it will be seen that these, too, bear definite ratios to one an-

Gametes from tabby *AaDd*

	AD	Ad	aD	ad
AD	AADD Tabby	AADd Tabby	AaDD Tabby	AaDd Tabby
Ad	AADd Tabby	AAdd Blue tabby	AaDd Tabby	Aadd Blue tabby
aD	AaDD Tabby	AaDd Tabby	aaDD Black	aaDd Black
ad	AaDd Tabby	Aadd Blue tabby	aaDd Black	aadd Blue

(left margin: Gametes from tabby AaDd)

FIG. 5. The construction of a checkerboard diagram for two pairs of assorting mutant genes. The expected ratio is 9 : 3 : 3 : 1 for the four classes of offspring. Note the various homozygous and heterozygous genotypes within each class.

other. For instance, the number of heterozygotes and homozygotes, with respect to any dominant gene, will be in the ratio of 2 : 1 for an F_2 generation precisely as noted earlier for the segregation of one gene.

It must follow that any individual which displays one or more recessive characters will be homozygous. Therefore, all of the non-agoutis must be *aa* and all of the dilutes must be *dd*. This is true whether or not the individual is a blue-agouti (*A-dd*) or a blue (*aadd*). The latter, moreover, shows two recessive characters and must be homozygous for both *a* and *d*. This is so. It is not possible to be equally explicit for individuals displaying one or more dominant characters. In the present case, for example, the blue-agouti may have either of the genotypes *AAdd* or *Aadd*. Following the remarks of the previous section, these ambiguities are represented by dashes in the genotype. Thus, the genotypes corresponding to the above F_2 would be written as: 9 *A–B–*, 3 *A–dd*, 3 *aaD–* and 1 *aadd*.

Gametes from tabby *AaDd*

		AD	Ad	aD	ad
Gametes from blue *aadd*	ad	AaDd Black	Aadd Blue tabby	aaDd Black	aadd Blue

FIG. 6. Expectations for backcrossing a double heterozygote to the double recessive; to illustrate the 1 : 1 : 1 : 1 ratio.

An instructive checkerboard is that representing the expectations from backcrossing the F_1 of *AaDd* to the self blue. The same four colours will be produced but in the ratios of 1 : 1 : 1 : 1 as shown by Fig. 6. The perceptive reader will no doubt observe that this result is a direct extension of the 1 : 1 ratio of the backcross with one gene. The reason for the ratio is that the four classes of offspring accurately reflect the random combination of genes which form the gametes produced by the F_1. This is so because the self blue is homozygous for two recessive genes. The blue can only produce the gametes *ad* and any F_1 gamete carrying one or more dominant genes will immediately reveal this fact by the colour of the expected offspring. It may be noted in passing that the genotypes of all these BC colours can be written out in full.

Gametes from tabby *AaDd*

		AD	Ad	aD	ad
Gametes from blue tabby *Aadd*	Ad	AADd Tabby	AAdd Blue tabby	AaDd Tabby	Aadd Blue tabby
	ad	AaDd Tabby	Aadd Blue tabby	aaDd Black	aadd Blue

FIG. 7. Expectations for a cross in which one gene is assorting in a 3 : 1 and another in 1 : 1; to illustrate the 3 : 1 : 3 : 1 ratio.

It is possible to have another type of backcross when two genes are involved. This arises where one gene is heterozygous in one parent but homozygous in the other. Such a cross will be of the type *AaDd* (tabby) × *Aadd* (blue-tabby). The offspring will be expected to occur in the ratio of 3 tabby, 3 blue-tabby, 1 black and 1 blue, as shown by Fig. 7. In effect, the 3 : 3 : 1 : 1 is a combination of the 3 : 1 and 1 : 1 ratios, as will be readily seen by those with an eye for such relationships.

A more extensive checkerboard is that of Fig. 8 which depicts the expectations for an F_2 generation involving the simultaneous assortment of three recessive genes. The third gene is *l*, a mutant allele which produces long hair and may be assumed to be inherited independently of *a* and *d*. The F_1 could be that of a cross between a tabby of genotype *AADDLL* and a blue long hair of genotype *aaddll*. The F_1 will be triply heterozygous (*AaDdLl*) and the F_2 offspring will be that shown by the body of the checkerboard. The eight classes will be expected to occur in the ratios of 27 : 9 : 9 : 9 : 3 : 3 : 3 : 1. The interesting aspect is that, while the diagram may appear formidable at first sight, inspection should reveal that this is not altogether so. Each sequence of genotypes and phenotypes are built up by simple duplication of the steps described for previous checkerboards.

The ratios discussed in this and other sections represent, of course, the theoretical expectations for the various matings. This does not mean that in a litter of four kittens, for example, three will be of the dominant type and one will be of the recessive. Or, after a total of sixteen kittens have been bred, exact 9 : 3 : 3 : 1 ratios will be obtained. Unfortunately, the factor of chance will intervene of the same nature as that which prevents an exact 50 : 50 ratio of head : tails for 100 tosses of a perfectly balanced coin. However, the ratios are approximated if a large number of young are bred. This is admittedly difficult for the cat but, in more prolifically breeding animals (e.g. mice or hamsters), the theoretical ratios can be closely realised. The fact that exact ratios cannot always be obtained with small numbers does not invalidate the usefulness of the expected ratios. Most events occur in this world as a matter of relative probabilities and animal breeding is no exception. The usefulness of the expectations resides in their value for planning experimental crosses and, in a wider sense, as a guide to breeding programmes.

As a check on the working out of checkerboards, it is helpful to know the maximum number of different gametes which are produced by an individual heterozygous for a given number of genes. An individual

Gametes from tabby *AaDdLl*

(left axis, rotated) Gametes from tabby *AaDdLl*

	ADL	ADl	AdL	Adl	aDL	aDl	adL	adl
ADL	AADDLL Tabby	AADDLl Tabby	AADdLL Tabby	AADdLl Tabby	AaDDLL Tabby	AaDDLl Tabby	AaDdLL Tabby	AaDdLl Tabby
ADl	AADDLl Tabby	AADDll Tabby LH	AADdLl Tabby	AADdll Tabby LH	AaDDLl Tabby	AaDDll Tabby LH	AaDdLl Tabby	AaDdll Tabby LH
AdL	AADdLL Tabby	AADdLl Tabby	AAddLL Blue Tabby	AAddLl Blue Tabby	AaDdLL Tabby	AaDdLl Tabby	AaddLL Blue Tabby	AaddLl Blue Tabby
Adl	AADdLl Tabby	AADdll Tabby LH	AAddLl Blue Tabby	AAddll Blue Tab. LH	AaDdLl Tabby	AaDdll Tabby LH	AaddLl Blue Tabby	Aaddll Blue Tab. LH
aDL	AaDDLL Tabby	AaDDLl Tabby	AaDdLL Tabby	AaDdLl Tabby	aaDDLL Black	aaDDLl Black	aaDdLL Black	aaDdLl Black
aDl	AaDDLl Tabby	AaDDll Tabby LH	AaDdLl Tabby	AaDdll Tabby LH	aaDDLl Black	aaDDll Black LH	aaDdLl Black	aaDdll Black LH
adL	AaDdLL Tabby	AaDdLl Tabby	AaddLL Blue Tabby	AaddLl Blue Tabby	aaDdLL Black	aaDdLl Black	aaddLL Blue	aaddLl Blue
adl	AaDdLl Tabby	AaDdll Tabby LH	AaddLl Blue Tabby	Aaddll Blue Tab. LH	AaDdLl Black	aaDdll Black LH	aaddLl Blue	aaddll Blue LH

FIG. 8. A complex checkerboard to illustrate the assortment of three genes. Despite the size of the diagram, it is built up in exactly the manner as that of simpler checkerboards.

heterozygous for one gene will produce two different gametes; for two genes, the number is 4; for three genes, the number is 8; for four genes, the number is 16; for five genes, the number is 32; the number of different gametes doubling for each additional gene. The number of progeny which make up the expected ratios for an F_2 generation is the number found above multiplied by itself. The respective numbers for the five cases enumerated are 4, 16, 64, 256 and 1024, respectively. This series of figures should be sufficient to indicate how the sizes of the successive F_2s would have to escalate in order to breed all of the expected animals. For more than a few genes, the task rapidly becomes impractical. This aspect, as a matter of fact, constitutes a serious problem in animal breeding, for it frequently means that it is not possible to obtain all of the results to be anticipated from particular crosses.

Dominant and Recessive Mutants

The majority of mutants of the cat are inherited as recessive alleles to the wild type gene. That is, to the gene normally present at the locus in the wild coloured animal. However, exceptions do occur and no account would be complete without a mention of the possibility of dominant mutant alleles.

The most clear-cut instance of dominant inheritance is provided by a gene which is responsible for the yellow-eyed white (often blue or odd eyed as well but this is another story). Typically, the coat is fully white or white but for a few small patches of colour. The symbol for the allele is W; the wild type gene being represented by w. The white cat may have either of the genotypes WW or Ww. If two of the latter animals are mated together, a ratio of three white to one coloured is obtained, regardless of any other coloured genes which may be assorting at the same time. This is shown by the checkerboard of Fig. 12.

Detection of the Homozygous Dominant

A practical problem of breeding which sometimes has to be solved is that of deciding whether or not a reputedly homozygous cat may be heterozygous for a recessive gene. In principle, the solution is clear. Suppose it is desirous to discover if a black animal is heterozygous for blue dilution. The procedure would be to mate the animal to a blue. If only black kittens are produced, the animal may be assumed to be a homozygote but if a single blue kitten is produced (regardless of how many blacks siblings) the animal is a heterozygote.

In practice, the problem is that a heterozygous animal may produce a number of black kittens by chance. The situation is analogous to that of tossing a coin and obtaining a run of heads. It is obvious that equal numbers of heads and tails are expected but this does not prevent a series of either heads or tails to occur occasionally. Similarly, with the breeding of only black offspring when equal numbers of black and blue are expected. The difficulty can be overcome, however, by stipulating that more than a certain number of black kittens are bred before it is accepted that the animal is homozygous. In this way, the risk of being wrong (the error as it is called) can be made as small as desired. Should 5 offspring be bred, and none are blue, the risk of error is 3 per cent. This is reasonable but not as stringent as might be wished if the establishment of homozygosity is held to be important. The breeding of 7 black offspring is better since the error is reduced to about one in a hundred. This is equivalent to mating 100 known heterozygous black cats, rearing 7 kittens from each, and finding that one individual has produced entirely black offspring. Column A of Table 11 gives the probabilities of being wrong for various numbers of black kittens per tested individual.

The black-blue example is purely illustrative. The same problem would arise if it is necessary to test a tabby for possible heterozygosity for black, or a normal coated animal for either long hair or one of the rex coats and so on. In each case, it is convenient to testmate the cat with the form which it is suspected of carrying. A test could be carried out by mating the animal with another, known to be heterozygous for the recessive gene in question, but this procedure is not very efficient and is not recommended for those cases where the direct test can be performed. Many more kittens have to be bred to reduce the error to minor proportions. Column B of the above mentioned table will exemplify this point.

Incomplete Dominance

All of the mutant alleles so far described share a common property. All of them are inherited as complete recessives or as complete dominants. This is certainly the usual situation but a small number of mutant genes exhibit incomplete dominance. In these cases, the usual 3 : 1 ratio is modified to a 1 : 2 : 1 because the heterozygous class comes into its own instead of being indistinguishable from the homozygous dominant.

The most frequently quoted case of incomplete dominance in the cat involves the piebald form of white spotting, as found in the Tortoiseshell and white or a large proportion of mongrel cats. The piebald allele is symbolized by S, as opposed to s for non-spotted. The heterozygote, Ss, is usually mildly or moderately spotted of grades 1 to 4 of Fig. 21, mainly on the stomach and fore parts of the body, while the homozygote is much more extensively marked with white (grades 4 to 7). When two cats of genotype Ss are mated together, the offspring will segregate into one extensively spotted, two moderately spotted and one non-spotted in accord with the production of offspring having the genotypes SS, Ss and ss, respectively.

Unfortunately, the inheritance of white spotting is not the best of examples of incomplete dominance. At least, not the best in the sense that the two phenotypes of Ss and SS are always readily distinguished. The expression of white is very irregular and this fact makes it difficult on occasion to decide if a white spotted individual is Ss or SS. Nevertheless, the principle should be clear. A somewhat better example is given in the succeeding section on multiple allelism, where the 1 : 2 : 1 breeding behaviour of the dark phase Burmese, light phase Burmese and the Siamese is discussed (see Fig. 10).

Multiple Allelism

A gene locus may mutate to produce a new allele on more than one occasion. Each separate mutation could give rise to the same mutant allele but this need not necessarily be so. Though each mutation is a rare event, if each one produces a distinctive phenotype, it would be possible for a succession of alleles of one gene locus to be brought together over the years. This process has actually occurred in the cat, with the result that several very popular breeds are created by one series of alleles.

The pertinent series is known as the albinistic. There are two reasons for the name of albinistic. Firstly, each allele engenders a characteristic colour, typical of albinistic alleles in several species of mammals and, secondly, the lowest member of the series is usually the all-white pink-eyed albino. A property of albino series is that the different alleles cause a progressive diminution of first yellow and then black culminating in the pigmentless albino. It is also not unusual for one or more of the alleles to be incompletely dominant to each other, especially those which produce the more drastic reduction in coat pigmentation. All of these features are displayed by the mutant alleles of the cat.

The number of alleles which have been reasonably established are five and these may be listed as follows:

Name	Symbol
Full colour	C
Silver	c^{ch}
Burmese	c^b
Siamese	c^s
Albino	c

The symbols used to denote members of an allelic series consist of the same base letter (to denote that all of the alleles belong to the same locus), with suitable prescripts for each allele. The names of the alleles are taken from those breeds which each one is primarily responsible. Briefly, the action of each allele is as follows. The normal gene is C and cats carrying the gene have a coat with full (normal) intensity of both black and yellow pigmentation. Animals with c^{ch} instead of C show no decided change from the black but a noticeable reduction in the intensity of the yellow. The intensity varies from a cream or tawny to pale beige or off-white. With c^b, the black pigmentation is affected, the colour becoming dark sepia brown, while the yellow pigmentation is probably tawny or beige. The body colour tends to be lighter than that of the head and limbs. With c^s, the dark sepia or beige colour is restricted to the head, limbs and tail. The body fur is pale sepia, varying in depth of colour over different regions. With c, no pigment is formed, the coat is white and the eyes are pink due to the blood being illuminated by light rays passing though the translucent tissues. The eyes of animals carrying the c^b and c^s alleles are partially deficient in pigment as evinced by their blue-grey to blue colour.

The dominance relationships between the various alleles are summarized by Table 3. The gene for full coloration is dominant to all of the others; as may also be the case for c^{ch} in relation to c^b, c^s and c. With respect to the c^b allele, the situation is different. This allele is not fully dominant to either c^s or c; in consequence, two phases can be distinguished, a dark (c^bc^b) and a light (c^bc^s or c^bc). It is very probable that c^s is not fully dominant to c but that the difference in appearance between c^sc^s and c^sc could be so slight as not to be fully reliable. Both forms will be Siamese but the latter may have less shading on the body than the former. It must be admitted that the effects of the c gene have not been investigated in these combinations but the c^s and c alleles are so close that it is doubtful if a radical phenotypical difference is produced by the replacement of c^s by c in any heterozygous genotype. If there is a significant difference, it will be in the direction of a colour somewhat paler than the corresponding c^s combination. Table 3 shows the typical expression of the alleles in all of the possible fifteen genotypes, either combined with agouti or non-agouti. The latter will no doubt be the most familiar phenotypes.

TABLE 3. PHENOTYPES PRODUCED BY DIFFERENT COMBINATIONS OF THE ALBINISTIC SERIES OF ALLELES

Genotype	Appearance	
	With agouti	With non-agouti
CC, Cc^{ch}, Cc^b, Cc^s, Cc	Tabby	Black
$c^{ch}c^{ch}$, $c^{ch}c^b$, $c^{ch}c^s$, $c^{ch}c$	Silver	Smoke
c^bc^b	Sepia Silver (dark)	Burmese (dark)
c^bc^s, c^bc	Sepia Silver (light)	Burmese (light)
c^sc^s, c^sc	Siamese (tabby)	Siamese (seal)
cc	Albino	Albino

No matter how many alleles may be known for a series, only two may be carried by a particular individual. This is in accordance with the principle that the chromosomes, which are present in pairs, can each carry only one allele. For example, a tabby heterozygous for silver or for Siamese will have the genotypes Cc^{ch} or Cc^s, respectively. It cannot be heterozygous for silver and Siamese simultaneously, since this would imply a genotype of $Cc^{ch}c^s$. However, circumstances may conspire to suggest that this may be so and this situation deserves to be outlined.

Gametes from tabby Cc^s

FIG. 9. Expectations for a cross involving three alleles assorting simultaneously. Note that only two of the three alleles can be present in one individual. The result is the 2 : 1 : 1 ratio.

A silver may be heterozygous for Siamese and will have the genotype $c^{ch}c^s$. If now, this individual is crossed with the tabby heterozygous for c^s, the following offspring will be expected: 2 tabby, 1 silver and 1 Siamese. Full details are shown by Fig. 9. The explanation lies in the random combination of the genes c^{ch} and c^s vis-à-vis C and c^s, and in the dominance of C and c^{ch} to c^s. This example should demonstrate the care which has to be exercised at times in the interpretation of breeding results.

Gametes from light
Burmese $c^b c^s$

FIG. 10. The expectations from mating two light phase Burmese; to illustrate the 1 : 2 : 1 ratio of an incompletely dominant gene.

Another cross between members of the series is worthy of attention. This is between two Burmese of the light phase. The genotype of this colour is aac^bc^s and, when bred together, the form will produce dark phase Burmese, light phase Burmese and Siamese in the ratio of 1 : 2 : 1. Fuller details are shown by the checkerboard of Fig. 10. The light phase, therefore, is a perpetual heterozygote and nothing can be done to alter this fact. Despite this, there is no reason why the colour should not be bred by those who find it of interest. The dark and light phases, in fact, are an excellent example of incomplete dominance. All of the three genotypes can be reliably identified by their appearance.

A second series of alleles is known in the cat. These are concerned with the production of various forms of tabby striping. Three forms are recognized as under:

Name	Symbol
Abyssinian	T^a
Mackerel	T
Blotched	t^b

The order of dominance is usually taken to be as shown. In other words, T^a is dominant to T and to t^b, while T is dominant to t^b. As far as is known, the dominance is complete. The series is of unusual interest because the T gene produces the mackerel type of tabby which is closely akin to, if not identical with, the *silvestris* pattern of the wild cat. This is the probable ancestral type and forms a convenient "wild type" designation for the species. The other two alleles have probably arisen from T by mutation. This is intriguing because, while t^b is inherited as a recessive to T, the T^a gene is inherited as a dominant. Mutations at the same locus, therefore, may be due to alleles which are either recessive or dominant to the wild type. There is no restriction in this respect. It may be noted that a dominant allele in this case is represented by a capital letter with a superscript to indicate that it is not the wild type.

Masking of Genes

An important phenomenon of gene behaviour must now be described. The term dominance has a special meaning in genetics. Its use is restricted to those cases where one of two alleles at the same locus predominates over the other in the heterozygote. However, the effects of some genes are so over-riding that they are able to conceal the presence of genes at other loci. This "masking" effect is known as "epistasis" and it is not the same as dominance. The distinction should be carefully noted since it is easy to confuse the two.

Easily one of the most remarkable cases of the effects of one gene masking those of another is that of non-agouti over the various tabby alleles. The masking is virtually complete, so that while a black cat must carry tabby alleles, one would scarcely think so to judge from the uniformly black coat. The reason why the tabby striping cannot be seen is because the striping occurs as a pattern of solid black hairs against a background of agouti. However, the non-agouti gene eliminates the agouti ticking to produce a black background. Hence the tabby striping is completely swamped and cannot express itself. Rather, it would be surprising if it could! Yet, the alert reader may object that this statement is not wholly true. A "ghost" pattern of tabby striping can often be seen in the coat of the young kitten and sometimes in the young adult under certain conditions of lighting. Sometimes, the type of tabby can even be distinguished. This implies that the masking need not necessarily be complete at all stages of growth or at all times. It also confirms the statement that the black cat does indeed carry one or two tabby alleles although their presence may not be obvious.

The masking of the effects of one pair of genes by another produces a characteristic ratio in the F_2. This ratio may be exemplified by the interaction of non-agouti and the tabby alleles. Suppose that a blotched tabby (AAt^bt^b) is mated to a black of genotype $aaTT$. The F_1 will be tabby (because of the dominance of A to a) and be of the mackerel form (because of the dominance of T to t^b). The genotype is $AaTt^b$ and four types of gametes will be produced, viz., $AT + At^b + aT + at^b$. It is necessary to compile a checkerboard of sixteen squares to show the full expectation in the F_2 as per Fig. 11. The expected offspring are 9 mackerel tabby, 3 blotched tabby and 4 black. This ratio follows from the necessity of having an agouti background for the type of tabby striping to be dis-

Gametes from mackerel tabby $AaTt^b$

		AT	At^b	aT	at^b
Gametes from mackerel tabby $AaTt^b$	AT	AATT Mackerel tabby	$AATt^b$ Mackerel tabby	AaTT Mackerel tabby	$AaTt^b$ Mackerel tabby
	At^b	$AATt^b$ Mackerel tabby	AAt^bt^b Blotched tabby	$AaTt^b$ Mackerel tabby	Aat^bt^b Blotched tabby
	aT	AaTT Mackerel tabby	$AaTt^b$ Mackerel tabby	aaTT Black	$aaTt^b$ Black
	at^b	$AaTt^b$ Mackerel tabby	Aat^bt^b Blotched tabby	$aaTt^b$ Black	aat^bt^b Black

FIG. 11. The $9 : 3 : 4$ ratio which results from the simultaneous assortment of two mutant genes, one of which masks the expression of the other.

cerned. Unless it is possible to determine the nature of the tabby carried by the black kittens, these will have to be lumped together into a single group.

Unless one is aware of the existence of genes masking the effects of others, certain results may seem mystifying. For example, in the cross of $AAt^bt^b \times aaTT$, the F_1 are mackerel striped ($AaTt^b$). It might be wondered how this result could be, since the only apparent tabby animal is blotched and this is recessive to mackerel. The difficulty is cleared up once it is realised that the black could carry the mackerel allele. The confusion may arise because of an erroneous belief that tabby is dominant to black. This is not strictly true and it could be a dangerously misleading half-truth at the best of times. It may be reiterated that it is the dominance of the agouti gene A to non-agouti a which could bring this belief into being. This is only part of the story and the complete situation is not obtained until the type of tabby is concurrently examined.

Crosses with the W form of dominant white can also produce some apparently baffling results unless one is alert to the fact that whites are not all genetically alike. Suppose a blue (*aaddww*) is paired with a white of genotype (*AADDWw*). The F_1 will be expected to consist of half tabby (*AaDdww*) and half white (*AaDdWw*). It might be wondered whence came the tabbies since the blue does not carry the agouti gene nor the gene for dense coloration. The answer, of course, is that both genes are introduced by the white parent. The white coat colour might produce the impression that the animal lacks the ability to carry any colour genes at all but this is entirely misleading. The animal is white because it carries a gene which prevents the expression of pigment (of any colour) on the coat although the genes themselves are present. This aspect can be further understood by contemplation of the expectations from crossing $AaDdww \times AaDdWw$. The expectations are : 9 tabby, 3 blue-tabby, 3 black, 1 blue and 16 whites. The reader should work out the expectations for himself; particularly to verify that, for every one of the 16 coloured individuals, there is a corresponding white individual of the same genotype but for the presence of a W gene. This should emphasize that white animals may have almost any genotype.

Should two heterozygous white cats, which are also heterozygous for another gene, be mated together, the 12 : 3 : 1 ratio of Fig. 12 will be obtained. In this example, the two cats are shown as heterozygous for non-agouti. Because of the epistatic nature of W, the assortment of the A and a genes can only be seen in the one quarter of offspring with coloured coats. The other three-quarters will be white animals except possibly for an occasional spot or two of coloured fur. As a matter of practical interest, it is often possible to determine from these spots which genes are carried. Those with tabby spots will be of genotype AA or Aa and those with black spots will be aa. This minor point is mentioned because it is wise to be continuously on the look-out for clues which can establish the genotype.

The phenomenon of the over-riding influence of some genes brings into focus a point made earlier in respect to dominance, namely, the importance of making a distinction between the genotype and phenotype. The animal's appearance is one thing but its breeding ability is something different. Appearance is often the only guide to the worth of an individual and full use should be made of it but, on the other hand, it is not entirely trustworthy. The genetic calibre of the individual lies not so much on appearance but on the quality of the offspring. For this reason, it is

Gametes from white $AaWw$

	AW	aW	Aw	aw
AW	AAWW White	AaWW White	AAWw White	AaWw White
aW	AaWW White	aaWW White	AaWw White	aaWw White
Aw	AAWw White	AaWw White	AAww Tabby	Aaww Tabby
aw	AaWw White	aaWw White	Aaww Tabby	aaww Black

Gametes from white $AaWw$ (left vertical label)

FIG. 12. The 12 : 3 : 1 ratio which comes into being from the masking effect of the dominant W gene.

advisable to supplement appearance by consideration of parentage and the adoption of a breeding system. It is well to recall the aphorism that animal breeding would be a greatly simplified pastime but for the existence of dominance and epistatis.

Mimic Genes

It is not uncommon for two or more independent mutant genes to have identical or closely resembling phenotypes. This sort of parallel behaviour is not due to coincidence but is connected with the fact that each character is governed by numerous genes. Any one of which may mutate to an allele bringing about a similar change in phenotype. Such genes are rather loosely called "mimics".

Gametes from normal *RrRere*

	RRe	Rre	rRe	rre
RRe	RRReRe Normal	RRRere Normal	RrReRe Normal	RrRere Normal
Rre	RRRere Normal	RRrere Devon rex	RrRere Normal	Rrrere Devon rex
rRe	RrReRe Normal	RrRere Normal	rrReRe Cornish rex	rrRere Cornish rex
rre	RrRere Normal	Rrrere Devon rex	rrRere Cornish rex	rrrere Devon- Cornish rex

*(left margin, vertical)* Gametes from normal *RrRere*

FIG. 13. The expectation for the F_2 generation from animals heterozygous for the two rex genes: to illustrate the 9 : 7 ratio of normal : rex.

That such genes can occur in the cat is shown by the occurrence of at least two rex mutants. These are the Cornish and Devon rexes, each of which are inherited as recessives. The test for similarity or independency of the recessive genes with the same phenotype is to inter-cross the two forms. If they are genetically identical, the offspring will resemble the parents but, if they are independent, the offspring will be normal. Crosses between the two rexes have produced normal coated kittens; hence, the two genes are genetically distinct. The symbols for the Cornish and Devon rex mutant alleles are *r* and *re*, respectively.

The cross between the two rex mutants deserves to be discussed in more detail. Symbolically, the cross will be *rrReRe* × *RRrere* to give the F_1 of genotype *RrRere*. Each parent has contributed a wild type gene (viz., *R* and *Re*) and this is the explanation for the abrupt disappearance of the rex coat. Should the F_1 be inbred to produce an F_2, the ratio of normal : rex will be 9 : 7. This curious ratio will occur because the two rexes are of similar appearance and it may be difficult at times to distinguish one form from the other. The double rex combination (*rrrere*) will be a rex and probably identical to one of the other rexes. The reader may like to work through the appropriate checkerboard (Fig. 13) to assure himself that the expected ratio is indeed that of 9 : 7 of normal and rex kittens.

Mimic genes are of interest to geneticists because meticulous examination often reveals subtle differences which are valuable in understanding how characters develop. In practical breeding, however, they can be a nuisance. For instance, unless careful breeding records are kept, it is possible for the mutant forms to become mixed up. Furthermore, it could be a serious mistake to cross the two forms and expect to recover each type at a later date. Their similarity may be conducive to errors which would be costly to rectify. If the descendants of such crosses are recklessly distributed, the occasion may arise when two animals of the recessive form are bred together, only to give offspring of the dominant phenotype. This is likely to cause dismay and even to cast doubt on the validity of the rule that recessive traits always breed true.

The rule is not contradicted, of course; it only seemed to be so because of the similar phenotype possessed by each gene. Actually, the genes belong to different loci, hence the reversion to normal is to be expected. Other cases of mimicking genes may wait to be discovered and an obvious candidate is blue dilution. In the mouse, several distinct diluting genes are known which, when inter-bred, produce wild type offspring. Some of these mimic blue dilution closely and could be easily confused. Suppose such a situation existed in the cat. The occasion will eventually arise when two apparently blue individuals are mated, only to produce black kittens. This could mean that one parent was homozygous blue dilution, but the other carries a different diluting gene. It must be emphasized very strongly, however, that few people may be willing to accept the existence of two independent diluting genes unless it can be convincingly shown that a mis-mating (or double mating) can be precluded. This is not always so easy to establish as one might think.

The Multiple Recessive

One of the features of genetics which intrigues some people is whether there is a limit to the number of mutant genes which can be combined together. Simply answered: not as a rule. There are perhaps two qualifications to be made in regard to this statement. Both involve practical considerations of what is possible and what is not. Some mutant genes confer a slight inviability on the individual which, while not being particularly noticeable in isolation, may reveal itself more obviously when in combination. Sooner or later, this reinforcement effect could bring the process of combination to a halt. However, no effects of this kind have yet been observed for the cat.

The second qualification has to do with the problem of lack of recognition of the combinations because of epistatis. This is especially true for colour mutants. In general, each additional gene will result in a reduction in colour until a nearly white or white animal is engendered. The cat with the greatest number of recessive genes is the lilac Siamese of genotype $aabbc^sc^sdd$. If to this is added the gene for long hair, the Lilac Colourpoint will result, of genotype $aabbc^sc^sssddll$. Or, a Cornish rex version could be produced, of genotype $aabbc^sc^sddrr$. From crosses between these, the Lilac Siamese long haired Cornish rex of $aabbc^sc^sddllrr$ could be derived. Phenotypically, this animal is of Lilac Siamese coloration, with the fine hair and curved whiskers of the long hair rex.

Expressivity and Impenetrance

One of the delights or nuisances of animal breeding, depending upon one's point of view, is that no two individuals are exactly alike. This variation affects both the wild type and the mutant form but, seemingly, more especially the latter. The existence of this variability has led to the concept of "expressivity" as a means of describing the situation. Some mutant phenotypes are relatively stable while others vary considerably. A character which shows wide variability is that of piebald white spotting as illustrated by Fig. 21.

Now, the interesting feature of the variation is that, while more than one gene may be involved, there is reason to believe that most of the variation is due to a single gene. The S gene is semi-dominant which means that the heterozygotes and homozygotes are different on the average and this fact will be contributory. Yet, even when this is taken into consideration, the variation in expression of the spotting is variable, particularly for the heterozygote Ss. This variation can be assessed by plotting the number of individual successive grades of spotting as a curve on a graph. This could be termed the "expressivity profile."

A curve for one strain of cats could be different for another and, thus, be indicative that the expression of the character may vary not only between individual cats but also between strains.

If a character is extremely variable, then it is conceivable that some individuals could fail to express the character at all and appear as normal. This curious phenomenon could even occur for a character which is not exceptionally variable. The special terms "impenetrance" or "partial manifestation" are used to denote this situation and it means that the character has failed to manifest although the genotype would indicate that it should. Fortunately, impenetrance is not an important factor for the colour genes known at present. All of these manifest regularly and to expectation. As an example of impenetrance, however, mention may be made of the probable existence of a minor spotting gene which produces a small white spot or clump of hairs on the breast or lower belly. The size of the spot is variable and it is possible that some animals, which ought to exhibit the spot, do not. These are solid in colour. Such animals are called "normal overlaps" because, though of normal coloration, they have a mutant genotype and will indeed breed as a mutant.

Though coat colour genes, as a rule, exhibit regular penetrance, this is not true for genetic anomalies. It is not unusual for these to display impenetrance. The inheritance of tail kinks or nodulation could be an example and doubtless other instances will come to mind. A possible reason for this is that the body of an animal shows surprising powers of self-repair. This is particularly true when a defect makes an appearance early in development, before the tissues are too well formed that timely and self-regulating growth cannot swing into action to rectify the defect. That is to say, to put the matter simply, the genetic disruption may persist and eventually produce a defective individual. In another individual, however, the disruption can be overcome with the result that an outwardly normal individual is produced. The varying severity of many anomalies is due to the same process, only in these cases, the self-rectification has only been partial. In both cases, the gene causing the disruption is present and, particularly in the case of the spuriously normal individual, this should not be overlooked.

Manifold Effects of Genes

Some genes seem to modify only one character while others appear to influence the expression of several characters simultaneously. In this latter case, it is said that the gene has "pleiotropic" action. The concept of pleiotropism is intimately bound up with the depth of analysis of gene action. To a superficial appraisal, many genes will exhibit pleiotropic effects to a lesser or greater degree. For example, if eye colour and coat colour are treated as separate characters, then the Siamese gene could be regarded as pleiotropic because of its effect on both eye colour and coat colour. Yet, if the pigmentation of the animal is treated as a whole, there is no pleiotropism, since the blue eye and whitish sepia coat are both due to the same cause. Namely, the severe impairment of pigment formation brought about by the gene.

Perhaps the above example is almost self-obvious but other cases may occur in which apparently unconnected characters are modified by the same gene. It is probable that no gene is truly pleiotropic. Some genes appear to be so because the analysis of their manifold effects has not probed far enough to reach the fundamental action of the gene.

Linkage

The cat has nineteen pairs of chromosomes and it is probable that each one contains some thousands of genes. While the number of known mutants are small, the chances are that these will be borne by different chromosomes. The inference for practical breeding is that the various mutants will be inherited independently of each other.

However, the situation is changed if two mutant genes happen to occur in the same chromosome. The inference of independent assortment will no longer hold and, in crosses, the two genes will tend to stay together as these are transmitted from one generation to the next. This "staying together" is termed "linkage" and the two genes are said to be "linked". Linkage is an attribute which cannot be forecast but only discovered by experimental breeding.

None of the mutants of the cat are known to be linked. Regrettably, this is not due to experimental tests for linkage which have proved to be negative but rather to a complete absence of tests. It is traditional to assume that genes are inherited independently until such time that evidence for linkage becomes unmistakable. As more mutants are discovered (such as, the recent addition of the folded-ears gene) and progress is made with cat genetics, the chances of finding a linkage will increase until the event becomes an almost certainty. For this reason, apart from general knowledge, it is wise to be aware of the possibility of linkage and to be on the look-out for possible instances.

Two phases of linkage may be recognised. In one, two genes may be located in the same chromosome, whence they are said to be "coupled". When the two genes are present in the same parent, they will be transmitted together far more often than they are separated. This is the criterion for this phase of linkage. In the other phase, the two genes are in different members of the pair of chromosomes. When the genes are present in the same parent, they will be transmitted separately far more often than they are together. The criterion in this case is that the genes are not recombining as freely as they would if they are inherited independently. The two genes are then said to be in "repulsion". It may be seen that the names given to the two phases indicate clearly what is to be expected in breeding operations. In the first, the two genes are behaving as if coupled while, in the second, they behave as if they are repelling one another.

It may be queried: what exactly is linkage and do linked genes remain permanently linked? The special cell divisions which lead to the formation of gametes require that the pairs of homologous chromosomes come to lie in extremely close proximity and to form intimate contact at certain points along their length. During this process, internal stresses are induced which are relieved by spontaneous breakage and rejoining. In a proportion of cases, the rejoining is between constituents of partner chromosomes, rather than between those of the same chromosome. The result is that the chromosomes have exchange segments of themselves with each other. In effect, the changes are a means of ensuring that the pairs of chromosomes have a common unity but this aspect is beyond the scope of this book.

The exchange of material between homologous chromosomes means that blocks of genes have been conveyed from one chromosome to the other; or, to use the appropriate term, have "crossed over". The separation of linked genes is known as "crossingover" and the term means that (1), for coupling, the mutant genes have been separated from each other and (2) for repulsion, the formerly separated genes are now combined in the same chromosome. Now, the chance of separation will depend upon the relative distance between the two genes. The greater the distances, the greater the chance of crossingover. Therefore, it is possible for two genes to be "loosely" or "closely" linked. When two genes are closely linked, the absence of random assortment is particularly noticeable.

The whole topic of linkage is of some import for both pure and applied genetics and most genetic textbooks discuss the subject in depth. However, in applied genetics, the event of linkage may be received with mixed feelings. For example, the intrusion of linkage is annoying when a breeder is endeavouring to create a new colour variety by the recombination of genes only to find that this is proving to be more difficult than anticipated.

Sex-linked Heredity

It may be remarked with some pride that the cat is one of the few mammals to boast of a case of sex-linked inheritance which dates from the dawn of genetics. The curious situation of the tortoiseshell pattern of the female and the great scarcity of tortoiseshell males has been cited in most books on animal genetics.

It is stated in a preceding chapter that the sex of the individual is determined by a pair of special chromosomes: the X and the Y. These chromosomes carry gene loci which can mutate, just as those borne by the ordinary chromosomes. However, there is a vital difference. A mutant allele carried by a sex chromosome will be associated with sex and display "sex-linkage".This is the situation for the mutant which produces "ginger" or red pigmentation and which is indirectly responsible for the mosaic pattern of the tortoiseshell.

The gene responsible for the ginger cat is known as orange and is symbolized by O. The colour is produced by an alteration in the animal's pigment physiology so that entirely yellow pigment is produced instead of a mixture of yellow/tabby for the tabby and black/tabby for the non-agouti. The word yellow, it may be interposed at this juncture, is used in a general sense to include all cream, yellow and red pigmentation. Yellow is the technical term for the pigment granule which produces all of these colours. The black tabby striping emerges as red striping of the same pattern and the intervening agouti areas become yellow or rich beige.

The sex linkage of O becomes apparent when the segregation of the gene is considered for the various matings. The O gene is borne by the X chromosome. Now, the male has but one X chromosome; consequently, they can only be either O (yellow) or o (non-yellow). On the other hand, the female has two X chromosomes; consequently, they may be one of three genotypes. These are: OO (yellow), Oo (tortoiseshell) or oo (non-yellow). The tortoiseshell, therefore, is the heterozygote and is unique in that its coat reflects the influence of both the O and o genes in different parts of the animal at the same time. The yellow areas corresponding to O and the non-yellow areas to o.

Gametes from tortoiseshell
Female Oo

		O	o
Gametes from yellow male OY	O	OO Yellow female	Oo Tortoiseshell female
	Y	OY Yellow male	oY Black male

Fig. 14. The assortment of the sex-linked O gene. Note that O can only be transmitted in half of the male gametes.

To predict the results of matings with sex-linked genes, it is necessary to know which colour is the male or vice versa. For convenience, all of the possible matings with the orange mutant are arranged in Table 4. The expectation for the table can be found by the aid of checkerboard diagrams, as shown by the examples of Figs. 14 and 15. The reader may find valuable exercise in working out the expectations for all of the crosses of the table. The point to remember with sex-linked genes is that the male can only transmit one gene (O or o) in 50 per cent of gametes; the other 50 per cent carrying a Y chromosome which does not possess a O locus.

In the table, the word black has been used to denote non-yellow, this usage being common practice. This policy is acceptable, provided it does

Gametes from tortoiseshell
female Oo

	O	o
o	Oo Tortoiseshell Female	oo Black Female
Y	OY Yellow male	oY Black male

(left axis label: Gametes from black male o)

FIG. 15. A second example of the assortment of the sex-linked O gene. Note that the wild type gene o can only be transmitted in half of the male gametes.

TABLE 4. EXPECTATIONS FOR THE POSSIBLE MATINGS OF YELLOW AND TORTOISESHELL CATS

Mating		Expected offspring	
Dam	Sire	Males	Females
Yellow	Yellow	Yellow	Yellow
Black	Yellow	Black	Tortoiseshell
Tortoiseshell	Yellow	Yellow	Yellow
		Black	Tortoiseshell
Tortoiseshell	Black	Yellow	Tortoiseshell
		Black	Black
Yellow	Black	Yellow	Tortoiseshell
Black	Black	Black	Black

Note: In the above table, black is used as an euphemism for non-yellow (e.g., black, tabby, blue, etc.).

not blind one to the fact that "black" can mean tabby, blue, chocolate and other colours; the common denominator of which is that they are "non-yellow". The mutant genes producing these colours will be inherited independently of O and the assortment of these may have to be taken into account for working out the full expectation for any cross or series of crosses. The procedures to follow are those for ordinary inheritance, as shown by the checkerboards described earlier, in combination with those for sex-linkage.

The conversion of black pigment to yellow is so effective that the non-agouti yellow of genotype aaO or $aaOO$ is identical in appearance to that of $A-O$ or $A-OO$. That is, gene O masks the expression of the A and a genes. This fact can be verified by crossing a yellow male of genotype AAO to a black female of genotype $aaoo$. The offspring will consist of tabby males and tabby tortoiseshell females. Since the black female cannot carry agouti, the offspring must have gained the gene from the yellow parent. As it happens, the patchwork colouring of the tortoiseshell provides direct visual evidence that the yellow gene can mask the expression of non-agouti. It is possible to have both tabby and black tortoise-shells of genotypes $A-Oo$ and $aaOo$, respectively, yet the yellow areas in the two cats are exactly the same. One could not ask for a better demonstration of the epistatic nature of O.

Partial Sex-linked Heredity

It could be argued that sex-linkage may be of two sorts: total, as discussed previously or, partial, where a mutant gene may sometimes be carried by the X and sometimes by the Y. The gene being transferred from one chromosome to the other by crossingover. Partial sex-linkage is possible because there is reason for thinking that the individual sex chromosomes are composed of two parts: (1) a special sex-determining segment (or segments) and (2) a segment which is not primarily concerned with sex and which can exchange material as an ordinary autosome.

The sex segments are transmitted as distinct entities. The segment on the X is never found on the Y and, conversely, the Y segment is never found on the X. Exchanges between them are completely inhibited for the good reason that the segments probably contain the sex determiners and these must be maintained intact. Any genes located in either one of the segments will display total sex-linkage, even although the function of the gene itself may be unrelated to sex. This is the situation for the O gene which, in the ordinary course of events, seems to be located in the X segment.

It appears to be a necessary function of pairs of homologous chromosomes that these should come together and exchange material as part of their life cycle. The sex chromosomes retain their character, yet conform with this requirement, by having a part capable of making such exchanges (the "pairing segment"). A mutant gene carried by the segment will display partial sex-linkage because the exchanges will ensure that it is carried by the X chromosome in a certain proportion of cases and by the Y chromosome in others.

It seems doubtful if partial sex-linkage is an event to be seriously considered for the cat. On the other hand, the topic is brought up because, on more than one occasion, it has been suggested that the rare tortoiseshell male could result from a crossover which has uniquely involved the piece of X sex segment containing the O gene. This explanation may still be a possibility for some of the tortoiseshell males although it seems that the explanation of abnormal sex chromosome combinations is more plausible. Anyone who delves into the older literature, will soon come across the partial sex-linkage hypothesis.

Sex-limited Expression

There is another form of sex associated heredity which, unfortunately, is sometimes mistaken for sex-linkage. This is where the expression of a gene is confined to one sex although the gene, itself, is carried by one of the ordinary chromosomes. No clear-cut instance of sex-limited expression of a gene affecting coat colour has been reported for the cat although examples are afforded by those characteristics which are clearly either paternal or maternal.

If it is supposed that cryptorchidism is due to one or more genes, this would be a character which is sex-limited to the male (at least, that aspect of the deformity which results in undescended testes). This defect is cited mainly as an example since, at this time, little is known of the extent to which it might be genetically determined. If the defect is due to a recessive gene (possibly with impenetrance), it would be a fine example. The lesson to be learnt from sex-limited inheritance is that while the trait will be inherited through both sexes, the trait will manifest only in one. This means that the breeding potential of the non-manifesting sex cannot be assessed directly, though some idea can be obtained from the manifesting sibs.

The type of maternal care a queen may lavish upon her kittens and the quality and quantity of her milk is determined in part by heredity. A female which neglects her young or rears weakly offspring should always be examined for a possible ailment which may be undermining her health or stamina. However, if this examination is negative, the possibility that these undesirable traits are caused genetically should be considered. Other factors being equal, she and her offspring should not be used for breeding. The point to be made is that it should not be imagined that these traits are inherited solely via the mother. A son from an excellent or poor mother is equally likely to pass on these desirable or undesirable qualities to his female offspring, as in a daughter from the same mother. A male cannot express any real forms of maternal instinct but, nevertheless, he will carry the genes for them.

Continuous Variation

The type of heredity described in previous sections is known as discrete or discontinuous because the characteristics involved are sharply defined. For instance, no one could confuse a tabby cat with a black nor, after a modicum of experience, a mackerel with a blotched striped tabby. Yet, not all variation is of this nature, many characteristics are known which vary continuously from one extreme to another. A good example, in the sense of being obvious to the eye, is the variation in intensity of yellow pigmentation, which can range all the way from light "ginger" to rich red. To be sure, a major step is required in the first instance to create the yellow cat but the variation of intensity is independent of this.

The question may be asked: is this continuous variation inherited and, if so, how? The answer to the first part of the question is, yes, very often a sizeable part of the variation is inherited, although the proportion may vary from character to character. In this respect, continuous variation differs from the discontinuous. With discrete heredity, the size of the step tends to swamp the incidental background variation, whether inherited or not. With continuous characters, on the other hand, the incidental background variation is included and it is not always wise to assume that all of the observed variation is inherited. It is also unwise to go to the other extreme and assume that none of the variation is inherited. The true situation lies in between, some of the variation is genetic and the remainder is not.

The answer to the second part of the question is that the heritable portion is due to many genes with similar effects, though the effect of any one gene is small relative to the total variation. Though the action of each is small, the total effect is cumulative, so that an individual which carries a number of these genes is phenotypically different from an individual which carries only a few. Because numerous genes with minor effects are involved, the inheritance of continuously varying characteristics is blending. The genes themselves do not blend, of course, but assort in the manner of genes with major effects. It is the phenotype which shows blending in the form of offspring which are generally intermediate to that of the parent, with the production of the odd individual which deviates from the average. Characters controlled by many genes are termed "polygenic" and the genes concerned are known collectively as "polygenes". The important point to remember is that many, rather than a few, polygenes are involved as a group and that the effect of each one is small compared with the cumulative effect of the group. Those genes with large effects (i.e., ordinary alleles) are "major genes" in this terminology.

It is convenient to speak of polygenes as possessing plus and minus effects with respect to the expression of a character. For example, take the variation of intensity of yellow. The ginger mongrel cat may be visualised as possessing minus polygenes, as opposed to the rich colouring of the exhibition Red Tabby which is brought into being by plus polygenes. Furthermore, these extreme forms breed relatively true; ginger cats rarely produce other than ginger young and red tabbies produce red tabbies. The colour may vary but, on the average, this is so. The reason is that they are at the extremes of the variation. Should the two forms be crossed, the offspring would be expected to be intermediate, richer in colour than the ginger but less so than the exhibition animal. Inbreeding these cross-breds would be expected to produce a generation consisting of very variable offspring. Most would be intermediate in colour but a number will approach either the ginger or the red of the grand-parents. Should the intensity of yellow be divided into grades and the parentage of animals of each grade be tabulated for a large number of offspring, the result could be similar to Fig. 16.

The checkerboard of Fig. 8 may be used to convey a mental picture of the behaviour of polygenes. Suppose that three polygenes are involved and that the plus alleles can be represented by capitals and the various minus alleles by small letters. Therefore, the ginger grade of yellow will have the genotype aabbcc and the red grade will be AABBCC. To keep the picture simple, assume there is no dominance and that the variation of intensity of yellow can be divided into seven grades (from 0 for ginger

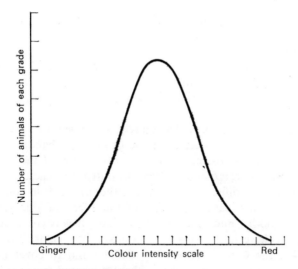

FIG. 16. Idealized curve to illustrate how the frequencies of animals, graded for intensity of yellow, might be distributed in the F_2 of a cross between a ginger and an exhibition red.

to 6 for the most intense red). The F_1 will be of an intermediate colour (grade 3) and have the genotype $AaBbCc$. When these are inter-bred, the polygenes will assort and combine at random to produce the totality of 64 genotypes as shown by Fig. 8 (by substituting the symbols A, B, C, etc. for A, D, L, etc. of the checkerboard). Let each plus polygene increase the intensity by one grade, so that the genotype $aabbcc$ will be of grade 0 and the genotypes $Aabbcc$, $aaBbcc$ and $aabbCc$ will be of grade 1, and so forth. Proceeding in this manner over the whole range of genotypes, the 0 to 6 grades will be found to occur in the frequencies of 1, 6, 15, 20, 15, 6 and 1, respectively. Figure 16 shows the expectation in a rather idealized form. The curve in the figure is of the general type which occurs when numerous factors are operating to determine the expression of a character. Even with a hypothetical example of 64 individual, the shape of the curve can be seen in a plot of the expected frequencies.

If the F_1 are backcrossed to the red, the expectation is a range of grades from 3 to 7, with the majority of offspring being of the intermediate grades 4 and 5. Similarly, if the F_1 are backcrossed to the ginger, the range of variation will be from grades 0 to 3, with the majority of offspring being of the intermediate grades 1 and 2. The average in each case will be that of a grade of yellow which is half-way to that of the parents. This is a typical result of continuous or polygenic heredity. Note that it is the average of the offspring which is intermediate. The majority will in fact be intermediate but there will also be some individuals which will be either paler or darker. Any breeder who has had occasion to breed together yellow cats of various intensities will probably have noticed this behaviour.

The above remarks have deliberately simplified the mechanism of polygenic heredity for, apart from the obvious probability that many, rather than a few, polygenes will be involved, any of the attributes of genes with major effects could be shown by polygenes. These could include unequal effects for different polygenes, either alone or in company with certain others, dominance, masking of the effect of one gene by the presence of another and other odd behaviour. It is beyond the scope of this book to delve into this sort of complex behaviour. This is not to suggest that the topic is impossibly difficult but to cover the subject adequately would be to expand this chapter beyond reasonable bounds. The complexities of polygenic inheritance has been competently tackled and anyone wishing for further information should read either Mather (1949) or Falconer (1960).

Polygenic variation may be conveniently divided into two sorts: (1) the "pure" state, where no major genes are involved, and (2) where the variation is due in the first instance to the presence of a major mutant gene. The heredity of body size and conformity falls into the first category. No major genes are known to effect either of these features. On the assumption that the diet is adequate and the cat receives sufficient exercise for full development, the size and shape of the body is due to polygenes. "Size and shape" is an abstraction, of course, encompassing many individual features. Apart from bulk, *per se*—as measured by weight—a cat may be thick-set or long-bodied, heavy or lightly boned, short or long legged and so forth. These items do not vary independently but are correlated, and it is this fact which gives a meaning to the concept of "type" as visualized by the breeder seeking to perfect an ideal animal.

By far the commoner situation, however, is where a major gene is also concerned. The example of variation in intensity of yellow is most striking but may be justifiably held that the variation is brought into prominence in the first instance by the presence of the *O* gene. This is true and, what is more important, it has led to the idea of the polygenes being regarded as "modifying" genes. That is, the yellow colour is due to

O but the expression of O is due to modifying polygenes or "modifiers" for short. The importance of this concept is considerable. In the first place, the concept is very general. For instance, long hair is primarily due to the mutant l but there is a great difference between the long haired mongrel and the exhibition animal. At present, there is no indication that the difference is due other than to polygenes modifying the length and texture of the long haired condition. Another example, which occupies the attention of breeders, is the variation of depth of colour of blue cats. The basic genotype is *aadd* but the blue colour can vary quite appreciably. This variation is due to polygenes. Now, black cats also vary in depth of colour but to a less extent than do blues and, therefore, it may be said that the polygenes involved are modifiers of the expression of the blue gene.

Some people have proposed that where the expression of a gene (particularly, a mutant) is dependent upon the presence of modifiers, these latter produce no effect on the alternative allele (particularly, the wild type). The variation in the shade of blue is a made-to-order example. Superficially, blacks are blacks and that's it! Yet, black cats do vary in intensity but certainly not to the same extent as blues and this fact provides a clue to the variation. The dilution modifiers probably modify the black phenotype but not so much as the blue. The action of the dilution polygenes are "damped down" where the former is concerned but "accentuated" for the latter. This aspect makes it rather difficult to assess the nature of any dilution polygenes carried by a black; whereas, it is fairly obvious that a light blue carries those polygenes lightening (minus alleles) the colour while a dark blue will carry those of opposite tendency (darkening or plus alleles).

In a similar manner, the coat length polygenes may have a greater effect in combination with l than with the type allele L. That is to say, their effects on hair fibre length is accentuated when the fibre has already been lengthened by the l gene. It is as if the normal stabilized development had been upset by the advent of l. Something of this nature is certainly conceivable. This would explain the relative minor effects of the polygenes on the wild type phenotype and yet the apparently greater effects on the mutant phenotype. The dilution polygenes in conjunction with d and the coat length polygenes in conjunction with l. On the other hand, the hair length modifiers may have some effect on the normal coat in view of the extraordinary full coat often shown by the F_1 between a normal coat animal and an exhibition type long hair. This result should be a warning not to generalize too readily with respect to the action of specific polygenes.

However, there is no reason why a definable group of polygenes should not be treated as a genetic entity in its own right. Especially where it can be shown that the group is combining or interacting with more than one gene, since this would mean that the concept of the group as modifiers of a specific gene or phenotype will no longer hold in a rigid sense. Those polygenes responsible for the intensity of yellow pigmentation apparently behave in this manner. In addition to their effects on the yellow phenotype, the quality of the yellow pigment shown by the exhibition Brown Tabby and the Abyssinian, compared with the mongrel tabby, could be ascribed to the group. Also, the variation of the yellowish or tawny suffusion in the mongrel silver and the amount of yellow shown by the Red Siamese could be part of the variation. The thread running throughout these observations is variation in the intensity of yellow pigmentation, whether or not this be against a phenotype provided by the O, C, c^{ch} or c^s genes. The c^{ch} and c^s alleles reduce the amount of yellow in the coat but they do not eliminate it completely and the amount remaining is variable. In this connection, the exhibition silver displays no suffusion. This implies that selection has operated against yellow pigmentation, decreasing the amount to the point of total elimination.

The polygenes decreasing the amount of yellow may reveal themselves in a manner which is interesting enough to be mentioned. When an exhibition silver is crossed with a normal tabby, the offspring are often unusually pale in colour. It is as if the yellow coloration has been diluted (the black pigmentation is normal), such as might occur if C is incompletely dominant to c^{ch}. Now, this is a possibility but, so far at least, it has not been proven. However, the interesting point is this. It is more likely that the polygenes carried by the silver are inherited in a typical blending manner. This means that although C is dominant to c^{ch}, the intensity of yellow pigmentation will be diluted by the action of the polygenes. This sort of polygenic behaviour is not unusual whensoever the phenotype of one of the parents has been selected for extreme expression of a particular feature. The present case involves a colour trait but it may be noted that it parallels the situation described above for crosses with the exhibition long hair.

Apropos colour inheritance, it is necessary to recognize at least three or four groups of polygenes. The first is the group affecting the intensity of yellow and named (at least provisionally) rufous. The second are those modifying the depth of blue pigmentation (dilution group). A third group could be those modifying the depth of chocolate pigmentation, as found in the Chestnut Brown. The variation here is akin to that of the blue since it is possible to have light and dark chocolate coloured animals yet the corresponding blacks scarcely differ. If the dilution and chocolate groups are identical, the dark blue and rich chocolate animals would carry identical polygenes which darken the colour. It is by no means certain that the rufous polygenes are independent of the dilution group. Those polygenes which deepen the yellow to red could be the same as those which darken the other colours. For most purposes, the rufous and dilution groups can be treated as independent, but it is wise to be aware that this may not be so. The last group to be mentioned is that controlling the amount of agouti ticking in the tabby areas of the coat. This is variable and controlled to some extent by polygenes. As far as is known, the ticking polygenes produce no effect upon a non-agouti background.

Almost any feature of the cat which can be sensibly analysed will be found to vary, although not all of the variation will be genetic. The genetic proportion will vary from feature to feature and from strain to strain for the same feature. This explains in part why successful results can be obtained with some individuals and strains but not with others. The genetic variation, in general, will be of a polygenic nature. It may be, in fact, that the feature being studied was created in the first instance by the major gene and all the breeding animals are homozygous for it. This means that the major gene or genes becomes the basic genotype and subsequent modification of the phenotype will depend upon manipulation of the various groups of polygenes. How to attempt this manipulation will be discussed in a subsequent chapter.

Threshold Characters

Polygenic inheritance is usually associated with character which vary smoothly from one extreme of expression to the other. However, it is possible for polygenic variation to be involved with discontinuous variation which, at first sight, may be thought to be under the control of a major gene. The simplest explanation is the concept of a build-up of polygenes which enables a process to be carried past a "developmental threshold" so that a new mode of expression appears. This sort of character is called a "threshold character".

Alternatively, it is possible that a developmental process may fail to be carried through to completion because there are insufficient plus polygenes. Possibly this is a more comprehendable situation. Figure 8 may be pressed into service to exemplify the principle. Suppose that a vital physiological reaction requires the presence of a certain number of plus polygenes for fulfilment and that a population of cats may be represented by the figure. In this figure any individual may contain from one to six plus polygenes, together with a small number of deficient individuals (the 0 class). If the presence of at least one plus polygene is sufficient for full completion of the reaction, then only the zero class individuals will not come up to scratch; in other words, the failure rate will be about 2 per cent. However, suppose at least two plus polygenes are required, then both the 0 and 1 classes will be involved and the rate will rise to about 11 per cent. Therefore, generalizing, if many polygenic loci are involved and the essential polygenic complement varies from strain to strain, it is obvious that the incidence of a threshold character could vary within wide limits. Usually, the incidence is low because most individuals have a gene complement which leads to normal development.

Cases of threshold heredity occur in most domesticated animals and this is the main reason why the topic is mentioned. No definite instance is known for the cat although there is an air of general suspicion that certain gross anomalies could be generated in this manner. Any feature which differs rather sharply from the normal and occurs at a low frequency could be a threshold character. It could also be due, of course, to a mutant gene which is assorting at a low frequency in the cat population at large. This is particularly true if the gene is only partially penetrant, so that the occurrence is not only low but erratic. It is difficult to distinguish between these two situations unless it is possible to carry out precise breeding experiments. In most cases, the genetic diagnosis has to rely upon the known behaviour of similar traits in other animals and a "feeling" for the likely mode of inheritance. This is not scientific, it must be admitted but, if experiments are excluded and an explanation is still sought, this is the only line of approach.

It is perhaps just as well that cat breeders are not likely to be called upon to deal with threshold characters, for their manipulation can be tricky. However, for those who wish to delve deeper, Falconer (1960) has devoted a whole chapter to the topic and this excellent account should be consulted.

IV. BREEDING PRACTICE

IT is entirely possible to breed cats without concerning oneself with quality nor complying with any particular system of mating. However, this sort of behaviour is not breeding in any worthwhile sense. It is scarcely removed from cat rearing since anyone can have a male and a few queens about the house and nature will do the rest. As cat breeders, it behoves us to do better than that. This means that certain animals are favoured to others and that no matings are allowed until careful consideration is given to the outcome. That is, the good and bad points of the individual cats are assessed and weighed against each other and the pairings arranged with the motive of improving the cats. With pedigree animals, the prime motives are usually two, improvement of the standard of the breed and success in the show pen against the best efforts of other breeders.

The skill of cat breeding resides in the choice of animals and how these may be mated with each other. Not everyone may regard these two acts as being separate but they should be so regarded, particularly if the subject is tackled analytically. True, they are complementary to each other and this is the correct way to view the situation. The choice of animal for breeding is embodied in the concept of "selection" and the mating of the selected animals as the "breeding system."

The main factors in the practice of animal breeding are shown by Fig. 17. The phenotype of the individual is made up of a large number of genetic characters of varying expression. The ideal animal is one in which the expression of each of these characters is just right in the eyes of the breeder. This means that an intermediate expression will be required for some but an extreme expression for others. The expression is controlled by selective breeding, of which there are several kinds. The simplest is choice of the individual but selection can take in whole families and extend into progeny testing. Side by side with selection and reinforcing the process, there is the system of mating, which includes inbreeding of strong or moderate intensity, the mating of like to like and

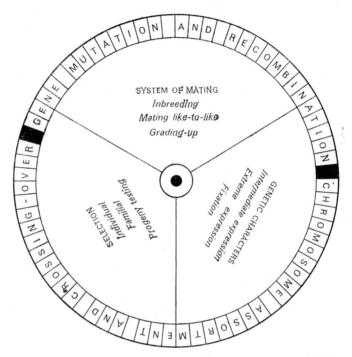

FIG. 17. The main factors of animal breeding portrayed as a wheel of chance.
The breeder's art resides in the skilful manipulation of these to bring together
genes which will engender the ideal individual.

the grading up of poor quality animals. These are some of the tools which
are at the disposal of the breeder should he so wish to use them. Just
how they may be used and which ones are most suitable for particular
problems is the substance of this chapter.

Selective breeding is by far the most potent factor, whether this be
straightforward selection with no frills or one of the more sophisticated
methods. The evidence for this is the existence of the various breeds of
cats. Not so much that of coat colour (this can be easily juggled around)
but that of body conformation which cannot be so easily manipulated
though it is the real basis of breed differentiation. Among domesticated
animals, the dog furnishes the finest examples of such differences. The
differences between the larger hounds and the diminutive toy breeds is
truly remarkable and testifies to the efficiency of selection. Yet selection

alone is not enough. Breeds of animal breed relatively true otherwise they would not be worthy of the name. It might be thought that selection is responsible for this property. This is true to some extent but it is doubtful if it is the whole truth.

Selection by itself is not very efficient in eliminating heterozygous genotypes (the producers of deviating forms). Inbreeding is consistently more efficient in this respect. Not necessarily close inbreeding but the moderate form which results from mating of not too distantly related animals. It may come as a surprise but some inbreeding is essential during the formation of a breed in order that the conformation should stabilize around a definite type. Later, there can be some relaxation, but not too much, otherwise phenotypic divergence will occur. Those individuals which diverge too much are either not bred from or are mated to a typical animal of the breed. In general, a breed stabilizes itself and moves forward as an entity because the majority of animals tend to be descended from, or are bred to, a small group of elite animals commonly regarded as the most outstanding specimens (rosette winners and champions of various kinds). Quite often these are inter-related to a greater degree than the ordinary members of the breed. In short, the breeders who have worked to produce these outstanding specimens are exceedingly choosy in their mating and bitter experience has taught them the inadvisability of straying too far from the basic blood lines of the breed.

Selection and the Total Score

Selection of breeding stock can take a surprising number of forms. However, these all have one object in view, viz. the raising of the general quality of the stock. It is methods of selection which differ and this is where the skill of the animal breeder can be taxed in an endeavour to choose between the various methods and to fit these in with other factors which have to be considered. Most people have an idea of what is meant by selection but probably only a vague idea of the methods which can be brought to bear.

An important factor in selection is its intensity. It is not always easy to assess the strength of selection for all traits but a very convenient measure is that of calculating the proportion of kittens kept back for breeding. For example, a round of litters from one male and four queens could produce 16 kittens, out of which it might be decided to keep two queens as replacements for two of the mothers. This represents a selection intensity of two-sixteenths or 6 per cent. However, suppose, a second round of 16 kittens is produced by the same parents and two of the best kittens from the first are kept back for comparison with the second. Selection of the two best females would now represent a 3 per cent intensity. It is very desirable to have as many young as possible among which to pick and choose since, in many cases, the amount of progress by selection is closely related to the intensity. This is common sense, but is sometimes overlooked when other (extraneous!) factors have to be considered, such as cost of feeding and housing.

The simplest form of selection is that of individual merit, based almost entirely upon appearance. This is basic, regardless of whatever refinements may be employed. The first requirement is that the animal should be healthy, as shown by good growth, freedom from disease and lively behaviour. If a male, he should be morphologically normal, display keen interest in the oestrous female and be persistent in coitus. He should have a high rate of fertile matings. If a female, she should come into heat regularly, have easy parturitions, bring forth normal and healthy young in average numbers, and be able to rear these unaided. Some of the above items can only be seen after the animal has been bred which means that certain parts of the selective process have to be deferred. Reproductive performance is so important that it may be thought superfluous to mention the topic. Unfortunately, in the sorting out of the many traits which have to be selected, reproduction is not always given the priority it deserves. It is scarcely good policy to breed a superlative strain only to find that it is held in low esteem because of either poor health or reproduction.

The most spectacular results are obtained where it is possible to select for a single well-defined character. These are situations which produce the nice arcing curves of the results of selection to be found in genetic textbooks. In most cases, the practical breeder may find that he has to settle for something less. There are several reasons for this, of which three may be singled out. The first is lack of facilities in terms of space and time. Many breeders plead this but not always convincingly. It is largely a question of making do with the best that can be provided. If a breeder intends to breed cats, the job may as well be tackled properly and full use made of the available facilities. The second reason is to have a clearly defined objective in mind from the start. For most people, this will mean cats excelling in all of the fine qualities of the breed of their choice. Fair enough, then this means a close study of the standard of excellence for the breed and of those animals judged to be the best available. One's own stock should now be critically compared with these animals. This is the moment of truth and, the more objective the comparison, the more quickly can something be done to correct any failings which are evident.

Thirdly, the breeder is rarely in a position where he can concentrate entirely on one character. All sorts of characters have to be considered simultaneously if all round excellence is to be achieved. There are three methods of setting about the problem. It might seem feasible to work on one feature at a time. Proceeding to the next only when the first have been raised to a sufficiently high standard. This is the so-called "tandem" method. The main objections to the method are the time required to produce worthwhile results for several characters and the real danger that the progress achieved with the early characters will be lost while the later ones are being dealt with.

A second procedure is to decide that any animal which falls below a given standard in any one character will be discarded. This is known as the method of "independent culling levels". The method is easy to apply and can be surprisingly effective, provided the breeder does not weaken in his resolve. As the culling levels rise with the improvement of the strain, so the selection becomes more stringent. Note, that the culling level need not be the same for each character. Some are not so important as others and some may need more drastic selection to realize the same results. All of these aspects should be considered. In fact, the more well thought-out the plan of action, the greater the overall improvement is likely to be.

An advantage of the method is that it necessitates a careful appraisal of the number of characters which can be dealt with and of their variation. The number of characters which can be effectively managed is limited and this implies that priorities have to be worked out. The manner in which the chosen characters vary individually has to be analysed in order to grade the animals as being above or below the culling level. The most serious objection to the method is that, on occasion, it may be too ruthless. It may be unwise to totally reject an animal possessing several admirable qualities just because it falls below a certain culling level in one character. To counter this argument, a third more flexible method has been devised.

The third method is that of the "total score" or "selection index" and it is the most efficient of the three. In company with the preceding method, it requires that the contribution of each character to the ideal cat be carefully assessed. The variation of each character should be graded by a convenient scale of points. The composition of the scale should be as accurate as possible without becoming unduly fussy. Even a simple grading of very poor (1), poor (2), average (3), good (4) and very good (5) gives a 5-point numerical scale. However, an endeavour should be made to do better than that and it is recommended that each animal should be scored against a 10-point judging scale, ranging from 1 for the lowest to 10 for the tip-top grade of expression of the character. The value of the scale will depend largely on the competence of the breeder in grading his charges. If in doubt, it may be wise to seek advice on this question from experienced judges.

Now, with the total score method, the problem of imposing a limit on the number of characters is not quite as important. In fact, it might be advisable to include as many as possible because it is difficult to foretell how a minor feature may turn out to be of first-rate importance. In this event, it is useful to be able to check on how the feature has been varying in past generations. In practice, a limit is set by the amount of time which can be devoted to the calculation of the index. The reason why a large number of characters can be considered is because the next step is to rank these by a system of "weights". These are numerical coefficients which reveal the relative importance of the various traits in the breeder's estimation. These are necessary because the points scoring of expression of each character cannot take this factor into account. This makes the total score two-tiered and this is a real advantage. The scale of points should be relatively unchanging, provided it is objectively drawn-up in the first instance, whereas, it may be necessary to change the coefficients from time to time in order to give greater emphasis to certain characters. For example, if a certain feature is showing no signs of improvement, the coefficient for it could be increased so that individuals with exceptionally good expression would score slightly higher. It must be warned, however, that the values of the coefficients should not be changed except for good cause.

The working of the method can probably be best explained by an illustration. There is no special virtue in the choice of characters considered nor in the values of the coefficients, since these must be chosen by the breeder for his particular cats and the task he has set himself. Suppose the following characters are graded: health (condition) (H), coat colour

(CC), coat texture (CT), body build (BB), head shape (HS), feet (F) and tail (T). Now, the relative importance of these seven features might be assessed as follows:

Total score $= 5\,H + 4\,CC + 3\,DT + 3\,BB + 2\,HS + F + T.$

That is to say, head shape is considered to be twice as important as either feet or tail and so forth. Health is ranked as the most important item and this is how it should be. All of the animals in the stud are doubtless healthy but giving it a high coefficient means that a weakly individual will be heavily penalized. To calculate the total score, each cat is appraised and graded on a 10-point scale for each character. The maximum total would be 190 but no animal would be expected to attain this exalted level.

Table 5 shows how eight cats might be evaluated according to the above formula. Cat A scores highly because it happens to be exceptionally good in the important character CC and CT although it is mediocre in other respects. Compare the score with that for cat C which graded highly for several unimportant traits but low on the important ones, thus producing a relatively low score. This shows how the coefficients will adjust the point rating in this respect. The best all-round cat is B, followed closely, perhaps by C. Individuals C, D and E tend to be similar, somewhat above average, animals, and, without the total score, it might be difficult to rank these in order of preference. This aspect reveals the discrimination possessed by the method. It should be noted that cat F is a fine animal except that it suffered an attack of undefinable sickness which makes its health suspect. This fact has reduced the total score rather

TABLE 5. AN EXAMPLE OF CALCULATING TOTAL SCORES AS AN AID TO SELECTIVE BREEDING. (See text for meaning of the character abbreviations)

Cat	Point grading for each character							Total score or Selection index
	H	CC	CT	BB	HS	F	T	
A	10	10	10	6	5	5	5	158
B	10	8	7	7	7	8	8	154
C	10	6	7	6	8	9	9	147
D	10	6	6	7	8	6	5	140
E	10	6	6	7	7	6	6	139
F	6	7	7	8	6	7	7	129
G	10	5	6	6	5	5	5	126
H	10	5	4	4	5	5	5	114

sharply; had the cat been fully healthy, its score would have been as high as 149.

The table indicates the ranking of the eight cats for potential value to the breeding programme in terms of the total score. If three animals are required for the next generation, these would be A, B and C. Now, it might be interesting to compare this choice with that obtained by the use of the method of independent culling levels. Since only three individuals are required, the culling level will have to be rather high. If all animals which score grade 5 or less are eliminated, cats B, C, E and F remain or if all animals which grade 6 or less are eliminated, only cat 3 remains. Thus, the method does not possess the fine discrimination shown by the total score. In this example, cat F could be eliminated on the grounds of its suspected health and this leaves the three wanted animals. However, this is an arbitrary choice, taken after the selective processes had been completed which should have properly assessed the health factor in the first place.

It may be particularly noted that cat A is totally rejected since it grades poorly in several characters, in spite of its exceptional rating in the important traits CC and CT. Also, cat D is possibly unfairly discriminated against, though admittedly this is a debatable point. A refinement would be to vary the culling levels, being more stringent against the important traits and less so against the unimportant. To do this, however, is to move the practical application of the culling method closer to that of the total score but without quite gaining the flexibility of the latter. It might be worthwhile to employ the total score without more ado.

The total score is essentially an aid to selection and its value is no greater than (a) the ability of the breeder in defining the characters which are important for the task in hand, (b) his skill in grading and (c) the correct balance between the weighting coefficients. Instruction in the calculation is necessary for a person taking up the method for the first time but a "feeling" of a soundly constructed score only comes from experience. The example given above is probably crude in that it may be advisable to consider more characters, such as eye-colour and temperament. Also, it should be feasible to sub-divide those considered as one becomes more adept at grading. Coat colour (CC), for instance, could be further analysed in depth of colour (shade), tone quality and evenness of colour over the whole body.

Those readers who are familiar with the construction of selection indices may query the arbitrariness of the choice of weighting coefficients for the total score described above. It is possible to derive coefficients which are related to the innate qualities of the total variation and which should maximize the hoped-for improvement. Unfortunately, the derivation of these coefficients is beyond the level of this book. Details of the theory which underlies the derivation and their practical calculation may be found in Lerner (1958), a book which has many interesting things to say on the whole topic of selection.

Family Selection and Progeny Testing

Selection is normally practised against the individual and this will always be the basis of selective breeding. However, selection may also be applied against a litter or a series of litters from the same parents. This is "familial" selection and, if it can be carried out, the effectiveness of the selection is enhanced. It can be applied regardless of the method employed, whether this be that of culling levels or the total score. The total score lends itself more easily to familial selection since it provides a numerical value from which to find an average.

Ordinary selection usually ignores familial relationships, the more superior animals being chosen from all litters. However, a critical appraisal would take into account the capability of certain pairings to produce better offspring on the average than others. The appraisal could take one or two forms, that of noting which pairings have the highest number of young above a certain level of excellence or that of deriving an average. Should the total score be in use, the latter can be calculated by summing the individual scores and dividing by the number of young. The parents with the highest average are clearly those producing the better offspring. These are the individuals upon which to concentrate. Further young should be obtained from these parents and preference should be given to their offspring. Indeed, to carry familial selection through to its logical conclusion, those parents which have produced the inferior litters should be discarded, together with their young. The effectiveness of familial selection stems from the fact that the selection is acting somewhat more drastically upon the genetic constitution than is possible by selection upon individual phenotype.

Quite often the same breeders are involved, the offspring being produced by different combinations of parents, some of which have resulted in better average offspring than others (a phenomenon known as "nicking"). In this case, those combinations which have produced the inferior offspring need not be repeated. This sort of difference can be deliberately exploited to reveal differences in breeding capability. Normally, queens cannot be examined in this manner because individually it is impossible to obtain enough young in a reasonable time. However, in theory at least, two or more stud males can be investigated. The procedure is to obtain a round of litters with several females from one male and a further round of litters with the same females from a second male. A comparison of the quality of each round of litters could be revealing as regards the breeding ability of the different males. This is "progeny testing" in one of its more direct forms, whereby the breeding worth of a male is determined by the average quality of his offspring.

Familial selection in conjunction with one of the systems of mating to be described in a subsequent section stand to give the maximum results. In particular, a comparison of the average total score for the offspring of two or more sib mating lines could indicate that one is consistently inferior. The breeder should consider abandoning this line and forming two separate lines from the superior. Two or more closed studs composed of a few animals could be similarly dealt with. This is "group selection". In both of the above cases, the procedure is to commence with more than one sib mating line or closed stud of a few individuals and, at an appropriate stage, make a comparison to ascertain if one line or group has made greater improvement than the other.

It is possible to combine familial selection with sib mating in the following way. A male can be mated with several sisters and the offspring for each litter be examined for the average score. The individuals for the next generation being chosen from the pair with the highest score. In any event, it is unwise to keep only two animals to continue a sib mating line since one may die and the line would come to a premature end. A male (or even two if so desired) and several sisters could be selected on merit for each generation and the availability of the extra animals put to good use. Be careful not to choose animals from different parents otherwise the mating would no longer be that of brother to sister.

The closed stud method of breeding is readily adaptable to progeny testing of the male when two or three are kept. This system requires a fairly constant number of females per generation and a point should be made of breeding a round of litters from each male in succession. Examination of the average score for each round of litters could indicate that one male is siring better (or worse) offspring than the others. It is also possible that certain combinations of male and female are producing exceptional litters, but this may not be easily established because of the small number of young per litter. A litter of exceptional young could be due to chance. It is probably better to rely upon the results from the whole series belonging to one male. Though litters may be procured from several males, it may be desirable to restrict the selection of animals for the next generation to those of one or two males. Obviously, the choice would be from the offspring of the male (or males) with the highest average score. In this manner, familial selection (by means of progeny testing) can be combined with some degree of inbreeding, with probably more fruitful results than if either is used alone.

The Stud Male and Grading-up

The stud male is the most important member of the cattery. Not because of his sex nor because characters are inherited more strongly via the male. The reason is statistical. A stud male can sire many more kittens than a queen can ever hope to produce. It follows, therefore, that a breeder should be particularly choosy in the choice of male. Fortunately, it is possible to be more selective of males because fewer are required. In general, this means insistence on at least as high a standard for the male as the best of the females or a higher standard whenever this can be managed.

For various practical reasons, not everyone can keep a male cat and the practice of placing exceptional animals at open stud has become common. This benefits the owner financially and the fancy as a whole by raising the overall quality of the breed. When circumstances warrant it, there should be no hesitation in taking advantage of the services of these males. The only problem which may doubtless arise is which male to use? The fact that the male is a well-known champion does not necessarily mean that he is the most suitable animal. For instance, he may have the same faults (despite his championship status) as the breeder is wishing to correct in his own stock. It is sound policy to visit shows and examine the various males on exhibition and to assess the good and bad features of each one. One or more should emerge as the appropriate mate for certain queens and arrangements can be made accordingly for a visit.

Queens may be sent to males at open stud for various reasons. Probably the more common is a desire for general improvement, especially if the queen is not outstanding in any way. Improvement in this manner is known as "grading-up", a term which may be used to denote most policies of mating mediocre stock to superior animals. The matings are usually repeated for more than one generation (i.e. backcrosses) in an attempt to firmly impress the superior qualities. This may not always succeed since this aspect is dependent upon the degree of purebreeding of the superior animal. This problem is discussed in more detail later since "pureness" of breeding is closely related to the amount of inbreeding which the superior stock has undergone. The backcrossing should be immediately halted should it become apparent that a general improvement is no longer occurring. However, leaving this aspect in abeyance, grading-up is the quickest method for the improvement of mediocre animals and one which can be recommended to the novice breeder. Superb exhibition stock is usually scarce and expensive, and the beginner often has to be content with lesser animals. These are not to be despised, especially if derived from a reputable strain and, correctly mated, could produce very good kittens.

Another important reason for sending queens to outside males is that of improvement of specific traits. If the breeder's animals have many good qualities already, extreme care has to be taken not to upset these while the new features are being incorporated. The whole situation has to be handled very adroitly, both the choice of mates and in the subsequent breeding. Unlike general grading-up these outcrosses are not necessarily repeated, since it is not a general improvement which is being sought. Much will depend upon whether the specific trait shows a desirable change and if this can be incorporated into the stock without either deterioration or less of the good points it now has. To do this, it may be better to inter-breed the offspring, rather than to outcross again.

It should be obvious that the next move does not lend itself to any worthwhile generalization. Only the breeder, with full knowledge of his cats, can decide. So much depends on the problem being tackled and the animal's response to the outcross. If the offspring show deterioration, this may be a sign that the outcross has not been successful and an outcross to another male might be the best policy.

Selection for Intermediate Versus Extreme Expression

Selection of characters falls into one of two categories; that of selecting for an intermediate degree of expression or selection for extreme expression. Now, since many different characteristics make up the ideal animal, this can mean that both sorts of selection may be operating at the same time. This is unfortunate, since the two forms of selection require different handling if each is to achieve maximum success. In the case of intermediate expression, the selection will be that of eliminating animals which deviate most from the optimum. More than anything else, it is a matter of fixing the character so that as many cats as possible will possess it. The quickest means of achieving this is by close inbreeding.

Selection for extreme expression, on the other hand, implies striving for something not yet obtained or found in only a few individuals. Extreme expression is displayed only by genotypes containing a large number of genes having either plus or minus effects with regard to the character (depending on which end of the scale is being considered). These genotypes are only formed by gathering together the appropriate plus or minus genes which are scattered throughout the general population. Something of this nature must be the situation otherwise the extreme expression would be common. This means searching for and breeding from any animal with a phenotype tending in the right direction in the hope that different polygenes are brought in and combined to bring into existence offspring of more extreme expression than that of the parents. This is the underlying mechanism, in principle at least. To achieve this, it is desirable to have individuals heterozygous for as many genes as possible, despite the fact that the selection will tend to pick out homozygotes. In other words, too early a decrease in the proportion of heterozygotes will hinder the free recombination of genes which is essential for the formation of the extreme phenotypes.

Here lies the conflict. For fixation of intermediate expression, the heterozygotes should be eliminated; for the realization of ever more extreme expression, the maximum number of heterozygous loci are required. A compromise must be found. This usually takes the form of a moderate amount of inbreeding—combined with intense selection—in the hope that there will be a steady fixation of intermediate characters but not too quickly so that there can be some progress towards extreme expression in other characters. The mediator is the breeding system which can be so arranged that the amount of inbreeding can be high, moderate or weak. How this can be managed is the main topic of succeeding sections.

Systems of Mating

As a prelude, it might be wise to consider what is meant by random mating, the antithesis of inbreeding. Most mongrel cats are representatives of random mating in the sense that there is an absence of control. With fancy cats, the situation is different. The matings are controlled and may in fact be carefully regulated in the choice of animal. Yet, as far as the array of genes is concerned and taking into account that the various breeders will be acting independently of one another, effectively, there will be random mating. Random mating in a strict sense implies the odd mating of brother to sister and other, less close, matings of related animals. Some of the closer matings may be studiously avoided by many people but perhaps not by everyone as an occasional event. Therefore, the assumption of random mating is not unreasonable.

Ordinarily speaking, inbreeding means the pairing together of closely related animals. This is so, though in practice the actual mating should be specified since this determines the relative intensity of inbreeding. Some forms of inbreeding can be regarded as close, others as less so, and still others as quite mild. The rate of inbreeding can be roughly assessed for most systems of mating and can be used as a measure of its strength. This is an advantage, since in some circumstances it might be desirable to inbreed closely and, in others, less closely.

Inbreeding may be the act of mating of individuals of various degrees of kinship but what does the process achieve? Briefly, if continued for generations, it will produce ever increasing homogeneity in the offspring. That is to say, genetically, the offspring will become more and more alike in appearance and general behaviour. This is because the common ancestry causes many of the same genes to be received by different individuals. The limitation in number of different ancestors and the absence of out-crossing are the key factors. Therefore, there is a tendency for the offspring to receive the same genes from each parent and to become progressively more homozygous.

The proportion of homozygotes in an inter-breeding group of animals is known as "homozygosis". Conversely, the proportion of heterozygotes is known as the "heterozygosis". These two terms are merely the opposite faces of the same coin but both are in use because some people like to speak of an increase in homozygosis while others of a decrease in heterozygosis. Crudely put, the proportion of homozygosis represents the "purity" of the group while the heterozygosis represents the "impurity". In this immediate context, group can mean either a strain or a breed.

One of the closest forms of inbreeding is that of mating of full brothers and sisters or sib mating for short. Since the inbreeding is intense, easily appreciated and can be quickly put into practice, the consequences of repeated sib mating have been carefully investigated. The breeding scheme is simple enough, the best individuals from the same parents (not necessarily belonging to the same litter, though it is an added convenience if they are) are paired together. The result is a decrease in the amount of heterozygosis as shown by Table 6. The interpretation of the table is as follows. After one generation of inbreeding, the proportion of heterozygosis is 75 per cent of what it was before inbreeding began, after two generations, the amount is 63 per cent and so on. After 10 generations, the reduction has reached 11 per cent.

TABLE 6. THE STEADY DECREASE OF HETEROZYGOSIS FOR SUCCESSIVE GENERATIONS OF SIB MATING

Generation	Percentage	Generation	Percentage
1	75	7	22
2	63	8	17
3	50	9	14
4	41	10	11
5	33	11	9
6	27	12	7

The figures given in the table are those expected, calculated for each generation starting from scratch. The successive values show that the decrease is a little unsteady for the first few generations but then the ratio of decrease becomes relatively constant. It is convenient to ignore the initial unsteadiness and to consider that the constant ratio of decrease will be characteristic of the type of inbreeding. The ratio could be regarded as an average over the generations and, for sib mating, the ratio is 81 per cent. This ratio somewhat overestimates the decrease for the early generations and this fact may be borne in mind. As will be seen later, the ability to describe the intensity of inbreeding by a simple ratio (an index, if you like) has certain advantages when the relative usefulness of close versus mild inbreeding and other problems are discussed.

There is one other system of pairing which is very similar to sib mating and its average effect on heterozygosis. This is where certain offspring are chosen to pair with the younger parent. That is, a given individual is mated twice, once to its younger parent and once to its offspring. For example, suppose the mother was the younger parent, then a suitable son would be selected as her next mate. From the offspring of this mating, a daughter would be chosen to continue the line and so on. The ratio of decrease of heterozygosis is 81 per cent per generation, as for sib mating. Although the two systems of mating have the same ratio, they should not be intermixed if the object of the inbreeding is to bring about the maximum amount of homozygosis in the shortest time. When the two systems are intermixed, the ratio is 84 per cent whenever a changeover is made from one system to the other.

Another regular system of mating is where a male may be mated to two half-sisters who are full sisters of each other. Three individuals are involved in each generation and two series of litters. The procedure is as follows. A male is paired with two females to produce two litters (or series of litters if a wider range of offspring are desired from which to choose the next generation, provided the same male and female are paired). From one litter, a male is selected while the other litter contributes the two females. The system is self-perpetuating, since it should not be difficult to find two females per generation, yet the rearing of two litters (or sires) allows a wider choice of offspring per generation than is possible with either sib mating or mating back to the younger parent (one litter or single series). The ratio of decline of heterozygosis is less than that for the latter systems but still respectable, with the value of 87 per cent.

The above methods of inbreeding are said to be regular, mainly because animals are paired according to set rules. A more flexible system may be held to be desirable in many cases. Many breeders will have at least one male and a variable number of females. Now, inbreeding may be practised with these, provided the stud is closed to outsiders. No new stock is brought in and no queens are sent out for mating. The animals for the next generation must be chosen from litters born within the stud. No rules need to be laid down that certain animals be mated to others. Indeed, these are purposefully waived to give the maximum freedom of pairing.

This is the "closed stud" method of breeding and is similar to that used by many people in their ordinary breeding. It differs from ordinary breeding, however, not only in the exclusion of outside influences but also in that there is no overlapping of generations. Each male and his retinue of queens are chosen afresh each generation. Any backcrossing of daughter to the father, for example, will result in a retardation of the trend towards homozygosis. In general, the matings will be between half brother and sister if the number of males are small.

The closed stud method will lead to a decline in heterozygosis because of the limited number of parents within each generation. In fact, the intensity of the inbreeding varies according to the number of parents as shown by Fig. 18. This gives values of the ratio of decline of heterozygosis for different numbers of males and females. It is worthwhile to study the values of the ratio since a decided tendency is apparent. The decline is only appreciable if the number of males and females are kept quite small. From a practical viewpoint, the number of males is the important item. With one male and one female, it is only possible to carry out sib mating, and the figure shows that this has the quickest decline of heterozygosis. With one male and successive additions of females, the decline can still be reasonable up to about six, and possibly not all that unreasonable for larger numbers. However, the situation changes rather abruptly even for the addition of one extra male. The value of the ratio rises until the decline is so small that very many generations are required to reduce the heterozygosis. In effect, the amount of inbreeding is so miniscule that it need scarcely be considered as such.

The decline of heterozygosis over the generations can be approximately calculated by successive multiplication of the appropriate ratio for any size of closed stud. In this way, a series of percentages can be derived which are comparable to that tabulated for sib mating. The use of the ratio probably over-estimates the decline for the first few generations but the decline is doubtless accurate enough to provide a comparison between studs of different sizes. For example, the decline for a typical stud of one male and five females will approximate the following pattern. After one generation, the amount of heterozygosis is reduced to 87 per cent of what it was formerly; after two generations, the proportion remaining is 76 per cent; and after five generations, it has fallen to 50 per cent. It is of interest to be able to judge the effectiveness of any size of stud and this can be gauged by finding the number of generations necessary to reduce the proportion of initial heterozygosis by 50 per cent. This is shown

FIG. 18. The ratio of decrease of heterozygosis for various numbers of males and females for the closed stud breeding system.

by Table 7 for sib mating and several studs composed of different numbers of males and females. The fewer generations required, the more effective the inbreeding. Sib mating is obviously the most efficient and the effectiveness of the other systems is inversely related to the number of animals involved.

TABLE 7. THE NUMBER OF GENERATIONS REQUIRED TO HALVE THE PROPORTION OF HETEROZYGOSIS WITH VARIOUS BREEDING SYSTEMS

System	No. gens.	System	No. gens.
Sib mating	3	1 M and many F	6
1 M and 2 sisters	5	2 M and 6 F	8·8
1 M and 3 F	4·6	2 M and many F	11·4
1 M and 5 F	5	Group of 4 cousins	8·3
1 M and 8 F	5·5	Group of 8 cousins	18·9

Note: M = number of males, F = number of females.

The question whether or not to inbreed can be a difficult one to answer. However, one aspect is certain: if a breeder wishes to found his own strain with its own particular characteristics and uniformity of offspring, some measure of inbreeding is essential. The reason is that a high level of homozygosis cannot be attained in any other manner. Selection cannot do it. It can do so spuriously in the sense that the parents may be alike in appearance because a certain type are selected. But what of the offspring? These may be variable, with only the odd individual tending to resemble the parents. In breeders' jargon, inbreeding is necessary to "fix" the characteristics which are being selected. The appropriate genetic term is "fixation" of genes.

There is little doubt that inbreeding is valuable in stabilizing the results of selection. Does this imply that the inbreeding should be deferred until the selective breeding has proved successful or should it accompany and perhaps even aid the selection? There is something to be said for deferring inbreeding for a few generations, largely because the most significant results of selection are usually achieved during the early stages. Later, it is often a case of consolidating gains and seeking to make improvements which are less easily realized. This is where the inbreeding could commence. The merit of this policy is that it is simple and straightforward. The selection is not relaxed and the inbreeding is initiated whenever the breeder decides it is most opportune.

However, this is not the whole story. It might be pertinent to examine more closely what inbreeding can do. In practice, there are two systems to consider seriously. These are sib mating and the closed stud method (the latter usually centering on one or two specially chosen males per generation). Now, sib mating is the most intense form of inbreeding and engenders the most rapid increase of homozygosis. From the viewpoint of fixing a characteristic, it would produce the quickest results. However, this fixing of characteristics is double-edged. While it is desirable to have fixation of characters, once these are fixed, further progress is impossible. The characteristics of the strain are frozen in one mould, so to speak, and further selective breeding will have little effect. Should the animals of the strain be of a high order of excellence, the fixation may be deemed an advantage. Yet the cost must be considered. It may be that the fixation occurred before the full potentiality of the strain had been realized. No matter how excellent the strain may be, some faults are likely to be present and these are fixed as well.

What has happened is that the rapid increase in homozygosis has fixed both good and bad points with fine impartiality. On balance, the good points may predominate because the selective breeding has picked out the better individuals and these have left their impact. Now, suppose the increase has occurred less rapidly? In other words, if a less intense form of inbreeding had been adopted, it might have been possible to emphasize the good features of the strain still further and have eliminated more of the bad points before too much fixation had occurred. This is indeed so. A balance has to be struck between a rate of increase of homozygosis which will bring about fixation of desirable traits yet allow scope for the elimination of the undesirable. This is where the closed stud system has an advantage, for the intensity of inbreeding there is invariably less than that of sib mating.

In the majority of cases, the closed stud system of breeding will centre around one or perhaps two males. More than two males may be used but then the rate of loss of heterozygosity is very slow; possibly too slow except for very long-term projects. Should one male and a number of females constitute the stud, the inbreeding will be moderately high; the actual level being determined by the number of females. The king-pin being the common father which tends to hold the stud together. Within each generation, the actual individuals retained for breeding will be determined by the method of selection employed and the number of females required. A fair number of kittens should be obtained from each pairing in order that the intensity of selection can be reasonably high. In this manner, the two main factors in animal breeding will be operating simultaneously, one shaping the general appearance and quality of the strain and the other tending to fix these characteristics.

With the stud system, the temptation may be to backcross the daughters to the father, rather than to chose a male for the next generation. This temptation should be resisted unless the male is especially outstanding in some respect. The approach to homozygosis will be held up, particularly if the backcross is made during the early stages. This could mean a hold-up in the establishment of the strain by a generation or two. It is difficult to generalize in matters of this nature since the key-note of breeding is the ability to be flexible and to balance the results of one action against those of another.

Sometimes it may prove to be impossible to maintain a constant number of breeding animals per generation. One individual may regretfully die or two or more may be of such a high standard that it is decided to retain all of them for breeding. Could this have much of an effect on the progress towards homozygosis? If the numbers do not vary very much, the answer is no; as might be seen by the roughly similar values of the ratio given by adjacent entries in Fig. 18. On the other hand, should the numbers fluctuate rather widely, then a significant effect will emerge. Over a series of generations, the smaller numbers will have a more than proportionate influence over the larger. The simplest method of treating the problem would be to obtain the appropriate ratio for each generation and to multiply these together. This procedure will give the approximate percentage of remaining heterozygosity. For example, suppose that over a period of seven generations, a stud had consisted of a single male and the following number of females: 3, 4, 5, 6, 10, 12 and 15. The remaining proportion of heterozygosis would be estimated at 39 per cent. Now, the same reduction would be achieved by a stud of one male and a constant number of six females for each of the generations.

The difference between repeated sib mating and the closed stud is that the former leads to rapid fixation of all traits (sometimes so quickly as to block further progress by selective breeding) while the latter allows greater scope for selection to do its work but requires more generations for the stud to become true-breeding. On balance, the close inbreeding of sib mating might appear to be too drastic. Yet, there is another aspect of this form of inbreeding which has not been considered. Sib mating only requires two individuals per generation and this means that it may be possible to have more than one sib mating line in the cattery. Three of four such lines could be bred concurrently without too much trouble, whereas, the keeping of two or more separate studs could be difficult unless the number in each stud is restricted or the cattery is large.

The keeping of two or more sib mating lines has its advantages. The stud system carries the breeding group along as a whole, each individual tending towards the general average. The situation is otherwise for a series of sib mating lines. The rapid approach to complete homozygosis often induces a greater exposure of latent variation which can be seized upon by selective breeding. The outcome is phenotypic divergence between the inbred lines, some of which could be superior to the general average. Some may emerge as better than the results obtained by the stud system. It is difficult to be certain of the latter, of course, but the point to be made is this: the full benefit of sib mating cannot be realized unless several lines are bred in parallel. Should one line fall behind the others in overall quality, it should be discarded and replaced by a splitting of the best line into two. In this manner, the number of lines are maintained and selection can operate at two levels, between individuals within each line and between lines. This may sound complicated but it is not; it is only making the fullest possible use of selection to raise the standard of one's cats.

Should the occasion arise that the ratio of decline of heterozygosity need be calculated more exactly than that given here or for numbers of males and females not given in the table, the following formula may be used:

$$\text{ratio} = \tfrac{1}{2}\left\{1 - 2A + \sqrt{(4A^2 + 1)}\right\}$$

where $A = (M+F)/8MF$ and $M =$ number of males and $F =$ number of females. If the number of generations to reduce the initial heterozygosis by half is required for this ratio, the following may be used:

$$\text{No. of generations} = \frac{0.301}{\log (\text{ratio})^{-1}}$$

The ratio of decline of heterozygosis which has been given for various systems of inbreeding should not be taken too literally for several reasons. The ratio is quite general in that it is independent of the initial proportion of heterozygosis, and of the total number of genes, for most practical purposes. It applies particularly to autosomal genes but less accurately to sex-linked genes. However, for some systems, the ratio is similar for both sets of genes and, in others, the discrepancy is small. Since sex-linked genes are in a minority, the error is negligible unless the inbreeding is continued for a very long period which is an unlikely prospect. Another discrepancy could arise from selective breeding favouring the most vigorous and healthy animals and this may select out the more heterozygous individuals. As a result, the progress towards homozygosity may not be as quick as the ratio would indicate. However, only in exceptional circumstances, would a large difference emerge and, therefore, the ratio may be regarded as a useful index to the amount of inbreeding which will be taking place.

Grading-up and Prepotency

The extremely useful process of grading-up by the use of an outstanding male has two facets. One is that of gaining the genes which make the male so outstanding and the other is to raise the average quality of the stud. The likelihood of success of the latter is dependent upon the degree of homozygosis of the male. Repeated backcrossing of the females is a form of inbreeding since the successive matings are that of daughter, grand-daughter, great-grand-daughter, etc., and this is contributing towards the grading-up. The repeated backcrossing alone, however, is not sufficient.

The decrease of heterozygosis is rapid but it does not lead to complete homozygosis unless the pivoted male is highly inbred. Initially, assume that the male is derived from an inbred strain and is largely homozygous. The decrease in the heterozygosis of the mediocre stock is 50 per cent for each generation. After only a few backcrosses, it would be expected that the offspring will come to take on some of the superior qualities of the male. Furthermore, should the male inadvertently die, another male (a son from the same strain, say) could be substituted and the backcrossing continued. The limit would be stock resembling the inbred strain in many respects. Since selection has been in progress at the same time, it is to be hoped the up-graded animals have gained most of the finer qualities of the strain but not the weaker. At some stage, before the characteristics of the male have become too fixed, it will seemingly be worthwhile to break off the backcross and to inter-breed, simultaneously maintaining or even intensifying the selection.

When the backcrossing is made to a male which is not derived from an inbred strain, the outcome is different. In appearance, the male may be a fine specimen of his breed but his heterozygous genotype will imply that he will not hand these qualities on to his offspring in a uniform manner. There is a decrease in heterozygosity as a result of inbreeding but the limit is 50 per cent of the proportion initially present and this is not attained for a very large number of generations. In the meantime, the male will have died of old age and there is no male of similar genotype to take his place. Hence, the backcrossing will come to an end. The value of an outstanding male of heterogeneous origin lies in the genes he may be able to pass on to a few offspring by chance assortment and it is usually worthwhile to endeavour to capture these genes by selective breeding. However, this is a far cry from a general grading-up in quality which one might expect from the use of a superior male. His heterozygosis would be a severe stumbling-block which will probably doom the attempt to failure at the onset.

It may be necessary to issue a warning against a breeding system which might trap the unwary into thinking that it represents grading-up. This is where a single backcross is made to a superior male and, from the off-spring, the best son is chosen and used for breeding with the inferior stock. From his offspring another son is selected, and so on. Reflection should reveal that this is backcrossing in the wrong direction and any good points which might have been gained from the first cross will rapidly be lost.

"Prepotency" is a term employed to describe the situation when a male or a female possesses the remarkable property of producing offspring bearing a strong resemblance to his or her self. Males are usually referred to in this manner partly in error (incorrectly, it is often thought that the male has an innate propensity in this direction) and partly because they have greater opportunity to reveal the ability. Bad, as well as good features, may be transmitted, a point which is occasionally overlooked. Usually, the reason is that the individual has become homozygous for a gene or group of genes with dominant effects. This can happen by chance, especially if selection and inbreeding is being practised at the time. Should the characteristics be desirable there is every likelihood that these may be fixed in the stock since the animals bearing them will be retained.

The interesting aspect is that the more inbred an individual may be, the more homozygous he will be, and the greater the chance that he will display prepotency. This is where the male from an inbred strain will score over the male of heterozygous origin even should the latter be phenotypically superior. The prepotency may not be derived entirely from dominance in the case of an inbred male since he will be transmitting a uniform set of genes in every gamete whereas the queens will not. Hence, on average, the offspring will tend to resemble the male. The prepotency may be less striking but still evident.

Mating Like to Like and the Converse

The breeding together of animals of similar phenotype is often advocated and is known as mating "like to like". The usual reason for undertaking such matings is a belief that this will lead to fixation of characters. However, these matings are valuable for perpetuating a character but not, as a rule, for fixation. Inbreeding is the key to character fixation and this, coupled with mating like to like, is the surest means of stabilizing a desired degree of intermediate expression. In other words, mating of like to like is a form of selection and, as a general policy, has much to recommend it. The total score method produces a high proportion of such matings for the various characters which contribute towards the score. The converse of the above is the mating together of unlikes. This policy is often urged as a means of compensating for faults in one animal against those of another. It is implicit that the mating of animals with similar faults should be avoided at all costs, otherwise there is the danger of fixation. However, this may not necessarily occur, unless there is inbreeding, in which case it is true that there is a risk. The drawback of mating unlikes is that it tends to be a negative policy. It may be useful to combat the chance fixation of faults but it does so at the expense of encouraging heterozygosity. Even if the bad features disappeared or are mollified in the immediate generation, they could reappear in those following. This is especially true should there be over-compensation. That is, animals exceptionally good or bad in some points are appropriately matched with the intention of producing offspring with average all-round qualities.

Anyone who looks ahead to later generations should be able to appreciate the problems which matings of unlikes may entail. In general, this form of mating should not be viewed as a settled policy but only as an expedient in a rather difficult situation which cannot be resolved by other methods. The total score method undoubtedly will cause some matings of unlikes but these can be accepted unless they recur rather frequently, in which case a review of the composition of the score or the genetic behaviour of the constituent characters may be advisable. It may be that an inverse relationship (see later) has been exposed, in which improvement in one character can only be achieved at the expense of another.

Limits to Selection

It is impossible to eliminate all variation because a proportion is due to non-genetic causes. That is, to idiosyncrasies in the development of the individual cat and to the influence of the environment. Little can be done about the former but the effect of the latter can be minimized by providing as constant an environment as possible conducive to sturdy growth. However, even under optimum conditions, it is not always possible to remove all of the genetic variation nor to achieve a given objective at the first attempt. These two aspects may now be discussed.

The problem of fixing an intermediate expression of a character is the removal of genetic variation. The mating of like to like can make some contribution to this end but relatively slowly compared with inbreeding. Close inbreeding can induce the genetic proportion provided it is maintained for sufficient generations. On occasion, however, the progress is not so quick as might be expected or, in practical terms, the variation still seems to be as great as before the inbreeding began. There may be several possible reasons for this. The genetic proportion of the variation is not the same for all characters and it may be that the proportion is low for a particular character. Inbreeding will reduce this but the effect may be negligible because the genetic proportion was not making much of a contribution in the first place. Another possibility is that the more heterozygous animals are the more healthy and these may be preferably chosen for breeding. Hence, the genetic portion of the variation may persist. Choosing the less vigorous but more homozygous animals could lead to a reduction in variation but at the risk of the onset of inbreeding depression. This is not a necessary accompaniment of inbreeding, of course, but it is wise to be on the alert for it or, more to the point, for factors which can bring it into being.

One of the peculiarities of selection for extreme expression is that the extreme phenotypes of some traits may remain tantalizingly out of reach. The odd individual may turn up but it is very difficult, if not impossible, to breed more of the same type. Again, there are several reasons which could be behind this. One is the same as that previously mentioned; namely, that the genetic proportion of the variation may be small. If this is the case, those few individuals which do turn up owe their appearance to non-genetic causes. Thus, it is not surprising that these cannot be produced by selective breeding; also, if the nature of the non-genetic factor is unknown, the appearance cannot be produced by manipulation of the environment. A rather similar situation is produced when the genetic proportion of the variation is small. Some progress may occur but this soon stops and further selection is unavailing.

Even when the variation is largely genetic, it may still be that the results fall short of expectation because the genes present in a particular stock are incapable of producing the extreme phenotype. The stock has not the genetic potential, despite the fact that another stock was able to reach the desired extreme. The solution in this case is to introduce genes from the successful stock by means of crosses. It is also possible for a stock to fail because, though it originally carried the necessary genes, some became homozygous and others were lost before they could become combined. Inbreeding could bring this situation into being. Once again, the solution is to outcross to a successful stud, either by the despatch of a queen to the stud male or by purchase of a suitable animal. It may be noticed that both of these solutions are forms of grading-up, by which advantage is taken of the availability of animals which apparently have the necessary genes to produce the coveted phenotype.

Another obstacle to selection for extreme expression is where an inverse relationship exists between the characters. This subtle phenomenon can occur, often unexpectedly, in a number of guises and it usually comes to notice because progress with selection in one character can hold back progress in another and vice versa. A fictitious example will illustrate the problem which could arise. Suppose a breeder of Longhairs is selecting simultaneously for very long hair fibres, especially in the underfur, and for coat density. He may find over a period that those animals with good long coats appear to lack density and those with dense coats appear to be wanting in length. Try as he may, it does not seem possible to combine the two. Though such a situation may not exist, this example should convey the principle of inversity between two characters.

Whenever an inverse relationship is encountered, it usually means that a third character is mediating the other two. In the above example, the extra flexibility of the coat in the very long-haired cats may produce the illusion of lack of density. Or, the long hair fibres may only be produced at the expense of fibre thickness; again resulting in the illusion of lack of density. In both cases, the number of fibres per square inch of skin may be unaffected (the usual criterion of density). However, on the assumption that the lack of density is not an illusion, the increase in hair length may only occur at the expense of number of hairs for a given skin area. This could happen if the supply of hair substance (a keratin precursor, say) was limited, so that fibre length could only increase if there is a corresponding reduction in number. In these circumstances, an increase in hair length, with no reduction in number, could scarcely be managed by other than a greater supply of hair building substance. This may not be easily achieved (though perhaps not impossible) by selection based on either hair fibre length or density because changes in a trait (keratin substance) only subject to indirect selection (upon hair length and density simultaneously) are usually more intractable than if selection can be applied directly. It may be remarked that the example is fictitious, as far as known, though it could have a modicum of truth.

Finally, limited progress may be made because the selective breeding is being sloppily or inconsistently applied. Half-hearted attempts at selection may produce results of a sort but it is more probable that they will not. Or, the achievement in one generation may be frittered away in the next. Illogical changes in the emphasis upon the selection of different characters could undo years of careful selection. If the total score method is used, it may be that it is badly constructed, either for the characters considered, their grading or weighting. These items should be checked.

Inbreeding Depression and Hybrid Vigour

The fear is often expressed that inbreeding will bring about a decline in vigour or general weakness. This is "inbreeding depression", as it is usually termed. The loss of vigour is due to the homozygosity of an increasing number of genes with deleterious effects. These are polygenes in as much that the effect of any one in isolation is small. However, the cumulative effect can mount up and become noticeable. In the ordinary random bred population, most of these genes will be present as heterozygotes and their existence may be unsuspected until exposed by the inbreeding. This is not to suggest that all cats carry these genes or that inbreeding must inevitably produce weakly stock. On the contrary, the inbreeding of innately healthy stock is usually quite safe.

On the other hand, some animals do carry deleterious genes and these may make their presence felt on inbreeding. For this reason, the nature of inbreeding depression should be known. Almost any feature of the normal cat may be affected. There may be a decline in birth weight, as shown by small, thin or lethargic kittens, poor growth in later life and below standard adult individuals. There may be a fall in average litter size, an increase in the number of still-born or abnormal kittens. It is not uncommon for the reproductive performance to fall off. This may be shown by a reluctance of the male to copulate, the female to come into heat or partial sterility in either sex. There may be a greater proneness to illness. Perhaps one of these features may be rather strongly evident or several may show a small yet detectable deterioration. It is impossible to foretell the form the depression may take. It usually comes on gradually, affecting some individuals and not others. This means it can be countered by breeding only from the most healthy animals. This is a general maxim, of course, but it particularly holds when inbreeding is practised.

Should inbreeding depression become established in spite of efforts to counteract its effects, there is little recourse but to outcross to unrelated stock. If the outcross is made wisely, it ought to be possible to preserve many of the better qualities of the strain or, at least, not to lose too many. However, this is a matter of selection and skill of the breeder. It may be desirable to inter-cross two inbred strains which are displaying signs of depression. This could occur when several inbred lines are being bred in parallel. Should this be done, the first-cross offspring may turn out to be exceptionally healthy and fertile. This phenomenon is known as hybrid vigour or "heterosis". It does not always occur, of course, but it occurs often enough that most breeders have heard of the phenomenon. Random bred animals rarely show heterosis because much of their taken-for-granted vigour is in fact heterosis of a less obvious kind.

Some strains of pedigree cats show mild signs of inbreeding depression (i.e. they are more "delicate" or "temperamental") as a consequence of generations of selection and their somewhat inbred ancestry. This is tolerated, provided it is not too severe, because to outcross would destroy their proved characteristics and possibly their pedigree status. The depression is very insidious and it is not unknown for it to pervade many individuals of a breed, particularly if a majority of animals are related in one way or another. Weak inbreeding is then difficult to avoid and every endeavour should be made to breed only from the most healthy stock in order to counter a possible worsening of the situation.

Maximum Avoidance of Inbreeding

The occasion may arise where it is necessary to maintain a small group of animals with the minimum loss of heterozygosis. Such a case could be where a stud has attained a high level of perfection but signs of inbreeding depression have become evident. An outcross would be the obvious remedy but this is judged undesirable. For practical or sentimental reasons, the owner may not wish to break-up the blood line or it may be that no outside stock is available of comparable quality. In this event, the decision whether to outcross or not may not be easy. One solution would be to increase the size of the stud so that larger numbers are available from which to select the most vigorous animals. However, if the selection is intense, as it should be in the circumstances, the number of parents will be reduced and the stud will be exposed to inbreeding which may lead to further deterioration. The position is aggravated if it is only possible to keep a small number of animals.

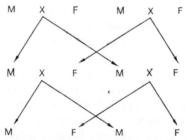

Fig. 19. Diagram of pairings for a group of four cousins. Two different males (M) and two different females (F) form the group in each succeeding generation. These must be paired as shown by the lines of descent. The pairings repeat for each generation.

A possible palliative would be to adopt a system of breeding in which the loss of heterozygosis is minimized. These take the form of groups of animals equally divided into males and females and are forms of cousin matings. Two of the simplest will be described, requiring only four and eight individuals per generation as shown by Figs. 19 and 20, respectively. In the first, two males and two females are so paired that the resulting two litters (or two series of litters) provide either both the males of females for the next generation. It is important that the sexes be chosen from litters with different parents otherwise the system reverts to sib mating which it is expressly designed to avoid. The ratio of decrease of heterozygosity is 92 per cent, a value which cannot be bettered by any other breeding system consisting of so few parents in each generation.

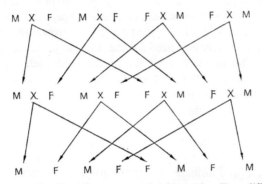

Fig. 20. Diagram of pairings for a group of eight cousins. Four different males (M) and four different females (F) form the group in each succeeding generation. These must be paired as shown by the lines of descent. The pairings repeat for each generation. Note the reversal of arrangement of the males and females in the two halves of the diagram; this is for clearer presentation of the lines of descent.

The second system requires four males and four females. The arrangement of pairing is more complicated and is best understood by reference to the Figure. Each of the four litters must provide two offspring for the next generation, a male and female. In the diagram, the letter M represents a male and the letter F a female, the lines of descent showing how the eight offspring must be paired for the next round of litters. Whence, the whole process is repeated. In practice, both for the previous system and the present one, it is advisable to make out a sketch-plan showing the lines of descent but filling in the names of the animals in the cattery instead of the M and F symbols. The sketch-plan should be completed for two generations so that the pairing of the kittens is definitely fixed. Later, it will only be necessary to add a row of names for the next generation. This can avoid the sort of mistakes which can occur, by trying to operate the system in the mind. The ratio for the second system is 97 per cent which is again larger than other systems for a similar number of parents per generation. The last two entries in Table 7 reveal how the two cousin groups preserve the amount of heterozygosis compared with other systems.

It is possible to propose a somewhat more flexible system of pairing than that outlined above for people who find it difficult to follow a set pattern. However, there are rules attached even to this system. The main one is that each pairing must contribute two offspring to the new generation. This is the same as before, of course, except that now there is no insistence that the pairs of offspring must be consistently of the same or unlike sex. Nor is there any need for the number of animals to be invariably 4 or 8. The numbers kept for breeding in each generation must necessarily be in multiples of two but this means that it is possible to have, for example, 6 or 10. However, there are certain rules which must be observed if the system is truly to be one of minimized inbreeding. Though the choice of sex is left open as regards individual pairings, the total number of cats per generation must be equally divided into males and females. Thus, strictly speaking, complete freedom of choice only exists for the initial animals. Later selection of animals must take into account that the sexes should balance.

The advantages of the present system is the greater freedom of choice for at least half of the animals and that the pairing between the selected individuals need not follow a defined pattern. This is true, provided there is no inadvertent brother-to-sister pairing for too many consecutive generations. In fact, for the system to function as minimized inbreeding, it may be necessary to arrange that some brother-to-sister pairings are deliberately interspersed among more distant pairings. This policy implies that pairing within the system is not entirely at random but ought to be planned to some extent. At least, the pairings in successive generations will have to be watched so as to avoid prolonged inbreeding, inadvertent as this may be. Similarly, care must be taken that a group of eight breeding animals, for instance, are truly interbreeding and are not by mischance actually divided into two lines of four. The two cousin systems described above, on the other hand, obviate these worries because all of the pairings are fixed beforehand.

Once inbreeding depression has set in, sooner or later it is difficult to avoid making an outcross if the strain is to be saved. It is possible that one of the present breeding systems may defer the event and it is just possible that ruthless selection within the system might counter the depression. It is a hope, if the avoidance of out crossing is that important. The usefulness of the two systems is that of a holding operation until suitable animals become available to which an outcross may be made.

Inbreeding and the Appearance of Anomalies

Some hesitancy may be expressed because it is felt that inbreeding can cause anomalies. This is not an unjustified feeling but possibly overemphasized and sometimes misplaced. In the first instance, inbreeding itself cannot induce anomalies, although it can bring to light genetic defects which may be latent in the stock. Random mating tends to keep defects hidden or prevents their recurrence except for the odd animal here and there. It is possible for a recessive anomaly to be brought into the stock, persist for a few generations, and be bred out without anyone being aware. Those heterozygotes which may carry the defect are likely to be fully healthy, hence there is no reason why anyone should be suspicious.

The chances of discovery of such a recessive defect will vary with the amount of inbreeding. The chances are small for weak and not very great for moderate inbreeding. However, the chances increase rather sharply for close inbreeding and this is the reason why inbreeding and the appearance of anomalies are believed to be associated. Only a minority of studs possibly carry a recessive anomaly and in most cases inbreeding will not produce anything abnormal. No one would be exactly pleased to discover an inherited anomaly yet should one be present in the stock it is wise to be aware of the fact and to take active steps to eliminate it. Fortunately, recessive defects can be removed and several methods are described in a later chapter. In some respects, inbreeding can be regarded as a cleansing operation, for if it has a propensity to bring recessive defects to light, it also leads to their eradication far more quickly than random mating. The chance occurrence of anomalies is not the same as inbreeding depression discussed earlier. This is a more vexsome and difficult problem to control.

The Meaning of Strain

Many people at some time of their life may feel that they would like to have a strain of their own. This is very natural and leads to the question "What is a strain?" In the cat fancy, all breeders may register a stud name and all kittens which are bred to previously registered parents. This introduces a small degree of control and ensures that a stud will become widely known when the animals from it are regular winners. Almost certainly, there will be demand for kittens and queens will be sent to the stud males. A certain amount of inbreeding may occur and it may be legitimate to speak of a blood line. Eventually, the word "strain" may be mentioned, perhaps in a general sense, but more specifically to those animals bred within the stud or from purchased animals not too many generations removed.

The terms "blood line" and "strain" are often used rather loosely in animal breeding, most commonly to indicate relationship rather than anything else. This is particularly true for blood line which in its most precise use means a line of ancestry tracing back to an exceptional animal or lineage of animals. Collateral descent is an important aspect of blood lines when it is desired to show that certain animals are related via a remote but common ancestor. Blood lines are held in high regard in the cat fancy, particularly when outstanding animals feature in the pedigree. Unfortunately, this must not be equated to genetic worth because animals of championship status may produce mediocre or downright inferior kittens. The appearance of the cat should always have first consideration and the pedigree examined with a critical eye. This is especially true when the names of champions are absent from one side of the pedigree or do not occur in the more recent generations. This could indicate that some grading-up has been taking place for the first case and that the stud has not been faring very well recently on the show bench for the second case.

In animal breeding, the term "strain" should not be lightly applied. Ideally, it should be used to denote a stock of animals of distinctive, if not exceptional, merit. It should represent a stud of relatively true breeding animals possessing unique features which tend to make them stand out. This sort of reputation is not achieved overnight and is the culmination of years of unremitting selective breeding. On a lower level, a group of closely related animals which have been inbred for several generations (e.g., beyond 5 or 6) would qualify as a strain, even if these are not of particular note in other respects.

The founding of a strain of elite cats should be the goal of all breeders. Not everyone may have the opportunity nor will everyone who attempts the task be able to succeed. Nonetheless, the attempt should be made just for the pleasure which animal breeding and tending can bring to people of all ages. Especially those who have to live in urban areas yet yearn for the company of animals.

Synopsis

Despite a risk of repetition, it seems desirable to summarize the main tenets of the foregoing sections. This may be expeditiously achieved by contrasting the effects of selection and inbreeding as follows:

Selection	Inbreeding
1. Small decline of heterozygosis	1. Steady decline of heterozygosis
2. Perpetuation of certain genes	2. Steady fixation of all genes
3. Increasing phenotypic similarity	3. Increasing genotypic similarity

A first reading of the tendencies induced by either selection or inbreeding might cause one to consider that the two processes are complementary and all one has to do is select the right animals and inbreed them. In very favourable circumstances, this might be feasible. The outcome would be (1) a low level of heterozygosis, (2) perpetuation of the desired phenotype and (3) both phenotypic and genotypic fixation. Unfortunately, in practice, it is usually impossible to obtain animals correct in all of the characters which should be considered and too much inbreeding could bring about fixation of bad points before these can be eliminated.

A compromise has to be found and, generally, this will have the form of selective breeding (using any method which seems best for the problem in hand) in conjunction with moderate inbreeding. The rationale is that this programme should bring together desirable combinations of genes and hold them until the inbreeding has led to the appropriate fixation. It must be emphasized that this is a general compromise. In special circumstances, selection with the barest inbreeding may be the correct policy or selection with intense inbreeding may be more fitting. In essence, the degree of inbreeding is the factor which cannot be decided without knowledge of the problems to be overcome or the ultimate goal of the breeder.

The concepts of animal breeding are firmly rooted in genetic principles and the two topics cannot be separated. In fact, most books on genetics touch upon animal breeding practice and may devote a chapter or two to it. However, the topic is worthy of serious study in its own right and a number of books are available which do just that. The previous sections present an introductory grounding which should assist breeders broaching the subject for the first time. Those who wish to extend their reading should consult Bogart (1959) and Hutt (1964) for elementary expositions. One of the best books ever written on animal improvement is that of Lush (1945). Lerner's (1958) account is more difficult but interesting in that it reveals just how involved the subject can become if one attempts to include almost every conceivable factor.

V. COLOUR AND COAT INHERITANCE

In almost all species which are subjected to scientific study, it is desirable to have a standard to which all deviating forms can be compared. In genetics, it is convenient to choose the type present in the wild and, in cats, this is the short coated mackerel striped tabby as found in the European wild cat *(Felis silvestris)*. Specimens of this type of tabby may be seen in almost all mongrel cat populations of the world. Doubtless this has been handed down from primordial wild ancestors, countless generations ago, persisting more or less unchanged to the present day.

Tabby Striping

The tabby pattern consists of dark melanotic striping apparently superposed upon a yellowish-grey ground colour. This ground colour is present in most animals and is known as agouti (so-called after a rodent of this colour). In particular, the hair fibres are not solid black from base to tip but are banded and/or tipped with yellow. It is the manner of the overlay of the fibres which produces the characteristic agouti coat. The colour is probably most well known for the wild mouse or rabbit. The cat, however, possesses a second system of pigmentation which these species lack, and this is responsible for the tabby striping. This striping is due to a marked reduction in the quality of the yellow band, leading to its elimination, with the result that a dark pattern is produced. The effect is to create the impression of one pattern imposed upon another; a coexistence of concealing colours which is seemingly basic to most members of the cat family.

The mackerel tabby may be observed in almost any mongrel population. It is characterized by the presence of vertical gently curving stripes on the sides of the body. These may be continuous or be broken into bars and spots, particularly low down on the flanks and on the stomach. A second type of tabby is also found in most mongrel populations. This is the blotched tabby. The head markings of this form are similar to those of the mackerel but the body pattern is very different. The even vertical striping is replaced by broader bands which form whorls and spiral arrangements. The legs and tail are relatively heavily barred. The actual blotched pattern is variable with respect to the width of the bands and the amount of fusion they may display. Where the coalescence is extensive, a very dark tabby is produced.

A third type of tabby is that found in the Abyssinian breed. This is an interesting form since the tabby striping is extremely evanescent (or should it perhaps be nascent?). In any event, little or no evidence of striping is normally present on the body, though some may be observed on the face, legs and tail. Usually, the barring is finer than that shown by the mackerel type, though this is not always so. In the Abyssinian breed, the legs and tail may be devoid of barring or, at least, can only be seen after careful scrutiny. The interest created by the Abyssinian type centres around the relative absence of the tabby striping. On the body, the colour is that of typical agouti. The depth of colour may vary from yellowish-grey to a ruddy-brown but this variation is independent of the Abyssinian gene. Thus, while the striping is usually regarded as an integral part of the tabby pattern (certainly in the popular mind and perhaps beyond), it is possible to find a genetic form which is largely devoid of it.

The three types of tabby appear to be inherited as an allelic series. It is generally accepted that the Abyssinian type is dominant to both mackerel and to blotched, and that the mackerel type is dominant to blotched. The symbols for the three genes are T^a (Abyssinian), T (mackerel) and t^b (blotched). The mackerel gene is the wild type as defined above. The phenotypes of the three alleles represent a series of increasing amount of melanoid pigmentation. The possibility that the homozygote T^aT^a shows less tabby markings than either of the heterozygotes (T^aT or T^at^b) should perhaps be entertained. The pure-bred Abyssinian rarely has tabby striping on the legs and tail, whereas the cross-bred Abyssinian almost invariably does so. This may mean either (1) that the pure-bred Abyssinian has been selected for complete absence of striping and that the crossing has upset this selective breeding or (2) that T^a is incompletely dominant to T or t^b. At present, the first alternative seems to be the most likely.

A fourth type of tabby may be mentioned at this point. This is the so-called spotted. This type could be a modified form of the mackerel, in which the vertical striping is much interrupted and appears as short bars or spots. As such, of course, the form may not be a new genetic type but could be the mackerel under a new guise. However, the form deserves to be noted since it has been suggested that it could be due to a mutant gene. The gene could be independent of the striping alleles or, possibly, be yet another member of the series. Against this, is the fact that this suggestion has yet to be proven by the appropriate breeding experiments. It may be mentioned that fanciers desire that their ideal mackerel tabby possess long unbroken stripes and that there is selective breeding towards this goal. The mongrel mackerel, on the other hand, shows a tendency towards a breaking up of the striping and the spotted form could be an extreme variant of this process. This variation appears to be due to polygenes which are independent of the tabby alleles.

Non-agouti

The gene responsible for the agouti-grey of the tabby has produced a mutant allele known as non-agouti. The resultant phenotype is the black cat. Though the animal is uniformly black in appearance, it will carry one of the tabby alleles. The presence of these can usually be seen in the coat of young kittens and sometimes in the adult under certain circumstances. The trick is to manipulate the animal so that the pattern can be seen by reflected light. Either the mackerel or blotched pattern should be discernible. If no pattern is observed, this could mean that the Abyssinian type is present but not necessarily so, of course. The non-agouti gene is inherited as a recessive and is represented by the symbol a.

Brown

This mutant gene changes the normal black pigmentation to brown. The colour change is most obvious when combined with non-agouti to produce the black versus chestnut brown. By analogy with microscopic studies on brown mutant forms in other species, the colour change is due to a reduction in size, shape and colour intensity (to a paler shade) of the pigment granules in the hair fibres. By a quirk of pigment physiology, the brown gene does not modify yellow pigment or, if it does, it is in the direction of producing a "brighter" or more richly coloured coat.

This effect can be seen in the cinnamon tabby (e.g., A–bbT–) which is more auburn than the corresponding black tabby (A–B–T–). The brown gene is inherited as a recessive and has been given the symbol of b.

Albino Alleles

The albino series of alleles are particularly noteworthy because, between them, the various members are responsible for many of the cat fancier's most popular breeds. In dominance order of ranking, the members are: silver, Burmese, Siamese and albino. In the same order, the recognized gene symbols are c^{ch}, c^b, c^s and c. All four are apparently fully recessive to the wild type (C) but not necessarily to each other. An exception may be silver, which seems to behave as a dominant to Burmese and Siamese. However, it is wise not to be dogmatic on this point since incomplete dominance between the lower members of a series of alleles is the rule, rather than otherwise. Further, what may be true for one series of crosses may not hold for others. It has been demonstrated that c^b is certainly not fully dominant over c^s.

It might be thought that the series is so named because the lowermost member is a gene producing the pink-eyed albino. In a sense, this is true but this is not the whole picture. Actually, the whole series has a unity which speaks volumes as an example of progressive gene action. Each mutant allele lower in the series, progressively removes greater amounts of pigment from the coat. The following account should make this clear. The silver gene removes much of the yellow, particularly in the agouti coloured areas between the tabby striping, but little, if any, of the black. The Burmese gene further depletes the amount of yellow on the body and also changes the black to a fuscous sepia. With the Siamese gene, the reduction in intensity of the black is continued. The body fur is either whitish or partially covered with pale sepia pigment. Yet, appreciable pigment may be seen on the "points", namely, the muzzle, ears, feet and tail. The albino gene completes the elimination, so that a pigmentless animal is the result. The eye colour displays a corresponding degradation, appearing successively for the mutants as topaz-blue, opalescent and pink, respectively.

The three alleles c^{ch}, c^b and c^s display a number of interesting features. All tend to produce a cat in which the extremities are more heavily pigmented than the body. This is most evident when the genes are combined with non-agouti to produce a more uniformly coloured animal than a tabby. The presence of dark coloured points is clearly noticeable for the Burmese and Siamese. The "ghost" tabby striping which often can be discerned in the juvenile coat of the ordinary non-agouti black ($aaC-$) is more clearly apparent in both the non-agouti silver ($aac^{ch}-$) and in the non-agouti Burmese (aac^b-) and, as a matter of fact, may even persist into the adult on occasion. When the long-haired gene is added to the above genotypes (to give the Smoke $aac^{ch}-ll$), an animal is engendered with pale or white undercolour. This could be an indication that the amount of pigment produced by c^{ch} is limited, apart from the impairment of the quality. This aspect is not always noticeable for the normal coat but becomes apparent when extra pigment has to be supplied for an unusually long hair fibre. It is probable that the long-haired Burmese (aac^b-ll) will have a white undercolour and, combined with the dark sepia, to give a variation on the Smoke phenotype. Alternatively, of course, the thermal factor (see later) could be responsible for the apparent drying up of the supply of pigment.

The tendency to produce dark points by the three mutant alleles could imply increasing degrees of thermo-sensitivity. This is most marked for the Siamese, where the phenomenon has been experimentally verified (Iljin, 1930). The young Siamese has a white coat and the typical pattern which develops with age is due to temperature gradients over the surface of the body. An important factor is the amount of heat loss of the skin. This is most noticeable for the extremities which probably have the greater heat loss and these show the most pronounced pigment. In one experiment, where an individual was left in a cold environment, the body became covered with light sepia fur and two new sites of intense pigmentation appeared on the shoulders and hips where the skin was stretched across the underlying bones. In another experiment, the bandaging of a small area of shaven skin caused the new growing hair to be white. After the removal of the bandages, subsequent hair growth was pigmented in the usual manner. That is, each fibre is dark tipped but paling to white towards the root. The long-haired Siamese ($aac^s c^s ll$) often shows less pigment than its smooth coated counterpart and this could be due to greater insulating properties of the long hair.

The silver allele reduces the amount of yellow pigment, though not entirely and to a variable degree. This variation is best seen when the gene is combined with the orange gene O. The silver yellow ($c^{ch}-O$) is whitish, with sandy-yellow to orange-yellow striping. The intensity of the striping and the amount of yellow in the areas between the stripes varies from individual to individual. In combination with Abyssinian tabby (c^{ch}–OT^a–), a pale tawny off-white colour is produced, depending how much yellow pigment is persisting. Incorporating d into the genotype (c^{ch}–$ddOT^a$–) pales the colour still further. A whitish undercolour is present in all of these forms and, in the long-haired versions, the white undercolour is very pronounced. The substitution of the c^b allele for c^{ch} in the above genotypes will probably not produce any great differences except for a general dilution of colour.

A gene for complete albinism is listed in this book as if fully proven genetically. It might be advisable, however, to make the point that this is not wholly true. No decisive experimental data has been properly recorded in a scientific journal. On the other hand, there are persistent reports of the breeding of complete albino in the United States of America under the name of Chinese White. Albino animals represent one of the most frequent of mutant forms and it would not be surprising to have one in the cat. Furthermore, there is ample reason for assuming that it would be inherited as the lowest member of the present series of alleles.

The suggestion has been made on several occasions that additional albino alleles may exist. As a general proposition this may well be true but no breeding data has been brought forward to support particular instances. The two situations which usually give rise to the suggestion are the following: (1) the observation of silver animals with variable amounts of yellow pigment in the coat and (a) the observation of Siamese cats noticeably different from usual. In both cases, the tendency is in the direction of increased pigmentation. In the case of silver, more yellow diffusion and in the case of Siamese, the occurrence of animals darker than the ordinary Siamese. However, these two features are just as likely to be due to modifying polygenes, which are independent of the albino series, as to further alleles. In fact, as a working hypothesis, the concept of modifying genes is probably the better approach.

Blue Dilution

In the blue diluted cat, the black is changed to blue (or slate) and the yellow to cream. The colour change is most obvious for each system of pigmentation by the production of the self blue and the cream. By analogy with microscopic work on similar mutants in other species, the colour dilution is probably brought into being by irregular formation of pigment granules within the hair shaft. The result is a hair fibre deficient in pigment interspersed with clumps of coalesced granules. The mutant gene is inherited as a recessive and is symbolized by d.

Pink-eyed Dilution

In addition to blue dilution, a second type of dilution occurs commonly in mammals. This is pink-eyed dilution, so-called because it imparts a characteristic pinkish or ruby glimmer to the eye. The coat colour is often a bluish-fawn. The genes responsible for this colour are usually inherited as recessives. A female cat of this general description is reported by Todd (1961). The eye is said to be pink and the coat a light tan in colour. Mated with a chocolate pointed Siamese, this unique animal gave birth to three kittens, born 10 days prematurely and none survived. However, it was possible to see that all three were typical tabbies. Therefore, if the colour of the female is due to a mutant gene, it could be inherited as a recessive and be independent of the albino alleles and of brown. The greater catastrophe was that the mother also died.

The amount of information is meagre indeed but it seems probable that a pink-eyed dilution type of mutant has at last been reported for the cat. The description would agree with expectation and, granting that the colour is inherited, recessive heredity is strongly indicated. Hopefully, it may be remarked that further instances may occur in the future. At least, it is now known that such a mutant is possible and an eager eye should be kept open for likely cases. The reward would be a whole range of potential new colours.

Dominant Black

The existence of a gene for dominant black is something of an enigma. Tjebbes in 1924 published a report on crosses between a Siamese and a tabby which indicated that the Siamese transmitted a gene which obscured the tabby pattern. The F_1 offspring were black but the tabby re-appeared in the F_2. Attentive reading of the report revealed that the black F_1 were probably the offspring of a single female Siamese. Only two Siamese cats are described and only the female was used in the cross-breeding. The two Siamese were stated to be descendants of a pair of

Siamese originally imported from Bangkok by a Dutch breeder about ten years previously. The Siamese strain has always been kept pure and has bred true to type.

In view of the apparent absence of the dominant black gene from the general population, the gene is not considered in the subsequent chapter on breed genotypes and other interesting gene combinations. There is no point in discussing combinations which may not be in existence. Should the gene be rediscovered, of course, the situation can be reassessed. On the other hand, the omission is not very great since the behaviour of dominant black in other mammals shows the gene to interact with other genes as would non-agouti. The only difference is that the gene masks the presence of agouti. Otherwise, the colour is changed to chocolate brown by b, to blue by d, modified to various smokes and sepias by the albinistic alleles and marked with white by S. It would be unwise to be too definite for the effect of O, but the most likely outcome is that the O gene will be epistatic. The dominant black gene has received the provisional symbol of Db.

Now, the intriguing aspect is that a dominant black gene has not been unequivocally discovered since. This does not mean that the gene may not exist but it does raise the question of how common it may be. There is no evidence that it is present in any other breed than the Siamese and it does not seem to be present in all strains of Siamese. Crosses between Siamese and tabby animals have produced tabby offspring on many occasions. The gene, therefore, may be restricted to a few or even one strain of Siamese. It may indeed have been lost had the Bangkok strain used by Tjebbes died out before crosses had been made with other Siamese.

Orange

Until recently, the gene responsible for the ginger or marmalade cat was known as yellow but the standard designation is now orange. It is unique because it is sex-linked, a statement which means that the gene is carried by one of the sex chromosomes. The chromosome is the X and a depiction of the principles of the heredity is shown by Figs. 14 and 15. A complete list of possible matings and expectations is provided by Table 4. The recognized symbol for the gene is O.

The action of the O gene is to eliminate all melanic pigment (black and brown) from the hair fibres. This is accomplished by a biochemical diversion of those substances destined to become dark melanism into the cognate compound phaenomelanin. The result is a lighter pigment granule, with different optical properties. The O gene removes the melanic pigment impartially from both agouti and non-agouti animals, so that the genotypes A–OO and $aaOO$ are identically yellow. That this is so is demonstrated by the existence of the two tortoiseshell forms: tabby tortoiseshell, with contiguous tabby and yellow fur and black tortoiseshell, with contiguous black and yellow fur. In the tabby tortoiseshell, it should be noted that the deeper tabby striping is carried through from the tabby areas into the yellow, where the barring is transformed into rich orange. Incidentally, the emergence of the tabby striping in the yellow areas of the black tortoiseshell is additional evidence that the a gene does indeed mask the presence of striping. All three tabby patterns are to be found combined with yellow. The mackerel and blotched forms can be readily identified but the Abyssinian is subtly changed. The contrast between the yellow and black ticking of the predominantly agouti coat is now lost and the yellow Abyssinian may seem surprisingly uniform at first sight.

An interesting feature of the orange mutant is that the heterozygous female (Oo) engenders the parti-coloured tortoiseshell. This patchwork pigmentation has often excited wonderment and speculation. An attractive explanation at the present time is that the X chromosomes are not so physiologically active in the female (where there are two) as in the male (where there is one). At an early stage of development, the decrease in activity leads to one chromosome being more inhibited than the other in different cell lineages. In those cells in which the X chromosome bearing the O gene is primarily affected, the tissue will produce black pigment; in those cells in which the o gene is primarily affected, the tissue will produce yellow pigment. The result is the tortoiseshell pattern.

The belief voiced by some breeders that tortoiseshell and white cats have a clearer pattern and larger patches of yellow or black areas than ordinary tortoiseshells, appears to be confirmed by the studies of Norby and Thuline (1965). The areas of yellow, black and white were outlined on a prepared chart of a cat. It was found that all non-spotted animals are brindled, having an intimate mixture of small areas of yellow and black. As the amount of white spotting increased, so the size of the patchwork areas increased, until in cats with much white, the coloured spots are usually of one colour. Just how this "segregation" is achieved is unknown, but it may be related to the fact that white spotting in cats has a tendency to remain whole. That is, the white areas are contoured, with little of the extensive breaks or runs into the coloured areas which are characteristic of white spotting in certain other species. Especially, in cats with a large amount of white, the impression is that the coloured areas are confined, as if they represent islands of pigmented tissue or descendents of a single cell lineage.

It is not uncommon for yellow pigmented mammals to vary very considerably in depth of colour. The cat is no different in this respect. The yellow cat may vary in colour from a sandy yellow to a rich red and all graduations of colour may be found between these extremes. This variation is almost certainly due to polygenes which enrich the colour independently of the O gene. This deepening of the colour has been termed rufism, meaning to redden. The variation is most noticeable in all-yellow phenotypes but is definitely not limited to these. The auburn coloration of the exhibition Brown Tabby and of the Abyssinian, and the variable tawny suffusion shown by many silvers are manifestations of the rufous polygenes.

The present section would be incomplete without a word on the tortoiseshell Tom cat. Theoretically, it would be held that these curious animals should not occur but they do, though at a low frequency, and an explanation must be sought. The fact that they occur only rarely is an indication that they must arise from a rather exceptional event. The number of explanations are legion, some fanciful and others obsolete, and there appears to be little advantage in recounting these old ideas. A full summary may be found in Robinson (1959) for those interested. The majority of tortoiseshell males are sterile, and a fertile animal is somewhat of a rarity among rarities.

Three possibilities for the occurrence of the tortoiseshell male will be outlined. The first is that of somatic mutation. Yellow animals occasionally have small spots of tabby or black hair on their bodies. Now, few people would presume to call these animals tortoiseshells, whether they be male or female. However, rarely, it is possible for the black markings to be more extensive and to simulate a tortoiseshell which is predominantly yellow. Little notice would probably be taken if the animal is a female but it could attract attention if it was a male. Such animals would be fertile and would breed as an ordinary yellow male. The reason for this is that a mutation has occurred in the body cells (from O to o) of a yellow cat, with the result that these now produce black pigment and not yellow. The size of the area would depend upon the development stage at which the presumed mutation occurred. The earlier in development, the larger the anomalous area would be expected to be. Somatic mutations may be likened to mistakes in development, for the germ-cells are usually not involved. Bamber and Hardman (1932) have described several curious animals under the name of "anomalous yellows" which, on the face of it, appear to be examples of somatic mutation.

The second explanation is based upon the possibility of crossingover between the X and Y sex chromosomes (Komai and Ishihara, 1956; Jude and Searle, 1957). Normally, the O gene is firmly located in the non-pairing segment of the X and the heredity is total sex-linkage. However, accidents do happen and the Y chromosome may come to bear either an O or an o gene. In each case, a potential tortoiseshell male could arise if these Y chromosomes are combined with an o or or O bearing X, respectively. These Y chromosomes are evidently exceptional and probably anomalous as well. This could mean that they bring about sterility, since fertility is dependent upon the relationship between a normally constituted X and Y. However, the sterility aspect is not obligate and this may be the reason why some tortoiseshell males are fertile.

The third explanation evolves around the proposition that when two X chromosomes are present in the same cell, the activity of each is reduced, one more than the other. The discovery that some tortoiseshell males have 39, instead of the normal 38, chromosomes prompted the suggestion that the extra chromosome could be an X. That is, their sex chromosome constitution is XXY. The sex is male because of the presence of the Y chromosome, whose influence is strong enough to over-ride that of two X's. The colour is tortoiseshell because one X chromosome bears an O gene and the other, an o. Independent of the presence of the Y, the X chromosomes are functioning differentially, just as if the animal is a female. Mammals with an XXY constitution seem to be sterile and this fact would lead one to expect that tortoiseshell makes of this type will be sterile. So far, several XXY tortoiseshell males have been positively identified and all seem to be sterile.

Further studies have revealed that the tortoiseshell male may result from other unusual chromosome constitutions. Two or more emerge as composed of a mixture of XX and XY cells, one of XX and XXY cells, one of XY and XXY cells, and one probably of XX, XY and XXY cells. These discoveries do not exhaust the range of possibilities. The tortoise-shell pattern becomes involved when one or more of the X chromosomes carry the O gene, together with the differential partial inactivation of the X. The fertility of some tortoiseshell males can be explained in a general manner by the presence of *XY* cells in the germ-cell tissue. Whereas, the *XXY* are outright abnormal and the *XX* abnormal for testis tissue, the *XY* are quite at home and these may be capable of producing functional sperms. The male may be fully or only partly fertile, depending how much of the testes are capable of producing viable germ-cells, among other factors. Now that chimaeric animals are known to exist, it has been conjectured that a tortoiseshell male of *XY* and *XY* cells could arise. The difference between the two cells is that the *X* in one could carry *O* while the *X* in the other could carry *o*. Paradoxically, the animals would appear to be uniformly *XY* under the microscope and be fully fertile.

The tortoiseshell male cat will almost certainly continue to feature prominently in research on abnormal chromosome complements. The *O* gene is sex-linked and the tortoiseshell male is not only a sex oddity but recurs at a low frequency, as do unusual chromosome combinations. Tortoiseshell tom cats, therefore, just call out for chromosome investigation. Comparable chromosome anomalies will occur in cats lacking the *O* gene but these will not be easily detected by ordinary external examination. It is only when the tortoiseshell pattern is found in the "wrong" sex that interest is aroused for a more searching examination. A report by Malouf, Benirschke and Hoefnagel (1967) may be recommended for further reading.

If the *XXY* male be responsible for some, if not all, of the tortoiseshell males, then the *XO* female could be responsible for some of the black females which have been reported for pairings in which they should not occur (Table 8). These animals do not excite attention because they do not represent such a unique phenotype as the tortoiseshell male but the fact of their exceptional occurrence is of genetic interest. If these exceptional females are sterile, it seems possible that they could be of *XO* constitution and a chromosome count could probably confirm this. If they are fertile, a chromosome count would be desirable, but it should be possible to check their suspected *XO* constitution by breeding tests. The exceptional black female should be mated with a yellow male. Should a yellow female occur among her kittens, it is likely that she is *XO*.

Although none have been reported so far, exceptional yellow *XO* females may be expected. These are yellow because the single *X* chromosome carries an *O* gene. Again, a chromosome count would be desirable. If the female is fertile, a breeding test could yield useful information.

She should be mated to a black male and if a black female occurs among her offspring, the chances are that she could be *X*O. It may be mentioned that with modern techniques, a chromosome count does not involve a major operation. Under favourable conditions, a skin biopsy should be sufficient.

TABLE 8. REPORTED OBSERVATIONS ON THE INHERITANCE OF YELLOW AND TORTOISESHELL; AND THE OCCURRENCE OF EXCEPTIONAL TORTOISESHELL MALES AND BLACK FEMALES

Mating		Offspring					
		Males			Females		
Dam	Sire	Yel- low	Tort.	Black	Yel- low	Tort.	Black
Black	Yellow	—	1*	58	—	53	13*
Tortoiseshell	Yellow	63	1*	44	58	46	6*
Tortoiseshell	Black	45	1*	43	—	29	24
Yellow	Black	23	—	—	—	19	—

Note: In the above table, black is used as a euphemism for non-yellow (black, tabby, blue, etc.) and yellow covers orange and cream. Exceptional or unexpected colours are marked with an asterisk.

The breeding data of Table 8 present an interesting picture of the inheritance of yellow and tortoiseshell and of the occurrence of the exceptional colours. The frequency of tortoiseshell males would appear to be about 0·6 per cent, while the black females would be about 3·6 per cent. These figures should be accepted with caution. It is probable that the frequency of tortoiseshell males is less than this, while the frequency of black females may be much over-estimated. Some of the black females could be tortoiseshell females in which the yellow areas have not been detected. Two other features may be noted. The number of exceptional black females is six times as great as that of tortoiseshell males whereas the two forms might be expected to occur with equal frequency. This is suggestive that the black females could be misclassified tortoiseshells. Also, no exceptional yellow females are recorded; though these would conceivably be expected to occur as frequently as the exceptional blacks.

Piebald Spotting

Piebald or white spotted cats are exceedingly common. The spotting may occur in company with any colour and, therefore, is an independent entity *per se*. The manifestation of the spotting varies from small tufts of white hair on the breast and on the belly to extensive white areas, with the pigment areas confined to the tail and to small spots on the head or body. The increase in amount of white is variable but is not without a certain regularity. With progressive increases, the belly becomes largely white, with the neck and chin becoming involved, together with the front paws. Later, the white extends up the sides and appears on the head and hind paws. From this point onwards, white is spreading all over the animal, breaking up the remaining coloured areas on the back into spots of decreasing size. Figure 21 is an attempt to portray the progression of white.

The genetics of white spotting are not exactly known. However, it seems to be inherited as a dominant in the sense that the breeding of nonspotted animals does not usually produce spotted offspring (unfortunately, there can be exceptions). Conversely, white marked kittens are usually produced whenever one or both parents are spotted (again, there can be exceptions). These results could imply that at least one dominant gene for white spotting is in existence. This seems to be generally accepted and the gene is symbolized by S.

In one series of observations by Kühn and Kröning (1928) the heredity of the spotting was that of an incompletely dominant gene. On the average, the spotting varied from grades 4 to 6 of the figure for Ss and from 5 to 8 for SS. Clearly, there is overlapping of expression for the two genotypes. Equally clearly, the variation could be different for other observations based on animals with different genetic backgrounds even if the same S gene is present. However, the same principle will doubtless apply. The main differences are likely to be that the Ss could range down into the low grades of 2 and 3 or the expression of Ss could be close to SS to give a more fully dominant mode of heredity.

If there is one thing which is certain about piebald spotting, that is its variability. Some of this variation will be non-genetic, being due to random eccentricities of individual development. On the other hand, some will be due to polygenes, although just how much is uncertain. This means by selective breeding it may be possible to stabilize (in so far as such an

FIG. 21. Variation of expression of piebald white spotting. Grades 1 and 2 show the typical location on the stomach while grades 3 to 8 show the progression increase in amount of white and the break-up of the coloured areas. Grade 9 represents the all-white cat. (Courtesy of the editors and publishers of *Bibliographia Genetica*.)

erratic character can be stabilized!) the spotting about certain grades. For example, the almost all-white cat of genotype *aaSS*, with a black tail and one or two spots of black fur on the head and body, is quite an attractive animal and one which some people consider should be recognized as a breed.

It may be that the postulation of a single gene for piebald spotting is a genetic oversimplification. There is in fact grounds for thinking that a second gene, which produces a very low grade of spotting (just a small spot on the breast or pubes) may exist (Kühn and Kröning, 1928; Dreux, 1967). The inheritance of this suspected second gene is not fully understood but it seems to be that of a semi-dominant with variable expression in some crosses or possibly as a recessive in others. It also seems possible that some cats which should show the weak spotting, by virtue of their genotype, fail to do so; a fact which complicates the issue. The presence of this second gene, interacting with *S* could be partly responsible for wide variation of the spotting.

Dominant White

The completely white cat, either with yellow, blue or odd eyes, is depicted in this book as due to a dominant gene symbolized by *W*. Since the coat colour is pure white it is impossible to ascertain by inspection which other genes are carried. In other words, *W* is epistatic to all other colour mutants. The only possible exceptions are those which have an effect on eye colour and there may be uncertainty even for these.

The results of crosses with dominant white, as reported in the literature, is indicative that the form is inherited as a simple entity (Robinson, 1959). This is important since it has been proposed that the all-white cat is simply an instance of the accumulative presence of several piebald genes. This is a plausible proposal but one which seems to be untrue. It has also been suggested that the dominant white gene is not independent of the main piebald gene but is an allele of it (Whiting, 1919). It may not be an easy task to experimentally examine the likelihood of this suggestion although it is a project which deserves attention. For the moment, however, it is assumed—purely on the useful premise that it is wise to adopt only the simplest assumptions that the data demand—that the *S* and *W* genes are inherited independently.

One of the problems surrounding the dominant white is the variation of eye colour, which may be either yellow or blue, or even one eye of each colour. It might be wondered if the blue-eyed form could be the homozygote (*WW*) white the yellow-eyed be the heterozygote. However, this does not seem to be so because a blue-eyed cat has been bred from a mating of a black female with a white male. The animal was completely blue-eyed. The existence of odd-eyed animals is suggestive that the blue-eyed condition is irregular in expression, either as an aspect of the dominant white gene or some other gene which might be interacting with it. Could another gene in fact be involved? An obvious candidate would be piebald spotting. It is not unusual for different types of white spotting to exaggerate the usual effects of each other so as to produce a more extreme phenotype.

Thus, the suggestion is that the blue-eyed condition is derived from the genotype *S–W–*; in particular from the genotype *SSW–* since the presence of two *S* genes greatly increases the amount of white in the coat (Whiting, 1919). The eye becomes blue whenever the white pattern of the *S* gene (necessarily unseen beneath the overall whiteness due to *W* but present none-the-less) fall across the eye region. The attractiveness of this hypothesis is that it could explain, both the asymetric eye colour of the irregular breeding of blue-eyed cats, in terms of the known variation of piebald. Not all *SSW–* animals need be blue-eyed since the head is often not fully affected by the spotting.

Associated with the blue-eyed condition is deafness. The association seems to be well-founded, though it is not complete. Again, there is irregularity of expression and, while many cats may be blue-eyed and deaf, others may be blue-eyed and yet hear quite well (Bamber, 1933). There has even been a report of a yellow-eyed animal which was totally deaf (Little, 1934). At this time, it is almost impossible to decide if the *W* gene alone is responsible for the blue-eyed condition and the deafness. That *W* is involved seems reasonably certain but it appears possible that *W* may only produce a yellow-eyed animal and that other genes interact to produce either the blue-eyed condition or deafness or both.

Rufism

This is a term given to denote the relative wide variation of yellow pigmentation, especially the deepening of the colour to engender the red found in the exhibition cat. This is the opposite to the "ginger" of the mongrel animals although this, of course, represents the "wild type" degree of colouring. The variation appears to be continuous from the lightest to the darkest colour and the heredity is almost certainly polygenic.

The range of variation is quite noteworthy. It is most obvious in the contrast between the ginger alley cat and the rich red of the exhibition Red Tabby. However, the same polygenes are doubtless involved in producing the warm ruddy-brown colour of the Abyssinian. Without these, the Abyssinian would be a drab and nondescript animal. The variation of amount of yellow pigment found in many silver animals probably owes its origin to the same group of polygenes. The implication is that variable quantities of rufous polygenes may be present in various exhibition breeds of cats.

The exhibition silver and the Chinchilla, on the other hand, probably represent breeds in which selective breeding has operated to eliminate the polygenes. The outcome is a phenotype exceptionally devoid of yellow pigment. It should never be overlooked that any polygenic complex has plus and minus polygenes (in a formal manner of writing) and that diligent breeding will result in accumulations of either one or the other type in specific breeds in an effort to approximate an ideal.

Eye Colour

The cat shows rather conspicuous variation of eye colour. The iris colour may vary from grey-green to yellow and from yellow to orange, the former occurring mostly in mongrels and the latter among exhibition animals. Despite claims to the contrary, there appears to be no reliable evidence for monogenic control of eye colour. The variation from yellow to orange is particularly distinctive and every graduation seems to occur. It may be assumed that the inheritance of this feature is polygenic.

A number of coat colour mutants have an influence on eye colour and, to this extent, it is possible to speak of monogenic variation. The most obvious effects are those produced by the Burmese and Siamese alleles. There is also the blue eye associated with the dominant white gene. It seems probable that the brown and blue dilution have a small diluting effect yet, if so, the amount seems to be swamped by the general variation.

Coat Composition

Before proceeding to discuss the distinctive features of the various coat texture genes, it seems opportune to give a general description of the hair fibres which make up the normal coat. Three main types may be recognized: These are (1) guard hairs, (2) bristle or awn hairs, and (3) down or wool hairs. The guard and awn hairs are sometimes called collectively, the over-hairs and, the down hairs, the underfur. All of the hair types are important to the animal, mainly as an insulating barrier against excessive heat loss for the down hairs and, in the case of the guard and awn hairs, as a protective covering to the soft underfur and for sensory purposes. The vibrissae or facial whiskers are extra stout hairs devoted primarily to a tactile function.

The three hair types are distinctive and their differences may be easily seen with the aid of a good lens. The guard hairs are normally straight and taper evenly to a very fine point. The awn hairs are thinner than the guard hairs and have a characteristic thickening in diameter (sub-apical swelling) near the tip of the hair before tapering to a fine point. The down hairs are the thinnest of the three types. They are of similar diameter throughout their length and are more or less evenly undulated or "crimped" as it is termed. The awn hairs tend to be variable. Some may approach the guard hairs in thickness and form; while others may approach the down hairs in thinness, even to the extent of becoming crimped and showing a barely perceptible sub-apical swelling. The latter have been called awn-down hairs. If necessarily, it is possible to distinguish three categories of awn hairs but it must be emphasized that all three grade into one another. The guard hairs are slightly longer than the other two types and the awn hairs are longer than the down. The difference may result, in part, from the crimping.

All three types of hair display a rather abrupt thinning in diameter at the point of entry into the skin but thickening again to form a slightly elongated club. This thinning and thickening probably enables the skin follicle which surrounds the hair to grip and hold the hair. The hair seemingly will lie in a sheath of flexible and probably contractile tissue which is of smaller diameter than that of the club. The club could function, therefore, as an anchor, apart from the likelihood that there is cell adhesion actually around the thickened region.

The coat of the long-haired cat contains all three types of hair fibre.

Their form appears to be unaltered except for length. The remarkable difference in length between the mongrel and exhibition long hair is due to modifying genes. The long hair fibres may arise from one of two causes (or both in combination if one wants to consider all possibilities). Firstly, the hairs may grow more quickly and attain a longer length before the growth phase is ended or, secondly, the rate of growth is unchanged but the period of growth is extended. Little serious effort seems to have been put in hand to distinguish between these alternatives but, if observations on other animals can be thought to be a guide, a longer growth period is the more likely cause. In contrast, if observations on other animals can be applied to the cat, the ultra short coat of the rex is due to a slower rate of growth. The period of growth being the same or similar in both the normal and rex animal.

It is a common fallacy that the rex genes completely eliminate guard and awn hairs. The typical soft rex coat being produced by abundant down hairs which are more or less normal. This is a very over-simplified picture of the changes which take place. More typically, the rex coat is produced because, while all of the various hair fibres are reduced in length and thickness, the guard and awn hairs are affected to a greater extent than the down. In some individuals, the stouter hairs may indeed be largely suppressed but, in most, the stouter hairs persist but so closely resemble the down hairs that a microscopic examination is necessary to distinguish the remaining differences. However, in some animals, the stouter hairs may be seen to be persisting above the underfur as mere shadows of their former selves.

The length of the rex coat is variable and this probably parallels to a great extent the variation to be found in the normal coat. The nature and degree of wave or curliness varies between different animals and is related to the length of the hair fibres, the presence of an exaggerated curvature to the rex hair and a tendency for the individual fibres to "lay" in a similar direction. This can cause a streaming effect and bring about a marcelled type of wave in contrast to a more randomized pattern of tight curls. Rex cats with these two extremes of curliness appear very different and different again from the rex with a smooth coat having a minimum of wave or curl.

Four of the various rex coats have been examined in detail. In three rexes (Cornish, German and Oregon) the guard hairs appear to be lacking or, if not lacking, reduced to the appearance of awn hairs. In some Cornish animals, even the awn hairs are missing but, in the majority, awn type hairs are present. Their numbers vary from cat to cat and many display the sub-apical swelling which is characteristic of the hair type. The relative thickening, however, does not seem to be as great as that shown by the normal awn hair. In fact, it is not unusual for the distal swelling to be absent or barely perceptible. In this event, the hairs appear as extra thick down hairs. It is not uncommon for a graduation in thickness to occur between the down hairs and the presumptive awn type hairs. This aspect may not have special significance because the awn hairs are variable in the normal coat and the present variation could arise from this. The inhibiting influence of Cornish rex gene having only a general effect.

The German rex coat contains awn hairs. More persistently, in as much as no individual has yet been found to be devoid of them, and more obviously. The difference in thickness between the down fibres and the awn hairs is more marked and the sub-apical swelling is a little more pronounced than that found in the awn hairs of the Cornish rex. The awn hairs in the German rex would seem to reach a higher level of development than the Cornish. This is revealed in another connection. Not only are the awn hairs more well formed but they seem to be more abundantly distributed in comparison with those present in the Cornish rex coat. It is of interest that, while the awn hairs vary in thickness, there is no real evidence for the presence of a third type which could be depicted as a guard hair. The observed variation is probably that typical of an awn fibre. The awn hairs in both the Cornish rex and German rexes are usually so bent and curved that they do not project above the general fur level as do the normal awn hair.

If the awn hairs are just that slightly more well formed in the German rex, compared with those of the Cornish, the awn hairs of the Oregon rex are somewhat more well formed and thicker than those of the German. In the Oregon rex, awn hairs are abundant in all fur samples examined, and showed unmistakeable sub-apical swelling. The awn hairs also seemed to project a little more above the general coat level provided by the down hairs. This is supported by the impression that the Oregon awn hairs are noticeably less bent and curved over than those of the Cornish and German rexes. Once again, though the Oregon awn hairs show variation, there is no indication that a guard hair type is present.

The coat of the Devon rex, on the other hand, appears to have three types of hair. Both guard and awn hairs seem to be represented by stouter hairs of two grades of thickness. These hairs, however, are more grossly abnormal than the awn hairs of the other rexes. Instead of being of even or smoothly changing diameter, they are strikingly uneven and given to excessive thinning in places. They also terminate abruptly in most cases, as if growth never commenced as a fine point or as if distal portions have been broken off. This latter possibility is supported by the observation of broken, but unparted, hairs on several occasions, something which has not been observed in hair samples of any of the other rexes. The Devon rex guard or awn hair could be more brittle than the ordinary hair or the irregularities of diameter noted earlier could produce weak points along its length. The constant grooming by the rough tongue of the cat could be responsible for the breakage. The Devon rex rarely has a full complement of whiskers, not even as young kittens. As older kittens or as adults, it is quite common for the whiskers to be absent or merely represented by a few bent stubs. This fact and the rapid loss of hair prior to the growth of a new coat distinguishes the Devon from the other rexes.

The burning question which now arises is how much of the observed differences is due to the action of the rex genes themselves and how much is due to the genetic background? Only extensive inter-crossing of the various rexes could provide a positive answer to this question. Alas, from a genetic viewpoint, such inter-crossing is not likely to occur. On the other hand, a little speculation may be in order. As will be discussed later, simple crosses between the Cornish, Devon and Oregon rexes have revealed that each one is due to a distinct mutation. Now, it is improbable that each gene will produce exactly the same effect and this implies that differences due to the type of rex gene may well occur. In general, however, the various rexes look grossly alike. Only the Devon differs rather sharply from the others in the often lack of whiskers and the premature moulting. Quite often, too, the coarse hairs present in the Devon rex can be felt by a sensitive hand.

The situation is different for the other three rexes. Judging from the relative development of the awn hairs, it could be that the Cornish rex will have the softest coat and the Oregon rex, the most harsh. However, this cannot be taken for granted, for other factors come into play in determining this feature (such as relative density) and it is doubtless unwise to generalize from awn hair development alone. From microscopic examination of hair samples, it may be possible to distinguish these Cornish individuals which lack awn hairs but it could be difficult should the awn hairs be numerous. In these cases, it may be impossible to separate those samples purporting to be from either Cornish, German or Oregon rexes. It is conceivable, of course, that the relative greater development of the Oregon awn hair may be a diagnostic feature (especially in comparison with the poorly developed Cornish) provided there is no trend towards the Cornish or German under the pressure of selective breeding. It is rather curious (not to say frustrating) that the German rex, which occupies an intermediate position as regards awn hair development and apparently may resemble either in its range of variation, has yet to be proven to be genetically distinct.

Long Hair

The long haired cat owes its unusually long coat to a recessive gene with the symbol *l*. The length of coat is variable enough in the normal cat and these differences are more noticeable for the long-hairs. The mongrel long hair has a shorter and coarser coat than that of the exhibition animal. In the latter, the coat is not merely longer but feels more silky. This could result solely from the increase in length, but it seems possible that there has been a greater proportional increase in the length of the down hairs. The effect of this would be to produce a "fuller" coat of exquisite texture. These differences of length and texture are due to polygenes and are the consequence of decades of patient selective breeding.

Cornish Rex

The first of the mutants to become popularly known was discovered in 1950 and is the Cornish rex (or rex—1, as it was formerly known). The rex coat is very different from the normal coated cat and, once seen, can never be forgotten. The coat is soft to the touch, mole-like, with an apparent absence of projecting guard and awn hairs. There is a definite tendency towards waviness in many individuals, either to produce a marcelled-effect or that of waves of tight curls. The whiskers are shorter than normal, more curved and often bent. This latter feature provides a ready means of identification of rex mutants from an early age. The coat density varies from a thin, limp covering to one in which the hairs form a thick even pelage. The Cornish rex is inherited as a recessive and has the symbol *r*.

The long-haired Cornish rex has been produced and the resulting animal is clearly rex as evinced by its bent whiskers. The coat fibres are longer than normal but shorter and seemingly thinner than those of the ordinary long-hair. The coat, therefore, has features of both hair types. This shows that the action of each gene is independent of each other and can function harmoniously in combination.

Devon Rex

A second rex mutant was found in Devonshire in 1960 and crosses between it and the Cornish rex soon revealed that the two are unrelated. The new form was known as rex-2 for a period but this ungainly designation has been discarded in favour of the more appropriate title of Devon rex. In appearance, the Devon rex is very similar to the Cornish. The coat is short and even in length, with a spurious lack of guard hairs by ordinary inspection. Again, there is a tendency towards waviness. There is a greater propensity for the Devon rex to lose its coat and to have bare areas, especially on the belly, which persist until the next moult. The amount of hair loss varies between different individuals and is seemingly due to genes inherited independently of the rex. The Devon rex gene behaves as a recessive and has been symbolized by *re*.

A notable and probably a distinctive feature of the Devon rex is that the whiskers of the majority of animals are lost at an early age and that many animals never seem able to retain more than a few stubs for any length of time. The existence of these stubs is suggestive that the whiskers are lost by breakage, rather than by a falling out of the hairs. Even at the best of times, the Devon rex cat never, or rarely, has such a full complement of whiskers as carried by other rex mutants. The effect is enhanced by the relatively greater crookiness of those which do remain.

In the early days of rex breeding, some confusion was caused by the unanticipated appearance of normal coated kittens from crosses between the two rexes. These are the results to be expected, of course, if the two rexes are due to independent recessive genes. Indeed, in the absence of such crosses, it would be impossible to ascertain that two different rex mutations had occurred. It is not entirely certain if the homozygous "double rex" animal has been bred of genotype *rrrere* but, if it has, it will be a rex possibly similar to the Devon form. On the other hand, it is possible for the *rrrere* rex to have an ultra-thin coat due to the combined action of the two rex genes.

German Rex

A third rex has appeared in Germany; in East Berlin to be precise. The coat is typically rex, the fur is soft and smooth, and there is the same tendency towards a waved effect. There is an apparent absence of coarse guard hairs and the whiskers are abnormally bent. The German rex is inherited as a simple recessive and has been provisionally symbolized by *rg*. The first rex individual was recognized as such in 1951 but the animal, a female, was then adult and there is circumstantial evidence that it was born a few years previously. Chronologically, it could be the first of the rex mutants.

Oregon Rex

One of the more interesting of the various American rex mutants is that known as "Oregon rex" after its place of origin. This rex was found in 1959 and is being bred by a band of enthusiasts. It is inherited as a recessive to the normal coat as in the case of all of the other forms. What is interesting is that crosses between the Oregon rex and both the Cornish and Devon rexes have produced kittens with normal coats. Thus, it would appear that three independent rex mutants are known for the cat. In fact, it is tempting to add the words "at least" to the last sentence. The symbol *ro* is proposed for the gene.

Other Rexoid Mutants

It is of interest to record that yet other instances of rex mutants have been observed. One occurred in Italy about 1951. Little is known of the Italian rex except that three rex kittens were bred from a normal mother. Without placing undue emphasis on this evidence, it could be surmised that the form is due to a recessive gene.

The Oregon rex of the United States has already been described but it is worth mentioning that other cases have been reported from this country. By all accounts, these have occurred at widely separated points. A form from Ohio was observed as early as 1952 but was treated very casually and was allowed to die out. Several rex animals were bred from the same normal coated parents and this would suggest that a single recessive gene has been observed.

Another instance occurred in California in 1960. On this occasion, apparently combined with long hair. Inter-breeding with normal coated animals indicated that the rex type was inherited as a recessive. Hearsay evidence has it that crosses between the Californian rex and the Cornish rex produced normal kittens.

Wire-hair

This curious coat type occurred in the United States within the last few years. In appearance, the coat is rough and unruly in contrast to the smooth even coat of the normal animal. The new form has been termed wire-hair. All three hair types are present but are abnormal. The guard hairs appear thinner than normal and are curved rather than straight. The awn hairs seem to be characteristically abnormal. These are thin but have the typical sub-apical swelling. Most of them show exaggerated undulation and a "shepherd's crook" type of configuration in the region of the sub-apical swelling. The down hairs also display exaggerated and irregular curvature; unlike the more regular undulation of the normal hair. The overall effect is a sparse, wiry coat, coarse to the touch.

The breeding data on the wire-haired condition is meagre at present. However, it seems to be inherited as a simple monogenic trait and, subject to confirmation, as a dominant to normal coat. The symbol Wh is proposed for it.

TABLE 9. KNOWN COLOUR AND COAT TEXTURE MUTANTS AND THEIR SYMBOLS

Symbol	Designation	Symbol	Designation
a	Non-agouti	S	Piebald spotting
b	Brown	r	Cornish rex
C	Full colour	re	Devon rex
c^{ch}	Silver	rg	German rex
c^b	Burmese	ro	Oregon rex
c^s	Siamese	T^a	Abyssinian tabby
c	Albino	T	Mackerel tabby
d	Blue dilution	t^b	Blotched tabby
Db	Dominant black	W	Dominant white
l	Long-hair	Wh	Wire-hair
O	Orange		

Note: The orange gene is sex-linked.

VI. GENETICS OF
COLOUR VARIATION AND BREEDS

THE raw material of the evolution of breeds of cats is gene mutation. In the main, these are mutants affecting colour and fur characters. A noteworthy exception, of course, is the Manx. If a mutant gene, or a combination of such genes, furnishes the raw material, the process certainly does not end there. Numerous finer points will contribute towards the ideal exhibition animal, which may differ quite considerably from a mongrel cat of equivalent basic genotype. An attempt will be made to indicate the more important differences; although it must be appreciated to delineate all differences is well-nigh impossible. Indeed, it may not even be necessary, for anyone who is keenly interested in one or more breeds of cat soon learns to detect—by an almost proverbial sixth sense—the subtle qualities of each.

This chapter constitutes a detailed discussion of colour variation; both, generally, as the genes combine to engender an ever increasing range of colour and coat forms, and, specifically, where a genotype or genotype has come to be a recognized breed. The chapter is largely self-contained, but not entirely so, and it should be read in conjunction with that of Chapter V. In particular, it sets out to clothe the bare bones of cat heredity described in Chapter III. On the other hand, the beginner would do well to master the elementary concepts before embarking upon the advanced discussion. This is a friendly hint to the wise.

Body Conformation and Coat Type

An established breed may be considered to have three distinct attributes: (1) general conformation, as shown by body structure and carriage, (2) coat type and (3) coat colour. The first attribute is probably the primary determinant of a breed since changes in coat and colour are usually trivial. This is not wholly true since the Long hair and Rex breeds owe their origin to simple coat mutants but, even so, the body conformation must still be regarded as of importance. On the other hand, although coat colour cannot be entirely disregarded, it must take tertiary place. This is shown by the recognition of several colours within the same breed, of which the Siamese is an outstanding example. In as much as it is possible to separate breed and variety in animal breeding, the various colours of Siamese are varieties of the same breed. The term "breed" is going to be interpreted rather widely to include certain breeds which are not officially recognized in Britain but are so regarded in other countries and certain varieties which are calling for attention as "emergent breeds".

Little is known on the heredity of body conformation. Two rather distinct types tend to stand out. A compact powerfully built frame, with a rounded head, and a sinuous lightly built frame, with a "wedge-shaped" frame. These tend to characterize the "British" versus the "foreign" short-haired breeds. It is not easy to define the two forms but Plates 2 and 8 show cats with the relatively compact body and rounded head of the first type and Plate 5 shows a Siamese with the slim body and more pointed head of the second type. A visit to a show and a chat with a friendly breeder is the best means of learning the difference. It is of interest that the two types can often be distinguished in mongrel cats. However, the difference is not abrupt, for animals of intermediate build are frequently seen and it is probably not a rash conjecture that the two types mentioned above represent the extremes of a continuum. Body conformation, whether due to general size or to variation in certain components (such as length or thickness of leg bones, head shape and the like) appears to be inherited in a polygenic manner. The conformation of the adult cat is the outcome of this polygenic control and the interdependent growth and development of all its organs and skeleton is influenced as diet and general care.

The Manx cat is in rather a special, if not a peculiar, position. The facts of life may as well be squarely faced as not and the adoption of the Manx as a breed means that an anomaly has been taken into the fold. The absence of tail is the hall-mark of the Manx, though this is not the only distinguishing feature. There has been selection for long hind legs which gives the animal a rather curious appearance, compared with other cats. The gait is curious, being rather stilted or stiff-legged which is suggestive of sacral or pelvic anomalies. Of greater genetic importance is that the Manx condition only exists as heterozygotes which dooms the breed as being perpetually impure-breeding. This statement should not be construed as a criticism. If the Manx is desired as a breed, the hetero-zygosity has to be accepted as part of the biological price of the tailless-ness. A number of defects are associated with the taillessness and it may be urged that only the most robust and healthy of animals be used for breeding. This injunction applies to all cats, of course, but is especially true for the Manx.

The soft hair of the long-haired cat is due mainly to the recessive gene *l*. The qualification mainly is used advisedly for the length and texture of the coat can vary. In the exhibition animal, the expression of the long hair has probably reached its peak of expression. The coat is long, full bodied and exquisitely soft, quite different from that of most mongrel long haired animals. In the latter, the coat is usually not so long, less dense and coarse in texture. These differences are due to polygenes which are inherited independently on the *l* gene. Most breeders of long-haired cats are aware that the coat of their charges can vary indivi-dually in length, density and texture, and the reason is the existence of these modifying polygenes. It is not always easy to assess exactly how these features may vary from animal to animal and this fact should be appre-ciated. For example, coat density, which means number of hair fibres per square centimetre of skin, may vary independently (or partially so) of texture, which could mean ratio of number of guard hairs to underfur or possibly the degree of "fullness" of the underfur relative to the guard hairs. A cat with a very low ratio may feel as if its coat is sparse, compar-ed with an animal with a high ratio, whereas, the actual density may be the same in both.

A recent addition to the range of coat types is that of the rex, in which the coat is shorter than normal and inclined to be wavy. When the rex first became available, some confusion was caused before it was real-ized that more than one genetic form was in existence. When the two forms are inter-bred, a reversion to normal occurred, much to the astonishment of some people. However, the situation has been sorted out and the two rex mutants which caused all the trouble have been given distinctive names. These are now known as the Cornish rex and the Devon rex. Unless the breeder has a definite objective in so doing, it is advisable to keep the two rex breeds apart and to refrain from inter-crossing. Each of the rexes are due to different recessive genes. There is a tendency for the amount of wave in the coat to vary between kittens and adults and between different individuals. An unwelcome propensity is that of loss of hair from parts of the body. In as much as some lose hair and others do not with the same diet and attention, this indicates an inherent weakness of the individual. Such cats should not be used for breeding.

The genetics of coat colour in relation to breeds of cat has proved to be a fascinating subject. Though the basic ground-work has been laid for decades, it is only in comparatively recent years that it has been possible to unravel the finer details. Despite this, however, the serious inquirer will probably still encounter many vexing unsolved problems. In a manner of speaking, this should be viewed as a challenge and an attempt should be made to solve particular problems by suitable crosses. The Short-haired breeds will be considered firstly, then the Long-haired, ending with the two rexes and the Manx.

The Tabbies

Three types (at least) of tabby striping must be recognized. Two of these, mackerel and blotched are common in mongrel cats of the town and country-side. They also define two breeds, namely the Mackerel-striped Tabby and the Brown Tabby, respectively. The Mackerel Tabby contains the wild type tabby gene T. As a breed, it differs (or should differ, shall it be said) from the mongrel mackerel in several respects. The vertical striping should be well defined, intense in colour and above all, as unbroken as possible. It is difficult to produce Mackerel Tabbies without some broken striping but particular attention should be given to this feature. However, the overall picture must always be kept in mind and this means that the definition and set of the striping must also receive due assessment in the final choice of breeders.

The Brown Tabby is homozygous $t^b t^b$. This breed, too, should differ from the mongrel blotched tabby in having a well defined pattern, as black as possible, and nicely balanced. The well defined pattern, of course, as well as the ideal placing of the markings on the body, legs and tail, can only be achieved and maintained by selective breeding. The main factor in the definition of the pattern is the relative absence of the agouti ticking which is prone to invade the tabby markings. This tendency is polygenically controlled and the remedy is that of unremitting selection of those cats with the least ticking. The same procedure is advisable for other breeds in which good solid tabby markings are desirable. Attention should also be paid to the tone of the ground colour. This should be rich and full; certainly not dull and lifeless as in the case of most mongrel tabbies. Again, the remedy is that of culling the worst offenders.

The Abyssinian is an interesting form of tabby. There is an absence of striping on the body but some may be seen on the head, legs and tail. The amount is variable especially in cross-bred or mongrel animals. The head and tail being particularly marked in these animals. In the purebred Abyssinian, the situation is quite different. Little or no striping may be seen in the legs or tail and that on the head is not so pronounced. This elimination of the remnants of tabby is almost certainly due to patient selective breeding. It is now "fixed" to the extent of being regarded as a breed characteristic. The tabby gene involved is T^a, and most Abyssinians seem to be homozygotes, though it must be appreciated that this need not necessarily be so. The coat colour of the Abyssinian is more ruddy than the other tabbies. This is due to a deepening of the yellow component of the agouti pattern. This feature is inherited independently of T^a; as shown by the often prompt disappearance of the rufous colour in cross-bred Abyssinians.

The Selfs

The black cat is due to the presence of the non-agouti gene a. It is unfortunate that the concept of non-agouti versus agouti versus tabby can be the cause of confusion. The situation may be briefly reviewed once again. The agouti colour is the yellow and black ticked hairs present between the tabby striping and is due to the gene A. When this gene mutates to a, the yellow disappears and the result is a black cat. The tabby striping is unaffected but is masked by the uniform black coloration In ordinary tabby animals, the striping is black pigmentation imposed upon the agouti but it is evident that it is not possible to impose black striping upon an individual which is already black. Therefore, in genetic symbols, mackerel tabby is A–T–, blotched tabby is A–$t^b t^b$, while black is either aaT– or $aat^b t^b$. If proof is required that black cats may carry either T or t^b, this can be found in two ways. Firstly, young kittens often show "ghost" tabby stripes and careful examination will soon discern that these may either be of the mackerel or blotched form. Secondly, a cross between the black mackerel ($aaTT$) and a blotched tabby ($AAt^b t^b$) will give mackerel tabby ($AaTt^b$) offspring. The Abyssinian allele may be combined with a to give the genotype aaT^a– and the result is a black, no different in outward appearance from the others,

The beauty of the black resides in its jet black colour; which should
be as absolute as possible with no trace of rustiness. This richness of
colouring can only be achieved by persistent selective breeding. Any cat
which has a persistently brownish tinge should not be used for breeding
unless it is positively outstanding in other respects. It must not be overlooked, of course, that strong light, particularly direct sunlight, is the
biggest enemy of a rich black coat. Continuous exposure will ruin the
best of colours. The presence of white hairs or even traces of white spotting on the chest or belly is a problem. The only solution is not to breed
from such animals if others of equal quality, but minus these blemishes,
are available.

The blue cat is a non-agouti plus the gene for dilute, namely *aadd*.
The depth of colour is somewhat variable and can be manipulated to
some extent by selective breeding. Cats approaching most closely to the
ideal breed colour should always have preference for breeding, provided
other factors are equal. The comment of the last paragraph on the black
cat with regard to over-exposure to strong light and the presence of white
hairs or minor white spotting are applicable to the blue. Two breeds
have the same basic *aadd* genotype. These are the British Blue and the
Russian Blue. The main difference between the two lies in their body type.
It is strongly recommended that the two breeds are not inter-bred. The
kittens of such a cross will be blue but will almost certainly be a blend
of each breed as regards type. Several backcrosses to the original breed
will restore the situation but a really compelling reason should exist to
make all this trouble worthwhile. In the ordinary course of events, it is
doubtful if one can be found.

The blue is a non-agouti animal which means that, as with the black,
any one of the tabby alleles may be present, though hidden by the uniformly coloured coat. Thus, to give an example, a cat of genotype $aaddt^bt^b$
would be a blue carrying blotched tabby. In combination with agouti,
the blue-tabby is produced. The two most frequently encountered are
the mackerel striped blue-tabby ($A–ddT–$) and the blotched striped
blue-tabby ($A–ddt^bt^b$). In these animals, the stripes are a slatey blue and
the agouti areas are cream or fawny. On occasion, it is difficult to make
out the type of tabby carried by some animals. The blue Abyssinian
($A–ddT^a–$) is a rarity but not unknown. The colour is a rather undistin-
guished bluish-fawn.

A point of genetic terminology may be remarked upon at this stage.
It may be noticed that in discussing the various non-agouti cats, the

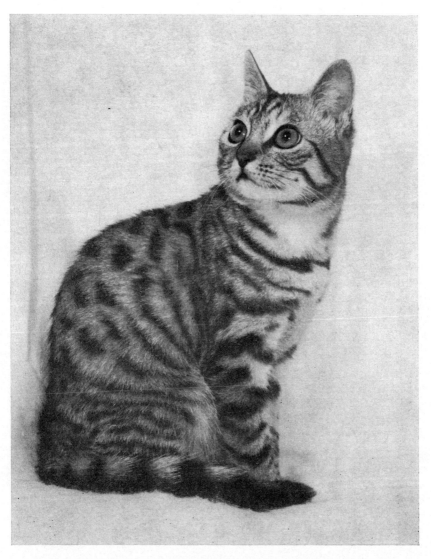

PLATE 1. A fine illustration of a silver mackerel striped tabby. In the silver, the yellow pigment is eliminated but the black tabby markings remain. On this individual, the mackerel striping is not continuous but tending to "break-up" into short bars or spots. The genotype is A–$c^{ch}c^{ch}$–T–.

PLATE 2. An ordinary blotched tabby. Note the irregular pattern on the side compared with the regular striping of the mackerel form. This is the so-called "classic" type of cat tabby pattern. The genotype is A–$t^b t^b$.

PLATE 3. A superb Abyssinian tabby. Observe particularly the complete absence of tabby markings on the body and fore-legs, and the virtual absence of markings on the tail. Cross-bred Abyssinians often show vestigial tabby markings on the forelegs and tail. The genotype is $A–T^a–$.

PLATE 4. A charming scene of four kittens enjoying a meal. The kitten at top left is a nicely marked mackerel tabby, with almost unbroken and evenly spaced vertical stripes; while the tabby at bottom right is the blotched form, with thicker and irregular markings. The kitten at bottom left is non-agouti black. The kitten at top right is a black tortoiseshell. Three of the kittens show small amounts of piebald white pattern (grades 3 and 4). The genotypes are, respectively, $A{-}T{-}$, $A{-}t^b t^b$, aa and $aaOo$.

PLATE 5. A typical tabby pointed Siamese. The tabby markings are clearly evident on the tail and nose but not on the legs. The genotype is $A-c^sc^s$.

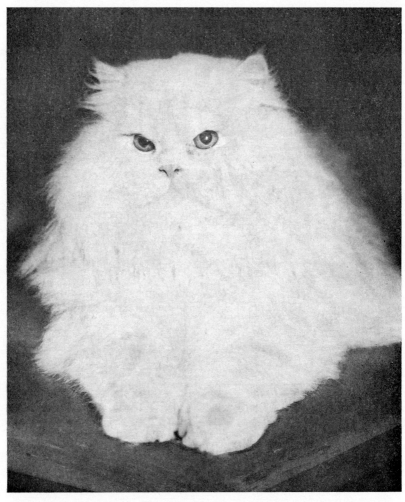

PLATE 6. A young long-haired cat, illustrating the soft fluffy coat of these breeds. The colour is red and the genotype, therefore, is either *llOY* or *llOO*.

PLATE 7. A delightful study of a normal coated queen, heterozygous for Cornish rex, and her two rex kittens. In addition to rex, these kittens carry the dominant white gene which produces a white coat and yellow or orange eyes. The genotype of the mother is $RrW-$ and that of the kittens $rrW-$.

PLATE 8. A Manx cat with several interesting features. The complete absence of tail can be clearly seen. The whorl of black pattern on the flank is characteristic of many blotched tabbies. The white markings are a typical expression of low-grade piebald, occurring on the nose and forehead in the shape of an inverted V and on the lower part of the legs (grade 4). The genotype is *A–MmSs*.

tabby alleles are omitted from the genotypes, despite the fact that at least one must be present. This is in accord with the practice of omitting all genes which are not strictly relevant to the discussion. It is true that one or more tabby alleles must be present but, since the a gene effectively "covers them up", there is no point in including them. Another not unimportant item to remember is that quite often, the actual tabby allele involved may be unknown. This means that the tabby allele cannot be given even if one so desired.

The Chestnut Brown (formerly Havana) is the true chocolate brown cat and has the genotype $aabb$. Most of the remarks on breeding self cats are applicable to the breed. The ideal colour can only be maintained by breeding from those individuals which approach most closely to it. The b gene appears to have originated in the Siamese as the Chocolate Pointed ($aabbc^sc^s$). Judicious crosses with the self black, and particularly with the Russian Blue ($aaB–C–dd$), eliminated the c^s allele and produced the Chestnut Brown ($aabbC–D–$). The cross with the Russian Blue was specially fortunate because the "foreign" body conformation emerged in a relatively pure state and was adopted as part of the ideal Chestnut Brown. Continuation of inter-breeding with the Russian Blue cross would in time produce the Lilac cat of genotype $aabbC–dd$. A very pretty animal, with a softer, more "warm" shade of blue. The colour has also been termed lavender. This is a colour which richly deserves to be established.

The combination of b with A results in three types of brown tabby. (A genetically brown tabby, *nota bene*, but, since the designation Brown Tabby has been taken as a breed name, it is proposed to denote the $A–bb$ animal as cinnamon, a good old-fashioned name for the brown agouti.) The blotched cinnamon tabby ($A–bbt^bt^b$) has chocolate brown tabby striping, interspersed with an agouti coloration somewhat brighter than the usual tabby. The mackerel tabby ($A–bbT–$) is somewhat similar. In both tabbies, the replacement of black pigmentation by brown reduces the contrast between the striping and the agouti areas. Of the two, this is more apparent for the mackerel tabby and one of the effects is to cause the striping to be broken up to a greater extent than normally. That is, the mackerel tabby takes on the appearance of being a spotted tabby; and a rather delightful one at that, with its bright yellowish-red ground colour freely dotted with brown ovoid "spots". The combination of $A–bbT^a–$ engenders the typical cinnamon cat. The colour is an orange-yellow with little resemblance to an agouti unless the coat is examined closely. Some Red Abyssinians appear to be of this genotype, the *b* gene interacting with the ruddy colouring of the breed to produce an extra-ordinary reddish-yellow colour.

Oranges and Tortoiseshells

One of the features of yellow cats is the range of shades in which they may be found. The common or garden names of "sandy", "ginger", or "marmalade" illustrate this point rather well. These are the typical forms and they cannot be compared with the intense splendour colouring possessed by the exhibition Red Tabby. In this breed, the depth of colour is at its greatest and the effect is enhanced by the presence of blotched tabby because, of the three tabby alleles, this type shows the maximum of deep red markings. It may seem strange at first sight that tabby strip-ing can be seen in yellow cats since it is obvious that they are not tabbies. However, the explanation is simple enough. The yellow colour is pro-duced by the gene *O* which converts all black pigment into yellow. It does this for all parts of the coat, both in the agouti areas and in the tabby striping. The fact that the striping comes through as a richer shade of yellow indicates that the amount of deposited pigment is greater. The equivalency of tabby striping in the tabby and of the dark markings in the yellow is shown by the behaviour of the pattern in the tabby tortoise-shell. The striping carries through from the tabby to the yellow areas without a break except for a change of colour.

Since the *O* gene converts black pigment to yellow, it may be wondered what effect the non-agouti gene may have. The answer is none at all. The yellow gene still carries on with the conversion, so that the yellow may be either *A–O* or *aaO*. Both are identically yellow in appearance; the *O* gene effectively masking the expression of both *A* or *a*. This aspect may be seen by examination of a black tortoiseshell. The black areas are black (as in a black cat) while the yellow areas are the same as those in a yellow or, for that matter, as those in a tabby tortoiseshell. Yet, of course, the genotype of a black tortoiseshell is *aaOo* and that of a tabby tortoiseshell is *A–Oo*. The *O* gene also masks the expression of *b* so that a yellow of genotype *bbO* is closely similar or identical to *B–O*.

This is explicitly shown by the brown tortoiseshell (*aabbOo*) which has brown and yellow areas. The yellow areas are the same in the two forms. There is one difference, however, which may be mentioned. Genetically brown yellow animals tend to be of a brighter and slightly richer colour than black yellows and this is apparent for the yellow areas of chocolate versus black tortoiseshells. This effect will seemingly hold for brown (bbO) versus black yellow (B–O) but probably not consistently enough for the genotype to be reliably identified by this means. On the other hand, anyone who is seeking to breed Red Tabbies of the richest possible colour might find it worthwhile to substitute gene b for B in the usual genotype.

The exhibition Red Tabby regularly has the genotype Ot^bt^b. That is, the deep red markings are those of the blotched tabby. It is unusual to see the OT– form of orange tabby although it would be readily recognized for the markings would be those of the mackerel tabby. The OT– is doubtless inferior to Ot^bt^b, as the markings will be less solid in appearance and there will probably be a tendency for them to merge with the paler background colour. The rich red colour of the Red Tabby is due to the concentration of modifying polygenes which deepen the yellow pigmentation. The Red Abyssinian of genotype A–OT^a– completes the trio of yellow tabbies. In this breed, the deeper yellow markings are absent except for the head and occasionally on the legs. The body colour is reddish-yellow, despite the lack of deeper coloured markings which are a contributing factor in other red breeds. This is due to the fact that the tabby Abyssinian has been bred to a rufous tone and the same polygenes which enrich the colour also intensify the colour of the Red. Some Red Abyssinians may be of genotype A–bbT^a– (the cinnamon Abyssinian mentioned earlier). In the United States, this form is sometimes referred to as the "Sorrel" Abyssinian to distinguish it from the Red Abyssinian. The brightest Red Abyssinian will probably be the result of combining the b and O genes in the same individual (A–$bbOT^a$–) for reasons given earlier.

The Cream animal is engendered by the combination of genes O and d. The dilution gene changes the yellow colour to fawn, or beige, in a comparable manner to the change from black to blue. The usual genotype for the exhibition Cream is either OT– or Ot^bt^b. The standard indicates that the animal should be devoid of bars and the former genotype would be superior to the latter in this respect. The contrast between the deeper cream markings and the ground colour is much less than that for ordinary yellow cats and, for this reason, it is fairly easy to diffuse out the markings by selective breeding to achieve a uniform colour. It is of interest that the OT^a– genotype would produce a cream coloured animal devoid of deeper barring. If the body conformation is correct, the animal would in fact be a cream Abyssinian of a delectable soft colour. In the above discussion, the various orange and cream genotypes are shown with a single O gene. This is how the genotype should be written for the male; the corresponding female will be OO and is phenotypically identical to the male. The reason is the sex-linked inheritance of O.

The exhibition Tortoiseshell has the genotype $aaOo$. It is self black, intermingled with intense yellow areas. The standard asks for the patches to be clear and defined and this is no easy task. Only by breeding from the best pattern animals is there much hope of any consistent success. The Tortoiseshell and white (Calico in the United States) has the genotype $aaOoS-$. It, too, is a patchwork of black and orange, with the addition of white areas. The white is due to piebald spotting and is never extensive as a rule. It is sometimes asserted that the tortoiseshell consists of three colours, namely, black, red and cream. This is not so, the red and cream difference is due to the tabby markings present in the yellow areas. The red corresponding to the deeper tabby markings and the cream to the lighter intervening colour. It is easy to imagine how the belief can be sustained when the red and cream are separated by black and thus appear as distinct patches of colour or even as adjoining patches which cannot be readily related to the underlying tabby markings.

It may be noted that the black is the only officially standardized colour at this time although a whole range of other colours do exist and, in fact, are often to be seen in mongrel populations. For example, the tabby tortoiseshell ($A-Oo$), either mackerel or blotched as the case may be, have already been mentioned and there is also the blue tortoiseshell or Blue-cream ($aaddOo$), the chocolate tortoiseshell ($aabbOo$) and the lilac tortoiseshell ($aabbddOo$). It seems remarkable that the colour quartet of black, blue, chocolate and lilac are not recognized within the general framework of the short-haired tortoiseshell standard in a similar manner as these colours are recognized for the Siamese.

Siamese, Burmese and Silver

The Siamese form of pigmentation (little on the body but much on the points) is due to the gene c^s. Basically, the reason is that of temperature dependency. The body temperature is just a wee bit too high for much pigment to be formed, whereas the points do so because their temperature is sufficiently low. This is not the whole story, for the amount of pigment can vary between different individuals kept under the same conditions. It has been suggested that more than one Siamese allele may be responsible for this variation. This is a possibility, of course, but it does not seem likely and, from a practical point of view, it is doubtless wise to proceed as if only one allele is involved. In general, part of the variation is due to fluctuations in the temperature under which the cats are housed and in part to modifying genes which are inherited independently of the Siamese allele. With Siamese breeding it is probably good policy to maintain the cats in a constant, reasonably warm, temperature. Not because they are more delicate than other breeds but to minimize any unwanted variation which might arise from sharp changes in temperature. Dark lines or light patches of colour in an otherwise smoothly shaded coat could be due to this cause.

The Siamese are known in a range of colours. From what has been said in previous paragraphs, it should be easy to comprehend the relationships between the four basic colours. For a start, all four are non-agouti. The Seal pointed is $aaB–c^sc^sD–$, the Chocolate Pointed is $aabbc^sc^sD–$, the Blue Pointed is $aaB–c^sc^sdd$ and the Lilac Pointed is $aabbc^sc^sdd$ (Frost Point in the United States). Since the body conformation is identical for each, it is possible to inter-breed the four colours without any real detriment to any single one. The Red Pointed Siamese is of c^sc^sO constitution; the points are patterned with orange markings against a white or cream coloured background. Altogether, the variety is attractive and is breaking new ground for the breed. The cream Pointed (c^sc^sddO) is a paler edition of the foregoing. Finally, the tortoiseshell Siamese (c^sc^sOo) has been produced; of which, the black (aac^sc^sOo), the chocolate ($aabbc^sc^sOo$) and the blue (aac^sc^sddOo) are probably the most distinctive and merit consideration.

Bringing the A gene into the genotype (*e.g.*, after initial crosses with one of the tabbies) will produce the tabby Pointed Siamese or Lynx Pointed as it is sometimes known. The type of tabby will depend upon the particular tabby allele involved. For instance, an animal of genotype $A–B–c^sc^sD–T–$ would be a mackerel tabby Siamese and the substitution of t^bt^b in place of $T–$ in this formula would give the blotched tabby Siamese. However, in view of the restricted expression of tabby, it may not be easy to distinguish the two. It is possible to have the tabby Pointed in four colours: black, chocolate, blue and lilac. The genotypes of these are the same as the four non-agouti colours, with the substitution of $A–$ for aa.

Should anyone wish to breed the tabby pointed, it would seem desirable to use the Abyssinian as the source of the agouti gene since the body conformation of the breed is very close to that of the Siamese. The points are silver patterned rather than tabby because the c^s gene allows little or no yellow pigment to develop in the lighter coloured agouti areas. This effect is also evident for the Red Pointed Siamese described earlier. A warning may be issued that it is possible for some non-agouti Siamese to display false "tabby" markings. The condition is analogous to the ghost tabby markings often discernable in young black cats. The difference in pigment concentration between the tabby and agouti areas reveals itself in a difference of colour intensity which simulates the tabby pattern. The absence of agouti ticking usually betrays the spuriousness of the pattern.

The Burmese is akin to the Siamese, not only in body conformation and a tendency towards darker points, compared with the body colour, but also genetically. The Burmese differs from the chocolate brown of the Chestnut Brown in being more of a sable brown or fuscous, with dark sepia overtones. The Burmese colour is due to a gene c^b which is an allele of c^s. The c^b gene is incompletely dominant to c^s, with the consequence that two phases of Burmese are possible; a dark aac^bc^b and a light aac^bc^s. The former is true breeding while the latter is not. In the light phase Burmese, the contrast between the body colour and the dark points is very evident, yet this animal is just as clearly not Siamese. In the United States, with a feeling for exotic terminology, the light phase has been variously called the "Golden Siamese" or the "Tonkanese".

The Burmese mutant has given rise to one interesting range of new colours. One of the first to be produced is the Blue Burmese of genotype aac^bc^bdd or aac^bc^sdd depending upon the phase. These are beautiful cats, obviously blue but lighter and more exquisitely coloured than their nearest counterpart, the Russian Blue. The combination of $aabbc^bc^b$ produces a *cafe au lait* colour, lighter than the ordinary Burmese and of a more subtle brown coloration. The points are now distinctly chocolate instead of dark sepia and the body fur shows a comparable lightening. The addition of d into the genotype ($aabbc^bc^bdd$) more or less completes the basic quartet of colours. This form emerges as similar to the Blue Burmese but of more pastel tone. When it is realized that both dark and light phases may exist for these varieties, it is easy to appreciate the fascination which they have for some breeders. In the United States, the brown and lilac Burmese have been called the "Champagne Burmese" and "Platinum Burmese", respectively, although the suitability of these euphemisms is perhaps open to question.

The Silver Tabby receives its name from the relative absence of yellow pigment from the agouti areas of the coat. Consequently, a cat is produced in which the black tabby striping stands out against a whitish or tawny background. The exhibition Silver has the genotype $A-c^{ch}-t^b t^b$ and a cat of championship standard is a beautiful animal. The agouti areas are white and the blotched striping is relatively devoid of ticking. Both the tawny tinge and the unwanted ticking has been eliminated by selective breeding. The situation is different for the mongrel silver which displays a variable amount of tawny pigment and ticking. This is perhaps most noticeable for the mackerel $(A-c^{ch}-T-)$, rather than the blotched, silver tabby because of the greater tendency for the striping to break up into bars and spots and to merge with the agouti background. The silver Abyssinian $(A-c^{ch}-T^a-)$ is a handsome cat, especially when the coat is devoid of the tawny tinge. The even black ticking set against a white background is reminiscent of *lanigera* chinchilla. The effect is spoilt, however, by the presence of the smallest amount of the undesirable tawny pigment.

The black Silver Tabby is the only one officially recognized as a breed at present but this does not mean that others do not exist. The blue silver of genotype $A-c^{ch}-ddt^b t^b$ has been produced, with bluish striping set against an off-white or tawny background. The latter could doubtless be eliminated by selective breeding. Similarly, the cinnamon silver $(A-bbc^{ch}-t^b t^b)$ could be bred if anyone is sufficiently interested; also the lilac $(A-bbc^{ch}-ddt^b t^b)$ to complete the quartet. The blotched tabby forms will probably be the most striking. The mackerel striped will probably appear to be too nondescript in colour to be worth breeding. Among the silver Abyssinians, the blue $(A-c^{ch}-ddT^a)$ could make an excellent foil to the black form mentioned in the previous paragraph.

The combination $aac^{ch}-$ is a black very similar to the ordinary black in appearance, except perhaps for the eye colour and possibly for a variable bluish-white under colour. No information seems to be available on the colours produced by other genotypes built around the $aac^{ch}-$ unit; as, for example, the colours produced by $aabbc^{ch}-$ or $aac^{ch}-dd$. Except may be for eye colour, it seems almost certain that these will resemble the corresponding $aaC-$ forms, namely, chocolate brown and blue, respectively. However, should someone believe that a novel colour will result from one of these rare gene combinations, an endeavour should be made to synthesize the genotype.

The bringing together of the genes c^{ch} and O results in the silver red; a cat with whitish or tawny ground colour and striping of orange-yellow. This phenotype indicates that, while the c^{ch} gene may inhibit most or all of the yellow pigment in the agouti areas, it does not have the same effect on the more intense areas. Some reduction in intensity occurs but not to the extent of effacing the pattern. The blotch pattern ($c^{ch}-Ot^{b}t^{b}$) is the most evident while the mackerel ($c^{ch}-OT-$) is variable depending on whether the stripes are well defined or are tending to break up. The Abyssinian form ($c^{ch}-OT^{a}$) is nearly white or tawny, flecked with darker yellow ticking. The analogy with the sequence of ordinary silver forms should be obvious; the difference is that a yellow tabby pattern or ticking, respectively, replaces black. Incorporating the d gene into the genotype, (e.g. $c^{ch}-ddOt^{b}t^{b}$) brings into being a pale cream and white animal with a somewhat blurred pattern. None of the colours of this paragraph are officially recognized nor, it would seem, bred intentionally. This may be a pity, for at least one (the blotched patterned silver red of genotype ($c^{ch}-Ot^{b}t^{b}$) appears to have potential as a possible attractive new breed.

Albino or Chinese White

The albino, with pink eyes and completely white coat, borders on the unknown in the cat. This is rather curious since albinism is one of the most common of mutants to appear in mammals. However, albinism is not entirely unknown, for there have been reports from time to time of such animals being seen. The latest information would suggest that a form of albinims is being established in the United States under the name of "Chinese White" or "Albino Siamese". The first name is rather fancifully derived from an early sighting of alleged albino cats in China; while the second name is based upon the stated origin of the present pale individuals. These are said to be bred from Siamese, especially from animals descended from one particular male. This has meant that the strain has assumed the "Foreign" type of body conformation, which is doubtless aesthetically pleasing but is of little significance in itself as a sign of oriental or other exotic derivation. The albino may be bred from Siamese parents, of course, but equally likely as a spontaneous mutation from those of any other breed or even among mongrel cats.

The All-Whites

The blue-eyed white is something of an enigma as regards the exact genetic status of the eye colour. The all- or almost all- white coat is due to a dominant gene W. That much seems to be reasonably established but it is the erratic heredity of the blue eye which is the problem. If breeders' accounts are accepted as reliable, *inter se* matings of blue-eyed cats do not invariably produce blue-eyed kittens nor do matings of yellow or orange-eyed cats never give blue-eyed kittens. In the face of this sort of information, there is only one course to follow, namely, to breed only from cats with two blue-eyes. Animals which excel in other features but with one or two orange coloured eyes may be used for breeding but only with the full acceptance that to do so may weaken the propensity towards the founding of a true breeding strain of blue-eyed whites.

The genetic basis for the blue-eyed condition has not been resolved to everyone's satisfaction. There are two main explanations. One is that the blue eye is part of the expression of W but that the manifestation is variable. The other is that another gene is involved which interacts with W. This is thought by some to be S. The amount of white produced by S is very variable and the erratic expression of the blue eye is considered to be related to this. It is clearly impossible to observe the expression of S in the W animal but, should it cover the head, the conjecture is that a blue eye will result. Whether or not, one or both eyes are blue, will depend upon the distribution of white in the head region. This explanation could be regarded as the "classic" since it has gone unchallenged for several decades. However, just recently, it has been proposed that the blue eye colour is due to a gene unrelated to S. This gene is depicted as being inherited as a recessive and does not produce any effect except in company with W. Moreover, it may not always find expression even then, hence the appearance of the odd- eyed individual and the errratic breeding behaviour.

The blue-eyed or orange-eyed white is not an albino, or a relation thereof, because it does not have the fundamental property of albinism: the pink or pigment-free eye. However, they share one aspect in common. The completely white coat must not be taken at its face value of an absence of all other colour genes. This false idea finds expression in the belief that the mating of a white cat with a coloured will produce offspring of the same colour as that of the coloured parent. This need not be so, for the reasons given in an early chapter. In general the W gene will mask the expression of all other genes which may be present. Only if another gene has an effect on eye colour may there be exceptions to this rule. An instance may be given. Suppose a cat distended to have yellow eyes carried the c^s gene (viz. $c^s c^s W-$), what would be the expected eye colour? In these situations, the expected eye colour is usually the palest; in the present case, this indicates the Siamese eye colour. The animal would have a white coat combined with the Siamese blue eye. This animal has in fact been produced and is known as the Foreign White.

White Spotted

White marked cats are very common among mongrel populations yet few breeds have white spotting as part of their make-up. The exception, of course, is the Tortoiseshell and white which displays fairly low grade marking. However, an attempt has been made in the United States to popularize a form under the name of "Chinese Harlequin", based upon an allegedly ancient chinese cat. This variety is mainly white except for small patches of black on the head, occasionally on the body, and a solid black tail. The spotting in fact corresponds to grade 8 and the animal's genotype would be $aaSS$. The form could conceivably breed relatively true for this amount of white.

The Long-hairs

The preceding sections have discussed the intricacies of colour inheritance as these relate to the normal or short-haired cat. However, quite a number of breeds exist which only differ from their normal counterparts in having long hair. These are the Long-hairs, known formerly as Persians and still earlier as Angoras. In fact, the whole compass of colours so far discussed may be found combined with the long-haired gene l. For the most part, the comparable long-haired version can be easily equated to the corresponding short-haired. This fact may be discerned from an examination of the columns of Table 9. On the other hand, there are certain differences which deserve to be specifically covered. These stem from two causes: (1) several colours are officially recognized as definite breeds as Long-hairs but not as Short-hairs and (2) the long hair, by virtue of its length, tends to obscure the form of several patterns or make their recognition less easy. This is perhaps not an important aspect for the experienced but it can be a hazard for the tyro.

The main factor to remember in considering the various long-haired animals is that the hair fibres overlap each other to a greater extent than in the normal coated cat and not always regularly. A much greater length of the hair shaft is also exposed, and, since this is less intensely pigmented than the tip, this often produces the effect of a spurious reduction of colour. The effect is probably more evident in mongrel long hairs than in exhibition animals where selective breeding has counteracted the effect to some extent, particularly for the black. The lack of definition of pattern applies specially to the tabby striping, both that of the Brown Tabby ($A-llt^bt^b$) and that of the Red Tabby ($110t^bt^b$). Very little is known how the officially recognized breed of Red Self differs from the Red Tabby. It could be surmised that there is no fundamental difference (except possibly in the substitution of T for t^b) but that, in the Red Self, the markings are excessively blurred and indistinct. As a point of interest, this aspect is taken advantage of in the conception of the ideal Blue Cream Long-hair. The genotype of this breed is $aaddllOo$ but, whereas the other Tortoiseshell breeds require the pattern to be well broken into patches, the Blue Cream pattern is required to be softly intermingled.

Whereas, it is desirable for the Black and Blue Long-hairs to have a solid undercolour, the reverse is true for the Smoke. The genotype for this breed is $aac^{ch}-11$ and the light or white undercolour is the outcome of an interaction between the c^{ch} and 1 genes, the longer fibres and the lay of the hair bringing the undercolour into prominence. The Blue Smoke is the dilute form and has the genotype $aac^{ch}-ddll$. The genotype of the Silver Tabby Long-hair is $A-c^{ch}-11t^bt^b$, comparable to the Short-hair of the same name. The pale undercolour is present under the blotched tabby striping, accompanied by white agouti areas from which the yellow has been removed. In the chinchilla, this process has been carried to the extreme. The white undercolour is pronounced and all of the yellow has been removed; both features presumably being the result of selective breeding. The coat is possessed of an overall covering of black ticked hairs which, however, is variable; the lightest ticked specimens being the most prized. Young Chinchilla kittens appear as silver tabbies until the hair growth obscures the striping and the white undercolour comes into prominence. The even ticking is more likely to be achieved by the presence of T rather than of the t^b gene. The amount of ticking can vary between individuals and this aspect is revealed in an indirect manner by the recognition in the United States of a "Shaded Silver" Long-hair, a breed which seems to be roughly half-way between the Silver Tabby Long-hair and the Chinchilla. Only the superb exhibition Chinchilla has the white ground colour; in most others and especially in mongrels, the ground colour is inclined to be tawny.

The exhibition Chinchilla is a remarkable animal and the genetic difference between the colour and that of the Silver has often been the topic of speculation. Both colours are devoid of yellow pigment and have the common features of a white undercolour. In the Chinchilla, the white undercolour extends almost to the hair tips. This effect is apparently due to selective breeding and the question may be asked: "Is the extreme white undercolour produced entirely by polygenes or could a major gene be involved?" So far, for the few crosses between Chinchilla and other colours which have been examined, no evidence for the existence of a major gene has emerged. The first-cross offspring usually have an undercolour which is more prominent than that typically present in a Silver but is far from being "Chinchilla." Unfortunately, these crosses have not been taken into an F_2 generation and this is the main reason why the difference between the two colours still has an element of mystery surrounding it.

The addition of gene O to the genotype ($A–c^{ch}–110$) gives the red Chinchilla, a form in which the black ticking is replaced by red. As in the black Chinchilla, the amount of ticking is variable. In the United States, these rather pretty animals have been called the "Shell Cameo" for the lighter, more delicate, ticked forms and the "Shaded Cameo" for the darker. As young kittens, these curious animals appear as red mackerel or blotched striped silver tabbies until such time as the hair growth obliterates the pattern. Other "Chinchilla" or "Shaded Silver" varieties are possible, such as the cream ticked ($A–c^{ch}Odd110$), which is rumoured as being bred in the States; the brown ticked ($A–bbc^{ch}–11$) and the blue ticked ($A–c^{ch}–dd11$). Whether or not these varieties are attractive enough to encourage people to breed them is perhaps a debatable question. This is a matter of personal opinion, which is true for almost all of the rare or unrecognized colours.

The conjunction of the Siamese pattern and long hair has produced the splendour of the long-haired Colour point. These cats are not simply long-haired Siamese, for the body type is that of the Long-hair, not that of the lithely built Siamese. This breed may be bred in all of the known colours, of which the following have all been realized to date: seal (aac^sc^s11), chocolate ($aabbc^sc^s11$), blue (aac^sc^sdd11), lilac ($aabbc^sc^sdd11$), and red (c^sc^sO11). In the United States, this breed is known as the Himalayan, with much the same range of colours.

A reference may be made at this point to the unusual but graceful Birman cat, now being bred in France, in the United States ("Sacred Cat of Burma") and latterly in Britain. The genotype is aac^sc^s11 and is a typical Seal Pointed Long-hair but with the addition of four white "gloves", one to each foot. These white markings represent a low grade of piebald spotting and the problem of breeding these cats is that of obtaining just the right amount of white. The white must be on all four feet and just sufficient to be a "glove" and not a "stocking". A cat with four evenly sized gloves is something of a novelty. A blue form (aac^sc^sdd11) is known for the breed and other colours could be synthesized by anyone so minded.

A rather exotic looking cat is that known as Van, introduced from Eastern Turkey of recent date. The animal is long-haired and is extensively marked with piebald spotting. In fact, only the greater part of the tail and areas as the head are pigmented. These are a rich auburn colour; showing clearly on the tail, especially, the alternating bands of light and dark yellow pigmentation of the tabby pattern. The genotype, therefore, is $110SS$. The precise nature of the tabby pattern is unknown since the pigmented areas do not normally occur on those parts of the body where the various patterns can be readily discerned. On the other hand, the t^b allele produces the more heavily barred tail and it is conceivable that this is the type of tabby possessed by the breed. The SS designation may be more symbolic than actual since the genetics of high grade piebald is not fully understood. However, if only one main gene is involved, the mostly white coat is indicative of homozygosity of S.

Rex

All of the colours known to occur in the normal furred cat may be found in, or can be produced in, any of the various rex breeds. It only requires patience and skill in manipulating the relevant colour genes in conjunction with the relevant rex gene. The combination of long hair and rex (e.g. $11rr$) has been produced; the phenotype displaying features of each coat type. The fur is longer than normal and very fine in texture, but not so long as that of the non-rex long-hair. The whiskers are bent which is a sure sign of one of the rex genes.

Manx

The Manx cat is bred in a fair number of colours, mostly the common ones as may be expected, since there has been few sustained attempts to extend the range. However, it will be apparent that any of those described could be combined with the Manx taillessness if anyone is so willed. The long-haired Manx (*llM–*) has been produced in the United States under the name "Cymric". Despite the name, the long-haired Manx has nothing to do with Wales. The synthesis of the rex Manx should not present any special problems; nor that of the triple combination of long-haired rex Manx, in a variety of colours, should this ever be considered a worthwhile undertaking.

Fundamental Genotypes

Table 10 presents the basic genotypes of the breeds recognized in Britain, the United States and those other countries which have largely adopted the breed standards of these two countries. Also included are the genotypes of various varieties and forms which are thought worthy of distinction. Colour is by no means the sole arbiter of a breed and for this reason the genotypes should be regarded as merely the genic backbone around which a breed has been moulded and developed. A number of breeds could conceivably have more than one genotype, with little or no change in their appearance. It would be a complex task to list these alternatives and one which would be of doubtful utility. The given genotype is that which either occurs most frequently or is most representative.

The genotypes of the table only lists those genes which differ from those present in the wild coloured cat. There are twelve gene loci which are of concern to the breeder and these may be written in symbols as follows:

A–B–C–D–L–mmooR–Re–ssT–W .

The dashes between each locus represent unknown genes which may be carried by the individual. The substitution of one or more mutant genes

TABLE 10. GENOTYPES OF NOTABLE BREEDS AND VARIETIES OF CATS

Short-haired	Genotype	Long-haired	Genotype
Abyssinian	T^a-	Birman	aac^sc^sllS-
Abyssinian, red	OT^a	Birman, blue	$aac^sc^sddllS-$
Abyssinian, silver	$c^{ch}-T^a-$	Black	$aall$
Abyssinian, sorrel	bbT^a-	Blue	$aaddll$
Black	aa	Blue Cream	$aaddOo$
Blue Tabby	ddt^bt^b	Brown Tabby	ll
British Blue	$aadd$	Cameo	$c^{ch}-llO$
Brown Tabby	t^bt^b	Chinchilla	$c^{ch}-ll$
Burmese	aac^bc^b	Chinchilla, blue	$c^{ch}-ddll$
Burmese, blue	aac^bc^bdd	Colourpoint, blue	aac^sc^sddll
Burmese, champagne	$aabbc^bc^b$	Colourpoint, choc.	$aabbc^sc^sll$
Burmese, light phase	aac^bc^s	Colourpoint, lilac	$aabbc^sc^sddll$
Burmese, platignum	$aabbc^bc^bdd$	Colourpoint, red	c^sc^sllO
Chestnut Brown	$aabb$	Colourpoint, seal	aac^sc^sll
Chinese Harlequin	$aaSS$	Cream	$ddllO$
Chinese White	cc	Red Tabby	$llOt^bt^b$
Cinnamon Tabby	bbt^bt^b	Silver Tabby	$c^{ch}-llt^bt^b$
Cream	ddO	Smoke	$aac^{ch}-ll$
Foreign White	c^sc^sW-	Smoke, blue	$aac^{ch}-ddll$
Lilac	$aabbdd$		
Mackerel Tabby		Tortoiseshell	$aallOo$
Red Tabby	Ot^bt^b	Tortoiseshell and	
Russian Blue	$aadd$	White	$aallOoS-$
Siamese, blue	aac^sc^sdd	Van	$llOSS$
Siamese, chocolate	$aabbc^sc^s$	White, blue-eyed	$llW-$
Siamese, cream	c^sc^sddO	White, orange-eyed	$llW-$
Siamese, lilac	$aabbc^sc^sdd$		
Siamese, red	c^sc^sO		
Siamese, seal	aac^sc^s		
Siamese, tabby	c^sc^s		
Siamese, tabby, blue	c^sc^sdd		
Siamese, tabby, choc.	bbc^sc^s		
Siamese, tabby, lilac	bbc^sc^sdd		
Siamese, tortoiseshell	aac^sc^sOo		
Siamese, tort., blue	aac^sc^sddOo		
Siamese, tort., choc.	$aabbc^sc^sOo$		
Siamese, tort., lilac	$aabbc^sc^sddOo$		
Silver Tabby	$c^{ch}-t^bt^b$		
Silver Tabby, blue	$c^{ch}-ddt^bt^b$		
Silver Tabby, choc.	$bbc^{ch}-t^bt^b$		
Silver Tabby red	$c^{ch}-Ot^bt^b$		

Short-haired	Genotype	Long-haired	Genotype
Tortoiseshell	*aaOo*		
Tortoiseshell, blue	*aaddOo*		
Tortoiseshell, choc.	*aabbOo*		
Tortoiseshell and White	*aaOoS–*		
White	*W–*		

in the above formula will produce one of the known forms of cat unless, of course, the effect of the gene is masked by another. The remainder of the genotype must be regarded as unchanged. The genotypes of the table may be viewed as the minimum change to produce the appropriate colour or coat type.

No Rex or Manx (or combination) are shown in the table since these typically partake of any of the commoner colours. For instance, the genotype of the black Cornish Rex is *aarr*, that of the Blue Devon Rex is *aaddrere* and that of the long-haired blotched tabby Manx is $11M{-}t^{b}t^{b}$. It is usual to write genotypes in alphabetical order of the gene symbols. Varieties displaying white spotting are shown as possessing a gene *S*. Since the genetics of white spotting are not fully understood, this should be taken as being at least partly symbolic. That is, the symbol denotes the presence of white spotting, rather than that of a definite white spotting gene.

VII. ABNORMALITIES

THE problem of the genetic anomaly is something which all breeders should be aware. This is not to suggest that such anomalies are common, far from it. Yet, on the other hand, the cat must be expected to have its quota of defects as in other fancy and domestic animals. The distressing aspect is that these anomalies will recur in subsequent litters and in subsequent generations if no remedial action is taken. In most cases, in direct defiance of improvements in husbandry, diet or veterinary practice.

To appreciate the problem of genetic defects, it is necessary to view the situation in perspective. Against a background of deficiency disease, bacterial or viral infection or straightforward injury, the true nature of a genetic abnormality could pass unrecognized. Indeed, an afflicted animal could be one of the first to succumb to a non-genetic ailment since many anomalies either lower the resistance of the individual or render it less able to compete with its fellows. Now, the deficiency disease can be prevented and veterinary safeguards erected against infection but what of the genetic defect? The occurrence of the anomaly is distressing enough but the real problem is its ability to recur in future litters of either direct or collateral descent.

The situation could perhaps be put more explicitly. Take a cattery in which the general housing conditions border on the lamentable, the food inadequate (as a result of ignorance probably more than anything else) and the conditions of hygiene indifferent, if not actually deplorable, it is small wonder that disease always seems to be lurking around the corner. Imagine, on the other hand, a cattery in which the housing is palatial, the food adequate and nutritious, and the hygiene attended to with scrupulous care. Here, most of the common ailments will be abolished and serious disease almost unknown. Yet, the breeder may find himself bothered with troubles of another sort. Those which seem peculiar to the individual and cannot be ascribed to bad husbandry, poor diet or neglect. These are the sort of ailments which could be due to genetic causes. Put another way, though genetic anomalies will occur in both bad and well-maintained catteries, it is in the latter that they will be most noticeable.

Genetic anomalies are usually grouped under the general term of "lethals" in genetic tests. However, various types of lethal action should be recognized. Firstly, there are genes which cause death prior to birth; this is the classical lethal. No homozygous anomalous kittens are even seen. However, the heterozygote usually differs from normal and is usually abnormal. It is the inter-breeding of these that will lead to the discovery of the lethality. Such a case exists in the cat in the form of the Manx. Manx cats have a deformed pelvic and caudal region and are almost tailless. The mating of Manx *inter se* results in a 2 : 1 ratio of Manx type and normal kittens (Fig. 22). The homozygote *MM* probably dies *in utero* and is absorbed. This fact reveals itself in a reduction in average litter size as well as in the kitten ratio.

Gametes from Manx *Mm*

FIG. 22. Expectations from mating two Manx cats: to illustrate the 2 : 1 ratio of Manx: normal tailed offspring. The homozygote *MM* probably dies *in utero*.

Secondly, there is the teratological lethal which produces monstrous young at birth. Quite often the "monster" is still-born as a result of various gross defects. In other cases, death usually ensues within a short period. Thirdly, there is the delayed lethal. Here, the animal is normal at birth but eventually dies of a late developing affliction. The onset may be delayed for months or even years. Fourthly, there is the semilethal or partial lethal. As the name implies, death is not an inevitable accompaniment but the individual is always either mildly or severely abnormal. These latter are responsible for a wide variety of mild defects. Thus, to summarize, not all congenital defects are of genetic origin although it is a fair assumption in most cases until the facts disclose otherwise. Conversely, not all late developing afflictions are necessarily due to the environment.

Several of the anomalies to be described in following sections fall into the category of semi-lethals. In some, the partial lethality is obvious, in others, it is not. Examples of the former are the hairless, ataxic, hare-lip and cleft-palate conditions, while examples of the latter are four-ears and urolithiasis. Even the Manx heterozygote cannot be depicted as one hundred per cent healthy since their pre-natal death rate is higher than that for cats with normal tails. The heterozygote, therefore, could be regarded as semi-lethal, regardless of the fate of the homozygote.

A frequent question is: "How are genetic anomalies discovered?" Or, to rephrase the wording, how can one be sure that an anomaly is inherited? It is true that most disorders occur in isolated events and this can give no indication of a genetic influence. However, suppose that the disorder shows a pattern, such as appearing in successive litters from the same parents or in different litters from parents which share a common ancestor. This is usually the first evidence that an anomaly has a genetic basis. The incidence is then said to be "familial". At this stage, it might be thought that it should be easy to obtain some idea of the mode of inheritance. Sometimes this is so, but, only too often among mongrel cats, the matings are uncontrolled and no information is available for the male parent; nor for remoter ancestors such as grandparents or great grandparents. Even when several cases of a particular anomaly occur in one neighbourhood, it is often next to impossible to connect these up in a common family tree.

With pedigree cats, the situation is different. Here, parentage is important, the matings are controlled and accurate records are usually available. It is among this group that anomalies with a familial tendency are likely to be discovered. Generally, the mode of inheritance will emerge according to the recognized laws of heredity. If necessary, special matings can be arranged to provide decisive data. In general, the mode of inheritance can be due either to a single gene (monogenic) or to the combined action of polygenes, possibly showing the threshold effect. If the inheritance is monogenic, it is essential to determine whether the anomaly is caused by a dominant or a recessive gene.

An effort has been made to include all instances of abnormality which are either known or suspected to have a genetic basis. There are two reasons why this policy seems desirable. The first is that veterinarians who are consulted for advice on how to treat the anomaly should be aware that the condition could be heritable. This may be helpful for cases where the advisability of breeding from the animal is sought. Secondly, knowledge that the anomaly could be inherited may encourage the collection of relevant data. Such information as is available at present is so scanty that additional data would be welcomed. Any anomaly which shows signs of being familial deserves to be energetically followed up. With this in mind, reference has been made to the pertinent research articles which treat the anomaly under discussion.

Elimination of Anomalies

Everyone is agreed that it is desirable to eliminate genetic anomalies. Yet, they appear to persist tenaciously. Why should this be so? The reason is two-fold: firstly, the problem can be more complex than appears on the surface and, secondly, the remedy may demand more drastic action than is acceptable. Somewhat different problems arise and different procedures should be followed according to the known or assumed mode of inheritance. That is, whether the anomaly displays (1) dominant, (2) recessive monogenic heredity or (3) polygenic heredity.

With dominant monogenic heredity, there is no problem when the disorder is readily apparent or is regularly manifested. However, this is not always the situation. For example, the affliction may not be evident until late in life. Until after puberty and the animal has been breeding for some time. This latter aspect can only be tackled by means of clinical analysis designed for early diagnosis of onset of the disease. Also, of course, the conscientious seeking and taking notice of such clinical reports. It is silly to ignore a positive report simply because an outstanding cat is apparently healthy. Eventually, it will not be and, meantime, the genetic damage it can do is considerable. The case of irregular manifestation is similar except that clinical diagnosis is excluded. Bodily, the animal is fully healthy and detection is probably best handled by the same methods as recommended for that of finding carriers of a recessive anomaly.

Theoretically, all dominant monogenic anomalies could be eliminated if all of the descendants of subsequently afflicted animals are prevented from breeding. This would be drastic action indeed when it is considered that about fifty per cent of the animal's descendants will be free of the anomaly. Unfortunately, the price to be paid is that the other fifty per cent will be handing on the anomaly until they are eventually detected. Fortunately, it is possible that the cat is not troubled with this sort of anomaly. It is to be hoped that this will always be so but, alas, this cannot be taken for granted. For instance, progressive retinal atrophy is a late developing genetic disease of the eye in the dog. In a few breeds, the disease is troublesome and the main factor for this is that the young dog can see perfectly but eventually becomes partially or totally blind. The late onset of the affliction means that the animal may have bred before the first symptoms are noticed. A similar disease could occur in the cat.

With recessive monogenic heredity, the problem is that of detection of the heterozygote or "carrier". It is not a question of clinical detection since these animals are fully normal. Their detection lies in another direction: that of test mating. This may be accomplished in one of two ways. If the anomaly is slight (undesirable, say, but not crippling) and does not interfere with reproduction, the animal to be tested can be mated to one or more affected animals. Provided sufficient normal kittens are produced, without the appearance of a *single* anomalous individual, the animal may be judged not to be a carrier. The number of kittens to be bred in each test will depend upon the level of acceptable error. It may be that a carrier animal could produce entirely normal young by chance. However, the chances of such an event become smaller as the number of kittens increases. This is, the error which must be made acceptably low by stipulating that a certain number of young be bred. Column A of the accompanying table gives the error for successive normal kittens examined. Two acceptable levels are 5 per cent (5 kittens or more) and 1 per cent (7 kittens). The latter is preferable to the former and there is a strong case for making it mandatory.

When the anomaly is severe, breeding from such individuals may be either unethical or impracticable. A different procedure should be followed. This consists of mating the animal to be tested with known carriers. Again, the matter of acceptable error must be decided. Since this procedure is more roundabout, the number of kittens required must be increased. Column B of the table shows the error for successive normal kittens examined. The two levels of 5 per cent and 1 per cent require the rearing of 11 and 17 kittens, respectively. It should be apparent that the kittens produced by these test matings should not ordinarily be used or sold for breeding since all of them will be carriers in the first method of testing and 50 per cent at least in the second.

Now, for various reasons, it may not be convenient to keep known carriers, yet it may be felt desirable to test certain animals. This still can be done by a method which is practicable for males. The procedure is to mate the male to a number of his daughters (which need not necessarily be from the same mother). The error involved here is a two stage affair, (1) that of not mating the male to a carrier daughter (only half of the daughters will be expected to receive the suspected recessive gene) and (2) that of not breeding at least one anomalous kitten. To calculate the error, it is necessary firstly to find the value for each daughter according to the number of kittens she has produced. This is shown by column C of the table. Then the error for the male is derived by multiplying each of these values together. Thus, suppose it has been possible to mate a male with four daughters and the various litters result in totals of 3, 5, 6 and 7 young per daughter. The values of C from the table are 71, 62, 59 and 57, respectively. The error for the male, therefore, is the product of these, namely, 15 per cent. For totals of this average size, it would require 7 daughters to reduce the error to below the 5 per cent level.

This last test is often the one carried out in practice. In terms of numbers of kittens required to attain a certain minimum error, the test does not compare in efficiency with the two described earlier. However, it has an advantage not possessed by these, namely, that the test would reveal *any* recessive anomaly carried by the male, not one in particular. This fact gives the test an added appeal. It may be objected that the test could not be performed by a small breeder or possibly not repeatedly by medium or large breeders. In this case, it might be advisable for several breeders to band together and form a breeders' cooperative as far as testing-mating of outstanding males is concerned. If this is not practicable, a breed society could take matters in hand and arrange a scheme of test mating. Certified males should commend (and deserve) increased stud fees. Adequate means of independent assessment would have to be devised to avoid deceit and to assure the correct operation of the scheme.

In practice, it is rarely possible to test mate females. This is unimportant if a male can be properly tested and pronounced free of genetic anomaly. No matter how many carrier queens he may mate, none of the offspring will be anomalous. Some of the carrier queens will produce carrier offspring but this cannot be avoided. It means, however, that stud males must be test mated in each generation before being passed into general service. This testing will have to be continued until such time as the breed is judged to be free of the anomaly. It is difficult to be certain how many generations will be required. In part, it will depend upon the prevalence of the anomaly before the test mating was instigated.

The values in the table are for recessive genes whose occurrence are up to expectation. Not all anomalies behave in this manner. Some so weaken the individual that they die before (for example, *in utero*) they can be recorded. Also, certain individuals may have the gene for an anomaly yet fail to show it. In these circumstances, the values of the table are too optimistic. There are methods of tackling this complication but they are beyond the scope of this book. Whenever such a situation is encountered, or even suspected, the remedy is to either lower the level of acceptable error or to breed several more kittens than would otherwise be necessary.

TABLE 11. NUMBERS OF KITTENS REQUIRED TO REDUCE THE ERROR
PERCENTAGE TO BELOW A CERTAIN VALUE
(e.g. below the 5 or 1 per cent)

No. of kittens	A	B	C
1	50	75	88
2	25	56	78
3	12·5	42	71
4	6·3	32	66
5	3·1	24	62
6	1·5	18	59
7	0·8	13	57
8	0·4	10	55
9	0·2	7·5	54
10	0·1	5·6	53
11	—	4·2	52
12	—	3·2	52
13	—	2·4	51
14	—	1·8	51
15	—	1·3	51
16	—	1·0	51
17	—	0·7	50
18	—	0·6	50
19	—	0·4	50
20	—	0·3	50

The situation may arise that none of the above techniques of test mating can be carried out. In this event, the elimination will have to rely upon selective culling. All affected animals should be banished from the breeding pen, together with their parents and sibs as far as this is consistent with the overall breeding plan. Familial selection is more efficient than individual selection. The appearance of a single affected kitten means that each parent is a heterozygote and two-thirds of the sibs will be potential heterozygotes. These are the facts to be borne in mind in coming to a decision whether or not to test mate or how ruthlessly to cull.

With polygenic heredity, the problem is that of detecting those animals which have a high propensity to produce anomalous kittens. Test mating is ruled out in any simple sense and even the determination of a high propensity for an individual means being wise after the event. If action is taken, it means being drastic because all of the healthy offspring will be potential "high producers", however excellent they may be in other respects. It is a question of balancing the quality of the individual offspring against the chances of passing on of the anomaly.

There are two main types of anomaly with polygenic heredity. The first is that where the severity of the anomaly is variable and the severity is determined by polygenes. This implies that culling of the most affected animals will bring about a gradual improvement. The extent of the improvement and the rate at which it occurs will depend upon the level of culling. In general, the more ruthless the culling, the greater the relative improvement. There are various complicating factors, of course, of which the most important is that certain of the mildly affected animals (which are not culled) will be capable of producing severely affected offspring. Against this will be the fact that the average level of severity should decline per generation of selection.

The second type of polygenic trait is where the anomaly is due to a threshold effect. Despite the underlying polygenic inheritance, there is no real inter-grading as formerly, the animals are either normal or abnormal. The degree of abnormality may vary and this may be polygenically determined but the normals are, to all intents, fully normal in appearance. Test mating cannot be easily performed and the only remedy is that of selective culling of abnormals and, as far as practical, all those individuals with a high propensity to produce affected kittens.

To be really effective, the amount of selective culling should be ruthless. Ideally, once an anomaly has been assessed as genetic, no further young should be bred from either parent, none of the sibs should be used for breeding (regardless of their apparent healthiness or excellence), and the culling should extend into their immediate collateral relatives. In other words, a clean sweep is necessary. Doubtless, this is counsel of perfection and intolerably drastic. However, if the culling is less than this, a price must be paid in terms of breeding a small proportion of affected animals in future generations.

Persistence of Anomalies

It may be wondered how the odd genetic anomaly apparently persists in spite of everyone being on record as "agin" them and patient selection being the art of cat breeding. The answer must be sought among a variety of causes, several of which may combine to reinforce one another. Genes producing anomalies cannot multiply throughout a breed of their own volition but they are "opportunist" to the extreme in the sense that given favourable circumstances, they can spread surprisingly.

A major factor in the spread of an anomaly is a relaxation of culling. This can come about should a breed become exceptionally popular. Breeding stock is scarce and demand for kittens is high. The temptation is to breed from every animal, even from those which would normally be discarded. This means that inferior animals can pass on their inferior qualities, even if an effort is made to secure the services of a good sire. The practice of selling unneutered kittens to people who promise not to breed from them is scarcely sound long-term policy and it may suddenly short-circuit in present circumstances. Under pressure, the promise may be conveniently forgotten.

Instances are known (specially in animals other than the cat) where a much admired and widely used stud animal has subsequently been found to be a carrier of a recessive anomaly. This was unknown at the time, of course, but becomes only too apparent after his offspring have multiplied and spread throughout the breed. Inter-breeding (not necessarily close inbreeding) will ultimately bring into being a rash of occurrences of the same anomaly. Breeders may suddenly find themselves confronted with the twin problems of preserving the reputation of the breed and of eliminating the gene causing the anomaly. It may be objected that this event must be uncommon. True, but this process is often behind the so-called mutant "epidemics".

A feature of this event is that the appearance of the first anomaly is usually delayed for several generations from the ancestral point of origin and that many years of effort is required to either eliminate the anomaly or to reduce it to such a low level that it is no longer a nuisance. Chance plays a major role in determining the type of defect which could be unwittingly spread in this manner, and the breed in which the process occurred. On the other hand, it may occur in any breed and at any time. The moral is perhaps not to place too much reliance upon one or a few exemplary sires. The process is usually mediated via the male since the female cannot produce enough offspring to influence the course of events.

Even in more normal periods of breeding where supply of kittens is roughly geared to demand, a particular defect may seem to strangely persist. Two possibilities may account for this. One is that the amount of culling may be reduced to a minimum because of a deliberate policy of not breeding more kittens than necessary to cover replacements and sales. The other is that of heterosis or hybrid vigour. Generalizing, there is a correlation between healthy vigour and the amount of genetic heterozygosity. It may be that when the amount of heterozygosity falls below a certain level, so-called "inbreeding depression" sets in. These animals appear sickly and "bad doers" and are culled. However, their more robust but heterozygous sibs are retained. Included among these may be carriers of a recessive anomaly; not because of the fact that they are carriers but because of their relatively high heterozygosity. Of course, should the gene producing the anomaly be associated with extra vigour when heterozygous (which is possible but not always likely), a ready answer is available for the persistence or even spread of the gene responsible.

A similar situation may arise in those circumstances where a breed standard encourages the breeding of a certain type of defective animal. The rise of the defect is inadvertent, of course, and quite rightly it is condemned. Yet the defect recurs because breeders are endeavouring to conform to the standard. A conflict situation may even come into being; as the breed moves closer to the standard, the incidence or severity of the defect may become greater. It has been suggested, for example, that the sinus ailment and running eyes of some long hairs is a consequence of selective breeding for a short nose.

Despite an avoidance of close inbreeding, many breeds of cats are inter-bred to some extent. Indeed it cannot be avoided if the breed is to be composed of a homogeneous group of animals of recognized breed conformation. In this sense, it is desirable. On the other hand, inter-breeding is more conducive to bringing out the latent anomalies in comparison with a truly random breeding population. Therefore, while anomalies are likely to appear in both pure-bred and mongrel cats, their presence is more likely to be discovered in the former.

It is extremely unwise to breed from animals with inherited defects which have been surgically corrected. Even if the defect is relatively minor, it could reappear in later generations in an aggravated form. This aspect is probably diminishing in importance as it becomes more widely appreciated that, while such surgical intervention may be desirable for the individual cat, the genes for the defect are still transmitted in the gametes, surgery or no surgery.

Achondroplastic Dwarfism

A short-legged condition is regarded by Schwangart and Grau (1931) as being inherited. No details are given for the mode of inheritance. This is unfortunate for such conditions are known to be inherited in a variety of domestic animals and, if the cat is to be numbered among these, it would be desirable to have precise information. As a general statement, of course, this sort of deformity could easily be genetic in origin.

Bent and Short Tails

Many cases of nodulated, kinked, bent or loss of the terminal portion of the tail are known to occur. In the majority, the defect is traceable to injury, possibly at parturition or at a later stage. Occasionally, however, the defect may occur in individuals of one particular strain or in blood lines. When this occurs, the likelihood of a genetic influence should be envisaged.

A form of partial tail loss is not uncommon in certain strains of Siamese. It has been thought for some time that the condition could be inherited although exactly how is unknown. However, Moutschen (1950) claims to have found that a shortened tail, observed in a strain of Siamese, is inherited as a simple recessive. There was variation in length for the affected animals but the tail was regularly shorter than normal.

In other strains, there may be little or no shortening of the tail. Instead, there are kinks or swellings such as would arise from a fusion of adjacent vertebrae. It is a debatable question whether these are an aspect of the same genetic situation which underlies the tail shortening or if an entirely different situation should be assumed. In the absence of critical experiments designed to probe this question, it is almost impossible to offer a worthwhile answer. The simpler explanation is that these are variable manifestations of the same genetic entity, the difference in expression being due to strain background. On the other hand, several different genetic tail anomalies may exist in the cat. At present, the only clue pointing in this direction would be differences of expression.

In most, and very probably in all, strains of exhibition-bred Siamese, there has been selection against deformed tails. The effect of this selection has been to reduce the frequency of occurrence and to alleviate the severity. Shortening of the tail is now rare but, not infrequently, the tail may be slightly kinked or firm nodules may be felt by palpation. When the manifestation of the deformity is slight it is conceivable that some impenetrance may occur. This could imply (1) that the descent of the deformity could be irregular and make accurate determination of the defect difficult, if not impossible, and (2) hamper elimination of the defect by means of simple culling of all affected animals.

Cerebellar Ataxia

There is a long history of congenital ataxia in the cat. Many occur in isolated cases and can contribute nothing of value in terms of genetic information. In other instances, the incidence appears to be familial, in which event, the possibility of genetic origin has to be considered as an aetiological factor. Only in one report is there definite evidence that the abnormal behaviour is inherited (Koch, Fischer and Stubbe, 1955). In this, the handing on of the anomaly from one generation to the next is unmistakeable. The heredity appears to be that of a dominant gene of variable expression which may, in the less severely affected cases, fail to manifest at all or so slightly as to be overlooked. The existence of this gene is not accepted by all cat geneticists (primarily because the experimental data are not conclusive) and for this reason the symbol (At) given to the gene is only recognized as provisional.

In spite of individual variation, which seems to be mainly in severity and duration, the ataxia is typically that of unco-ordinated and exaggerated movement. No symptoms are apparent while the kitten is at rest but, upon walking, the gait and posture can only be described as awkward. The legs may be held apart and there is much staggering which often ends in a fall. Some head weaving and a tremor may be noticed. Feeding is difficult because of rather violent head movements. The cat may repeatedly strike its head against the feeding dish, when attempting to eat solid food, or plunge its nose below the surface of the fluid when drinking. The ataxia may persist as long as ten to twelve weeks and sometimes into adult life. Prolonged survival is largely a matter of careful nursing unless the symptoms are relatively mild.

The cause of the behaviour is a marked underdevelopment of the cerebellum. Affected cats have a cerebellum which is a fraction of normal size. Though this aspect can only be discovered by post-mortem examination, the brain underdevelopment is the most significant and constant feature, and serves to place any given case of ataxia into the present category.

Abnormal ataxia behaviour may arise from a variety of factors and, even when it is found to be genetically determined, the same mutant gene and the same mode of heredity may not apply in every case. This aspect is probably appreciated but it seems worthwhile to underline the point. In other species where several different ataxic conditions are known it is often difficult to make a reliable separation without post-mortem examination and breeding tests. Some types, however, may have peculiar behaviour by which they can be readily identified while others may have ataxic behaviour of a rather generalized pattern.

Cryptorchidism

A few people have surmised that the failure of either both testes to descend properly (bilateral cryptorchidism) or merely one (unilateral cryptorchidism; strictly, monorchidism is terminologically correct) could be genetically determined. Unfortunately, there is no evidence one way or the other. Perhaps the statement is not quite true, for there are rumours that certain breeds are more prone to the affliction than others. However, reliable data to support the rumours are scanty; although such evidence could build up a preliminary case for genetic determination. Bilateral cryptorchidism can be a real misfortune since such animals are usually infertile. Unilateral cryptorchids are usually fertile but there should be great hesitation in placing these at stud.

The likelihood that cryptorchidism could have a genetic basis introduces an intriguing principle of causation. The defect is the outcome of failure of the testes to pass through the inguinal canal into the scrotum and, therefore, is a condition at least once removed from the primary cause. The inguinal canal may be imperfectly formed or not large enough to allow the passage of the testes or there may be a maladjustment of development, so that the testes are not ready to descend at the appropriate time. These are the factors which would be genetically determined, rather than the phenomenon of cryptorchidism. A thorough study would require a post mortem examination of all affected individuals and probably of the testes in normal brothers to ascertain if they are truly normal.

It may be wondered if there is a practical reason for distinguishing between the primary and secondary factors. There is, the reason is that while the primary defect may be present in every affected individual, the secondary defect (here, the cryptorchidism) may not be shown by every individual. Spuriously normal animals could have the primary defect and yet appear intact because testes descent had not been interfered with. The fact that the cryptorchidism can be unilateral could be an indication that something of this nature could be occurring. The cryptorchidism, therefore, would show impenetrance and anyone who was studying the heredity of the defect without recourse to autopsy would find the task more complicated. If such animals do exist, they would doubtless be used for breeding in the belief that they were perfectly normal. This is one means by which the anomaly could be passed on to future generations.

However, the main factor in the persistence of the defect is that cryptorchidism is an example of sex-limited inheritance. Only the male can have undescended testes. Whether, or not, the female may show a comparable primary defect to that presumed to occur in the male is something yet to be discovered. Externally, the female is normal although she may carry the propensity for cryptorchidism and be fully capable of transmitting the condition to her sons. In this respect, the carrier female is as big a menace as the unilateral cryptorchid. If a policy of selective culling is in progress, it would be wise to be wary of the apparently normal brothers and sisters of affected individuals. Other factors being equal, the sensible course would be to eliminate these.

Deafness

The deafness which is a possible aspect of dominant white may be briefly noted. This disability does not seem to greatly inconvenience the cat and it may probably be regarded as of minor import. The defect has been studied anatomically, however, and details may be found in the recent paper of Bosher and Hallpike (1965). Characteristic degenerative changes are reported for the cochlea and saccule of the inner ear, with marked underdevelopment of the organs of Corti.

Dwarfism

Most cases of dwarfism can usually be attributed to a deficiency diet or to a disease which severely interfered with the growth rate at a critical age. However, against this are two reports (one in Germany and the other in England) which are suggestive of a genetic dwarfism. It seems that the cats are true miniatures (i.e. not achondroplastic) and that the condition is probably due to a recessive gene. However, the circumstances are such for the English case that deliberate stunting cannot be excluded. This sort of malpractice cannot be too strongly deprecated.

Folded-ears

The ears of the cat are normally carried in an upright or "pricked" condition. The ears of the folded-eared animals, however, are bent forward in a characteristic manner. At birth, and until about four weeks of age, the ears appear to be normal. From this age, the tip of the ears tend to turn inwards and the fold is fully formed by about three months. When fully developed, the apexes of both ears are folded forward and downwards. The condition is inherited as a simple dominant and the responsible gene is designated by the symbol F. Although the condition can be held to be anomalous, it is not severe and the hearing does not seem to be impaired. Attempts are being made to establish the form as a breed.

Four-ears

A curious head anomaly is described by Little (1957). It is termed "four-ears" because of the presence of a small extra pair of "ears" in affected animals. The eyes are reduced in size and the jaw is slightly undershot. In all, the head is said to be of a peculiar shape. Growth and size do not appear to be abnormal but the animal seems to be relatively inactive and lethargic. This latter could imply that the functioning of the brain is affected. The condition is inherited as a recessive and the responsible gene is symbolized by *dp*. The data show a deficiency of four-ears which implies that the gene could be a semi-lethal.

Hairlessness

Every so often an account of a hairless cat appears in the literature. These odd, if not bizarre, looking creatures cannot avoid attracting attention, for the condition is rarely lethal. The loss of hair is not usually total. More often than not, various parts of the body may be nude while the remainder (e.g. muzzle, feet) is covered by fine down or fuzzy hair. Quite often the condition worsens with age, the fine covering of the young adult giving way to bare wrinkled skin and complete hairlessness over much of the body. This progressive loss usually distinguishes the true hairless animal from a temporary loss which may be due to a variety of factors. No improvement of feeding or nursing can produce a normal coat on the true hairless cat.

Hairless individuals may turn up spontaneously in any part of the world. Reports have come in as far apart as Australia, Canada, France and Morocco. There is even a description of a "Mexican hairless cat", given as if these curious animals were a breed in their own right. Anyone, of course, is at liberty to take this view since the condition is presumably inherited.

Two of the hairless conditions have been investigated, those of Canada and France (see Letard (1938) with regard to the latter). It is clear that the hairlessness in each case is due to a recessive gene (symbolized by *h*). It is a reasonable assumption that the majority of other cases are inherited in a similar manner. There is no means of knowing, of course, if the same gene has mutated on each occasion (this could, of course, be so) or if more than one loci could give rise to alleles producing a hairless animal.

It is a disputable point whether hairless cats should be kept. The lack of hair could mean that they will suffer from debilitating heat loss during cold weather. It would seem humane to have them destroyed at an early age. However, if this seems unnecessarily heartless, they should certainly be kept in a warm environment and be provided with a knitted woollen "over-coat" in very cold spells.

Rex cats have a tendency to lose their fur, sometimes in the form of a prémature moult or sometimes more permanently in old individuals. This may be represented as a hairless condition, although it is not a true independent loss of hair. The condition is part of the rex syndrome, for the rex coat itself is anomalous. The guard hairs are abortive and the down hairs are thin. In some animals, the anomaly is possibly intensified to cause a deficiency of the down hairs or to produce a baldness where the thin hairs either break off or are pulled from a weakly gripping hair follicle by the habitual incessant grooming of the cat. The Devon rex is the more prone of the two English rexes to baldness and the reason seems to be that the Devon rex hair fibres are particularly fragile. The loss of hair in the rex is termed baldness to distinguish it from the hairless condition due to the h gene.

Hare-lip and Cleft-palate

These two often associated anomalies are mentioned by Schwangart and Grau (1931) as being probably inherited. The basis for this statement seems to be that of a female cat with a slight hare-lip which produced kittens with a similar defect. One kitten was undersized and possessed a cleft-palate. The animals' ability to suckle was impaired and it eventually died. This information is interesting but scarcely sufficient in itself to more than hint at a genetic basis. As an isolated observation, little more can be expected but if a number of such familial associations are reported, perhaps a more positive conclusion can be reached.

Hydrocephalus

Hydrocephalus is a morbid condition associated with a swelled oedematous head region, often with other defects. Such animals occur at odd intervals, usually as a result of developmental mishaps. However, such conditions can be inherited and a case has been reported for the cat (Silson and Robinson, 1969). The breeding evidence indicates that a single recessive gene is involved. The mutant gene has been symbolized by *hy*.

The abnormality is readily identifiable at birth. The affected kitten is always very large and bloated in appearance around the head and limbs. It may also have various degrees of hare-lip, cleft-palate or talipes. However, it is uncertain if these abnormalities are strictly a part of the hydrocephalus condition.

"Kangaroo" Cat

A number of extraordinary animals are described by William-Jones (1944). These possessed unusually short front legs but otherwise appear to be normal. The gait of these creatures tends to resemble that of a ferret in their smooth but hunched-up movements. When induced to sit back, the posture is that, if anything, of a miniature kangaroo. The peculiarity is said to be inherited in that affected animals are observed in at least four litters. Unfortunately, precise details are lacking which might have established the mode of inheritance. This curiosity has occurred at least twice in widely separated localities, hence it is possible that it may turn up again.

Manx Taillessness

The Manx cat is well known as an established breed but it is also famous as a genetic anomaly. In fact, over the past few years, a flurry of interest into the effects of the Manx gene has taken place. This has revealed that the mutant has profound effects upon the whole spinal column, apart from the absence of a tail. A number of visceral organs also seem to be affected in one way and another (Todd, 1964; Howell and Siegel, 1966).

It has been known for some time that Manx taillessness is inherited as a dominant trait, with the symbol *M*. This has been confirmed and, what is more important, the accumulation of breeding data makes it highly probable, if not certain, that individuals homozygous for the Manx gene die prior to birth. The evidence for this is: (1) an apparent absence of pure-breeding strains of Manx and (2) a decrease of the average number of young per litter for matings of Manx to Manx. The reduction is from an average of about four to three living offspring per litter.

Thus, the Manx seems to be lethal when homozygous and, apparently, semi-lethal at all times. One aspect of this is a preponderance of females among the viable Manx offspring, as if the males are less likely to survive. Also, examination of Manx still-born kittens, and those which died before the age of twelve months, revealed a greater number of both skeleton and organ anomalies than was shown by those Manx cats which lived beyond the twelve months.

The absence of a tail is readily apparent although careful examination has shown that the loss can be relative. In all, four types of Manx tailless-ness have been distinguished. The true Manx is known as "rumpy", in which no tail vertebrae can be observed. Indeed, there is often a small dimple where the vertebrae would normally issue. A second type is "rumpy-riser", in which an extremely small number of tail vertebrae can either be seen or felt as an upright projection, usually immovable. The third type is "stumpy". Here, the tail is longer and usually moveable although often deformed, nobbly and kinked. The fourth type is the "longie" and possibly is the rarer of the four. The tail is longer than many of the above (though shorter than normal) and is of more normal ap-pearance. One series of experiments are suggestive that the various expressions of the Manx taillessness are controlled in part by modifying polygenes.

The influence of the Manx may be observed for the whole length of the vertebral column. In the fore-part of the column, this seems to be little more than a slight decrease in the length of the individual vertebrae but, in the hind-part, there is also a decrease in number and, particularly, fusion of vertebrae. The sacral and pelvic bones are also drawn into the general fusion and maldevelopment. In a number of cases, variable de-grees of spinal bifida has been found upon autopsy. Occasional or recur-rent bowel stoppage may occur because of a narrowing of the anal opening. This may be observed when the kitten takes to solid food. The firm faecal boli may tear the rectal linings and the region becomes inflamed.

Osteodystrophy

The basis of this disease is a skeleton which is seriously and cripplingly deficient in calcium. X-ray photography reveals distinctly rarified bones. The external symptoms are reasonably consistent and are as follows: the kitten often develops a lameness and is unable to stand. In severe cases, the hind limbs may become paralyzed. Limping or paralysis usually results from jumping from a low height. The cat may resent being handled, especially if gently manipulated in the lumbar region. Affected animals may or may not be undersized. Provided the disease has not progressed too far, an apparently spontaneous recovery can occur round about the time of normal recession of growth. A full description of the disease may be found in Scott, McKusick and McKusick (1963) and in Wilkinson (1966).

While the disease may be clearly congenital, there has been some disagreement whether or not a genetic factor is involved. Some investigators have thought not while others have hypothesized that the condition is due to recessive genes. However, the work of Scott, McKusick and McKusick has shown that the disease is due primarily to a diet low in calcium. In practice, this has meant that diets consisting almost exclusively of meat are specially conducive to the onset of the disorder; the more so, if milk is also withheld. The provision of a suitably corrective diet usually brings about a fairly rapid improvement and a disappearance of the worst of the distressing symptoms. Consistent with the above conclusion, is the fact that a study of the pedigrees of the affected animals failed to disclose any simple mode of inheritance.

It may be noted that a familial incidence could be simulated because the same deficient diet has been fed to successive litters or even generations. However, the decisive test is whether the skeleton dystrophy responds to corrective feeding. Scott *et al.* are careful to point out that a genetic influence cannot be entirely excluded since it is possible for certain strains or breeds of cats to have a particularly high requirement of calcium. In these animals, the propensity for the dystrophy could be higher than in the general population. The Burmese and Siamese breeds are mentioned as possibly falling into this category since the disease seems to recur rather often in them.

Polydactyly

If the number of separate reports is anything to judge by, the presence of extra toes on the foot is something that attracts attention. This anomaly has been noted as early as 1868, if not earlier, and on many occasions since that date. The distinguishing feature is, of course, the presence of extra toes, most noticeably on the front feet. There is considerable variation from animal to animal in the number of extra toes and how perfectly formed they may be.

The variation in this respect may range from an enlargement of the inside digit to resemble a thumb to the formation of three apparently well formed extra toes. Making a total of seven toes on one foot! This variation in expression may occur between different feet on the same cat. In fact, the hind feet are never, or rarely, affected unless the front are abnormal. Despite the marked variation, it seems to be rather rare for a genetic polydactylous cat to be normal, as could so well happen with anomalies of this nature. Different cases may vary in this respect, however.

Reviewing the various reports of polydactyly, it is remarkable how many give either direct or indirect evidence of a dominant mode of heredity. This aspect is remarkable since not all of the separate cases need be due to the same mutant gene. It is possible, of course, for the same gene to have arisen by mutation in different localities, and at different times, and this is an explanation which could account for the similar heredity. However, doubtless it would be wise to remember that other cases of polydactyly might behave somewhat differently. At the moment, only one polydactyly gene is recognized which is symbolized by *Pd*. Those veterinarians who may wish for anatomical details, the papers of Danforth (1947) and Chapman and Zeiner (1961) should be consulted.

Porphyria

Porphyrins are precursor substances for the production of haeme, a major component of haemoglobin. These substances arise in the bone marrow and, should they be produced in excessive amounts, are deposited in the body tissues such as the skin, bones and teeth, as well as being void in the urine. When this occurs, the teeth may appear to be unusually discoloured and the urine turns bloody. These symptoms are usually expressed from an early age. The diagnosis of the porphyric cat may be easily accomplished by examination of the teeth or bones under ultraviolet light. The impregnated teeth and bones exhibit a bright pinkish-red fluorescence.

Glenn, Glenn and Omtvedt (1968) have presented data which indicate that the condition is due to a single dominant autosomal gene. No symbol has been proposed for the gene but the designation of *Po* would seem appropriate.

Retina Degeneration

A naturally occurring degeneration of the retina has been observed as a rare anomaly in cats. There is a progressive loss of the cones and rods and a thinning out of the outer layer of the retina. Externally, the iris is dilated and appears circular instead of the normal ovoid. The cats are blind and exhibit great reluctance to jump any distance. No information is available on the heredity of the lesion but the fact of its spontaneous nature has caused speculation in this direction (Barnett, 1965). A study of the ancestors or progeny of future cases may uncover data which has a bearing on the possibility. Comparable defects are known to be inherited in other domestic animals.

Split-foot

The typical manifestation is that of a central cleft of either one or both fore feet. Other disturbances may be present, however, such as an absence of toes or fusion to produce double claws and abnormal foot-pads. X-ray photographs disclose considerable disorder of the bones, particularly the metacarpals and carpals. The defect did not appear to interfere with normal activity except that of climbing. The hind feet did not appear to be involved in those animals studied (Searle, 1953).

The split-foot condition is inherited as a dominant trait and the responsible gene is symbolized by Sp. The number of defective animals is observed to be less than expected and it is suggested that this may mean that a proportion of the genetically split-foot individuals may appear normal footed. This could easily occur as a result of the variability of expression of the gene.

Squint

The Siamese breed is sometimes regarded as possessing a convergent squint as a breed characteristic. This may be true for some strains of Siamese but it does not seem correct as a general statement. Whatever may have happened in the past, there are many strains in existence at the present time which do not show this affliction. It will be appreciated, of course, that a squint may occur in any individual or breed in addition to that of Siamese. Both the works of Kirk (1956) and of Wilkinson (1966) show photographs of the squint condition.

The situation is complicated to some extent by the fact that a kitten may display a mild squint while young which is slowly corrected as it becomes older. This means that genetically squint animals may appear as normal if the early life of the cat is unknown. Only one report on the condition in Siamese has made any attempt to interpret the mode of inheritance (Moutschen, 1950). However, the results of a number of crosses have not yielded clear-cut results. The condition seems to be inherited but seemingly as the outcome of the interaction of two or more genes. It seems possible that the squint is inherited as a polygenically controlled threshold character; alternatively, of course, it could be determined monogenetically but with impenetrance.

Umbilical Hernia

Two research veterinarians (Henricson and Bornstein, 1965) have observed a particularly high incidence of umbilical hernia among the Abyssinian breed in Sweden. The precise mode of inheritance could not be determined but the influence of heredity is unmistakeable in their data. For example, the chances of the offspring being herniated is about 75 per cent when one parent is known to have an hernia, against 3 per cent for the offspring of parents which are known to be normal or are unknown. These figures are cited merely as a guide and must not be taken too literally.

The fact of the high incidence among the progeny, when one parent is known to be herniated, prompted the suggestion that the predisposition towards the occurrence of an hernia might be inherited as a dominant. This may be the case, and the data is certainly suggestive in this respect, but it may be wise to be cautious. When the breeding data are closely examined, too many individuals are marked as "unknown" for positive conclusions to be drawn.

Umbilical hernia is usually due to an inherent defect in the umbilical ring. A weakness can result in a part of the abdominal contents being extrude as a soft bulge. However, even if the musculature is defective, a hernia need not always develop or the development may be so slight as to escape notice. This means that if attention is focussed entirely upon the presence or absence of hernia the fundamental or primary defect will not be detected in some cases. The hernia condition is a "secondary" manifestation of a probable anomaly of the umbilical region. The descent of the hernia from one generation to the next could appear to be irregular, in spite of the probability that the primary defect is inherited along regular lines. A similar situation may exist for cryptorchidism, where the problem of causation and detection of this sort of defect is discussed.

Urolithiasis

Livingston (1965) has outlined a case of urolithiasis which reveals a familial tendency. A male cat showed the disease and so did three kittens out of four from matings with his sister. Full details of the urolithiasis are not given except the statement that the disease failed to respond to any treatment, including surgery. The affected animals are otherwise healthy and no other cats in the neighbourhood have developed obvious symptoms. It is proposed that a hereditary influence may be involved.

Though intriguing, these observations would carry little weight, standing alone, but they are the sort that could contribute towards something tangible should a number of similar reports come in over the years. For this reason, if no other, Livingston's note deserves to be cited. It is quite likely that a predisposition towards the formation of urinary calculi could be determined to some extent by heredity. A genetic propensity towards urolithiasis is suspected in the dog.

VIII. RECORD KEEPING

A SIMPLE yet efficient system of record keeping is a vital adjunct of animal breeding. Indeed, it might not be too much to say that the art of successful breeding derives from the possession of reliable records and the use to which these are put. Alas, to some people, the writing up of breeding results and notes on the appearance of each kitten is a chore to be put off to a later date. Such an attitude is understandable when there is work to be done with the animals but it would be idle to pretend that it is good enough for well organized breeding. Fortunately, the majority of breeders appreciate the value of records—even those of the most simple kind—as a log of past achievement and as an aid to future breeding.

Record keeping in animal breeding is required to fulfil three functions: (1) to present an accurate record of familial relationship, (2) to provide information upon the phenotype characteristics and breeding performance of every animal and (3) to be a source of data from which to make future decisions. Accordingly, it is easy to sketch out the minimum of data which ought to be kept but less easy to set an upper limit. Clearly, if record keeping is not to be a burden, the chosen method should be simple to operate. On the other hand, the amount of information it is desirous to collect will depend upon the breeding programme which the breeder has set himself. It will also depend upon the temperament of the breeder. People's opinions differ on the relevancy of information for a given task. In general, however, it is advisable to record as much data as possible, provided it appears to have potential value and it does not make the whole business too onerous. It is convenient if all of the information can be brought together in one place: the stud book.

It is essential that each cat should be individually and readily identifiable once it has been entered in the stud book. When only a few breeding queens are kept and all of the animals receive regular attendance, it may be wondered if a means of individual identification is worthwhile. Possibly not, if mistakes can be definitely ruled out. With a large colony and new litters of kittens arriving at frequent intervals during the peak of a breeding season, a reliable method may be desirable. A simple method is to have metal or durable plastic tags attached to collars. Two sizes of collar may be necessary, one for kittens and one for adults, the tag being transferred from collar to collar. Frayed collars should always be promptly replaced and a careful watch kept for animals which develop a habit of worrying or slipping their collars. Metal tags may have to be engraved while plastic tags could be written upon in water-proof ink. With latter, it would be wise to be on the *qui vive* for rubbing or straining which could lead to illegibility of the wording.

A day-to-day record for breeding queens may be kept in the form of ordinary small filing cards. A supply of these, together with specially made boxes to contain them, can usually be bought quite cheaply from stationers. These cards are for dates of visits to the stud cat, parturitions and preliminary details of the litter. A separate card is made out for each female. The name and/or reference number in the stud book (see later) should be written at the head of the card. Every visit to the male should be listed, giving name and reference number of male, not forgetting the date. Should the mating fail, this should be noted and, if a reason can be adduced for the failure, this can be entered.

When the female conceives, the date of birth of litter and the number of kittens should be written down. Brief details should be given whether the kittens look fully healthy and if the queen had an easy parturition. These cards are a check on the reproductive history of the queen. Whether or not she conceives readily and produces the average number of kittens per litter can be seen at a glance. When the time arrives for the kittens to be examined and be entered in the stud book, the details of the litter are transferred at the same time. The litter reference number in the stud book can be written on the card for purposes of cross-reference. All of the cards should be preserved even after the queen has ceased to breed.

The stud book should be made the permanent repository for all information and most systems of recording revolve around it. The book may range from an ordinary note book, with a board cover for greater durability, to a spring back binder. A loose-leaf binder permits the insertion of extra pages and the need for these can recur with surprising frequency when the breeding programme is going well and new aspects are subsequently found to merit consideration. A recommended system of recording rests upon the successive numbering of litters. Commencing with the first page of the stud book, a number should be prominently written in the top right hand corner, beginning with 1, 2, 3, ..., etc. It may be found convenient to always have the number at the top right-hand corner of the next available blank page, according to the amount of space required. This could be as little as a page or could extend over several pages depending upon the amount of information to be entered. Each succeeding litter is assigned the next unused number in the book.

Since certain details will be the same for all litters, a number of headings could be written in beforehand or, if practicable, the pages could be obtained already mimeographed. An illustration of the possible arrangement of the basic details are shown by Fig. 23. The main headings are those on the left and consist of Queen, Male, Number of Matings to conception, Date of Mating and so on. The figure shows an example for a litter designated as 42 (the number at top right). This litter is produced by a mating of a queen with stud book reference 17d with a male of reference 9a (their stud names are also given in parenthesis). She was mated on the 12th of February and gave birth to five young on the 18th of April after a normal parturition.

One of the kittens died at birth but the other four were successfully reared. The kittens were weaned and recorded for coat colour and length. Two were normal coated self black, one a normal blue and the last a long-haired black. Each kitten is given one of the first few lower case letters of the alphabet and the above details listed for each one; together with the sex and genotype as shown. Each kitten has now been precisely designated by a number (42) and a letter. At this stage, a note may be added whether the mother has or has not nursed the litter satisfactorily. Finally, space may be left for subsequent history of the kittens. That is to say, whether they were sold (if so, to whom), died from disease (if so, state the disease) of from senility (if so, give date). After a while, the procedure soon becomes a matter of routine.

The main genotype can usually be appended to the colour description of the kittens similarly to that shown. However, it will also be highly desirable to record variation of polygenic characteristics, either by description or by grading on a suitable scale. On earlier occasions, the advantages (if not the necessity) of employing a suitable scale has been emphasized. These were for analysing a polygenic character and for the calculation of a total score. If the total score method of selection is being employed, there is no reason why this should not be used as a succint method of describing the variation. Additional supplementary

Queen   17d   (Abigal)

Male   9a   (Racine)

NO. OF MATINGS TO CONCEPTION   One

DATE OF MATING   February 12th 1968

DATE OF BIRTH   April 18th 1968

PARTURITION   Uneventful

No. of YOUNG BORN

     LIVE   4

     DEAD   1

DETAILS OF LITTER

     a   Male black   *aaD–L–*

     b   Female black   *aaD–L–*

     c   Male blue   *aaddL–*

     d   Female black LH   *aaddll*

CONDITION at WEANING   Excellent

GRADING OF CHARACTERS

KITTEN	H	CC	CT	BB	HS	F	T
a	10	9	9	6	6	4	4
b	10	8	8	7	4	5	4
c	10	–	7	6	5	6	4
d	5	5	–	5	6	3	3

Fig. 23. A specimen page from the stud book, showing the basic data which should be recorded for each litter and a proposed layout of the entries.

notes can always be given, though this ought not to be necessary, since every effort should be made to ensure that the scoring is as accurate and relevant as possible.

The figure shows how the grading of the four kittens could be arranged for the same seven characters as defined in the section on the construction of a total score. Suppose that the breeder is interested in the self blacks. Though the blue SH and the black LH will be discarded, all of the other characteristics for these cats should be graded as conscientiously as possible. These will vary independently (with the possible exception of CC because of the long hair in kitten d could interfere with accurate grading) of each other and no opportunity should be neglected to obtain data on the variation.

The nature and amount of data which is recorded will depend entirely upon the interests of the breeder. For instance, it may be that the breeder is seeking to create a particular form of spotted tabby which cannot be easily graded. In which case, the pattern for each kitten may have to be described in some detail if the breeder is to have an adequate record. Photographs would be useful, especially if the posture of each kitten can be standardized in order to minimize distortion. The employment of sketches should not be despised, particularly if outlines can be prepared beforehand and it is simply a matter of filling in details.

The advantage of having a reference system based upon consecutive numbering of litters is that it facilitates cross-reference. All the information on litters and individual cats are to be found in one book. At any time it is desired to check on any animal, it is only necessary to turn to the appropriate page number (viz. litter number) and consult the pertinent letter. For example, the mother is 17d, indicating she is the fourth kitten of litter 17. The composition of litter 42 might provide additional data on her genotype. Suppose she is a normal haired black; hence the colours of the kittens show that she must be heterozygous for blue dilution and long hair. If the heterozygosity was unknown (or only suspected) at the time of writing up of litter 17, the pages may be turned back and the relevant data added to that already entered for kitten d. Similarly, any new information on the male 9a can be added. In this respect, the comprehensiveness of the stud book will increase as the entries mount up. After a number of years, the stud book may consist of a number of volumes. However, the principle of consecutive litter numbering still applies, the numbers being carried on from one volume to the next. The numbers contained in a volume could be written on the spine for easy location.

The incorporation of purchased stock into the system can be accomplished by either of two methods. One is to treat the animal as a "litter" and assign a number to it at the time of purchase (but recording that it had in fact been purchased). Or, to designate those animals by simple numbers or capital letters (or group of capital letters which may be so composed as to act as a mnemonic for the origin of the cat). If the second procedure has been adopted, a whole page should be given over to each animal for recording any data which may be available. The seller would no doubt be pleased to supply such basic details as date of birth, parentage and litter sibs. These pages may be inserted in stud book at any convenient position, such as in serial order prior to the home-bred litters.

It will be appreciated that the use of the rather impersonal combination of litter number and lower case letter in no manner replaces either pet names or formal names under which cats are usually registered. The reference numbers are primarily for quick and easy location of individual animals in the stud book and for tracing parentages or ancestral lineages extending through successive generations. The system has been proven to function very well in this respect. When this is linked up with records of reproduction of the individual and the quality of the kittens produced, it forms a serviceable system of permanently recording breeding data.

IX. FURTHER READING

A SPECIALIZED book has the advantage that it can deal with its chosen subject in detail. On the other hand, if the text is to be kept within reasonable bounds, it cannot do more than cover the salient aspects of ordinary genetics. For a fuller account, a general work should be consulted. Most libraries carry one or more of the recognized texts and these should be read with the intention of gaining a more general picture. For instance, it is often useful to have knowledge of the heredity of comparable variation in allied species. The cat is a bit isolated in this respect but the genetics of the domestic rabbit, for example, duplicate that of the cat to a surprising extent.

However, even general books differ among themselves and some are more recommendable to cat breeders than others. The more suitable are those which lean towards the genetics of mammals. Most genetics books devote at least one chapter to the techniques of animal breeding. That is, the application of genetic principles to breed improvement. This is rather a specialized subject and those books which really reach the heart of the matter tend to be heavy going. It's the old story of the treatment being forced to match the complexity of the subject. With cat breeders primarily in mind, the following books and papers are respectfully suggested for further reading.

Elementary General Books

CASTLE, W. E. (1930). *Genetics and eugenics.* Cambridge, Mass.: Harvard University Press.

CASTLE, W. E. (1940). *Mammalian genetics.* Cambridge, Mass.: Harvard University Press.

COLIN, E. C. (1956). *Elements of genetics.* New York: McGraw-Hill.

DUNN, L. C. (1965). *A short history of genetics.* New York: McGraw-Hill.

GEORGE, W. (1956). *Elementary genetics.* London: McMillan.

HUTT, F. B. (1964). *Animal genetics.* New York: Ronald Press.

MÜNTZING, A. (1967). *Genetics: basic and applied.* Stockholm: Lts För lag.

SRB, A. M., and OWEN, R. D. (1952). *General genetics.* San Francisco: Freeman.

Advanced Books and Works on Animal Improvement

BOGART, R. (1959). *Improvement of livestock.* New York: MacMillan Co.

FALCONER, D. S. (1960). *Introduction to quantitative genetics.* Edinburgh: Oliver and Boyd.

LERNER, I. M. (1958). *The genetic basis of selection.* London: Chapman and Hall.

LERNER, I. M., and DONALD, H. P. (1966). *Modern developments in animal breeding.* London: Academic Press.

LUSH, J. L. (1945). *Animal breeding plans.* Ames: Iowa State College Press.

MATHER, K. (1949). *Biometrical genetics.* London: Methuen.

SEARLE, A. G. (1968). *Comparative genetics of coat colour in mammals.* London: Logos Press.

Research Papers of Interest and Literature Cited

BAMBER, R. C. (1927). Genetics of domestic cats. *Bibliogr. Genet.*, **3**:1–86.

BAMBER, R. C. (1933). Correlation between white coat colour, blue eyes and deafness in cats. *J. Genet.*, **27**:407–413.

BAMBER, R. C., and HARDMAN, E. C. (1932). A report on the progeny of a tortoiseshell male cat, together with a discussion of his gametic constitution. *J. Genet.*, **26**:115–128.

Committee on Standardized Genetic Nomenclature for Cats (1968). Standardized genetic nomenclature for cats. *J. Hered.*, **59**:39–40.

DREUX, P. (1967). Gene frequencies in the cat population of Paris. *J. Hered.*, **58**:89–92.

GILLASPIE, T. H. (1954). Cats–wild and domestic. *Scotsman*, 27 Nov. 1954.

HAMILTON, E. (1896). *The wild cat of Europe.* London: Porter.

ILJIN, N. A., and ILJIN, V. N. (1930). Temperature effects on the color of the Siamese cat. *J. Hered.*, **21**:309–318.

JACKSON, J. M., and JACKSON, J. (1967). The hybrid jungle cat. *Newsletter Long Island Ocelot Club*, **11**:45.

JUDE, A. C., and SEARLE, A. G. (1957). A fertile tortoiseshell tomcat. *Nature*, **179**: 1087–1088.

KEELER, C. E., and COBB, V. (1933). Allelomorphism of silver and Siamese coat variations in the domestic cat. *J. Hered.*, **24**: 181–184.

KOMAI, T., and ISHIHARA, T. (1956). On the origin of the male tortoiseshell cat. *J. Hered.*, **47**: 287–291.

KÜHN, A. and KRONING, F. (1928). Uber der Vererbung der Weiszchung bei der Hauskatze. *Zuchtungskunde*, **3**: 448–454.

MALOUF, N., BENIRSCHKE, K., and HOEFNAGEL, D. (1967). XX/XY chimerism in a tricolour male cat. *Cytogenetics*, **6**: 228–241.

NORBY, D. E., and THULINE, H. C. (1965). Gene action in the X chromosome of the cat (*Felis catus L.*) *Cytogenetics*, **4**: 240–244.

POCOCK, R. I. (1907). Cross between *Felis silvestris* and *Felis ocreata ugandae. Proc. Zool. Soc. Lond.*, (1907): 749–750.

ROBINSON, R. (1959). Genetics of the domestic cat. *Bibliogr. Genet.*, **18**: 273–362.

THOMPSON, J. C., COBB, V. C., KEELER, C. E., and DMYTRYK, M. (1943). Genetics of the Burmese cat. *J. Hered.*, **34**: 119–123.

TJEBBES, K. (1924). Crosses with Siamese cats. *J. Genet.*, **14**: 355–366.

TODD, N. B. (1961). A pink-eyed dilution in the cat. *J. Hered.*, **52**: 202.

ULLMAN, E., VON, and HARGREAVES, A. (1958). New coat colours in domestic cats. *Proc. Zool. Soc. Lond.*, **130**: 606–609.

WEIGEL, I. (1961). Das Fellmuster der wildebenden Katzenarten und der Hauskatze in vergleichender und stammesgeschtlicher Hinsicht. *Sangetierk., Mitt.*, **9** (*Suppl.*): 120 pp.

WHITING, P. W. (1918). Inheritance of coat colour in cats. *J. Exp. Zool.*, **25**: 539–570.

WHITING, P. W. (1919). Inheritance of white-spotting and other coat characters in cats. *Amer. Nat.*, **53**: 433–482.

ZEUNER, F. E. (1963). *A history of domestic animals.* London: Hutchinson.

Abnormalities

BARNETT, K. C. (1965). Retinal atrophy. *Vet. Med.*, **77**: 1543–1560.

BOSHER, S. K., and HALLPIKE, C. S. (1965). Observations on the histological features, development and pathogenesis of the inner ear degeneration of the deaf white cat. *Proc. Roy. Soc. B.*, **162**: 147–170.

CHAPMAN, V. A. and ZEINER, F. N. (1961). The anatomy of polydactylism in cats with observations on genetic control. *Anat. Rec.*, **141**:105–127.

DANFORTH, C. H. (1947). Morphology of the feet in polydactyly cats. *Amer. J. Anat.*, **80**:143–171.

GLENN, B. L., GLENN, H. G., and OMTVEDT, I. T. (1968). Congenital porphyria in the domestic cat (*Felis catus*): preliminary investigations on inheritance pattern. *Amer. J. Vet. Res.*, **29**:1653–1657.

HENRICSON, B., and BORNSTEIN, S. (1965). Heredity umbilical hernia in cats. *Svensk. Vet. Tid.*, **17**:95–97.

HOWELL, J. M., and SIEGEL, P. B. (1966). Morphological effects of the Manx factor in cats. *J. Hered.*, **57**:100–104.

KIRK, H. (1956). *The cat's medical dictionary*. London: Routledge and Kegan Paul.

KOCH, P., FISCHER, H., and STUBBE, A. E. (1955). Die kongenitale cerebellare Ataxie bei *Felis domestica* als Erbleiden. *Berl. Munch. Tierarztl. Wschr.*, **68**:246–249.

LETARD, E. (1938). Hairless Siamese cats. *J. Hered.*, **29**:173–175.

LITTLE, C. C. (1934). White cats and deafness. *Nature*, **133**:215–216.

LITTLE, C. C. (1957). Four-ears, a recessive mutation in the cat. *J. Hered.*, **48**:57.

LIVINGSTON, M. L. (1965). A possible hereditary influence in feline urolithiasis. *Vet. Med. Small Anim. Clinic*, **60**:705.

MOUTSCHEN, J. (1950). Quelques particularites herediatires du chat siamois. *Nat. Belges*, **31**:200–203.

SCOTT, P. P., McKUSICK, V. A., and McKUSICK, A. B. (1963). The nature of osteogenesis imperfecta in cats. *J. Bone Jt. Surg.*, A, **45**:125–134.

SCHWANGART, F. and GRAU, H. (1931). Uber entformung, besonders die vererbbaren Schwangmissbildungen, bei der Hauskatze. *J. Tierz. ZuchtgsBiol.*, **21**:203–249.

SEARLE, A. G. (1953). Hereditary "split-band" in the domestic cat. *Ann. Eugen.*, **17**:279–282.

SILSON, M., and ROBINSON, R. (1969). Hereditary hydrocephalus in the cat. *Vet. Rec.*, **84**:477.

TODD, N. B. (1964). The Manx factor in domestic cats. *J. Hered.*, **55**:225–230.

WILKINSON, G. T. (1966). *Diseases of the cat*. Oxford: Pergamon Press.

WILLIAM-JONES, H. E. (1944). Arrested development of the long bones of the fore-limbs in a female cat. *Vet. Rec.*, **56**:449.

INDEX

Abnormalities 153–176
Abyssinian 106, 135
Achondroplasia dwarf 162
Acinonyx jabatus 21
Acquired inheritance 11
Age records 14–15
Agouti 28, 105
Albino 43, 108–110, 144
Albino alleles 42–43, 108–110
Albino Siamese 144
Alleles 27, 41–45
Angora 146
Anomalies 101, 153–176
Assortment 31
Ataxia 164–165
Average litter size 14
Avoidance of inbreeding 98–101
Awn hairs 123

Baldness in rex 133, 169
BC 29
Bent tail 163
Birma 149
Black-footed cat 21
Black self 135–136
Blindness 174
Blotched tabby 106
Blue Abyssinian 136
Blue Birma 149
Blue Burmese 142
Blue-cream 147
Blue dilution 110–111
Blue-eyed White 145
Blue self 136
Blue Siamese 141
Blue tabby 136
Blue tortoiseshell 140

Bobcat 8, 21
Body conformation 131–132
Breed genotypes 131–152
Breeding systems 69–104
Brother-to-sister mating 83, 87, 89
Brown 107
Brown tabby 134
Burmese 43–44, 109, 142
Burmese allele 42, 108–109

Californian rex 130
Cameo 148
"Carrier" animal 157
Cerebellar ataxia 164–165
Champagne Burmese 143
Characters 26
Checkerboards 33–38
Cheetah 21
Chestnut Brown 137
Chinchilla 147
Chinese Harlequin 146
Chinese White 144
Chocolate Siamese 141
Chocolate tortoiseshell 138
Chromosomes 18–25
Chromosomes of cat species 21
Cinnamon tabby 137
Cleft-palate 169
Closed stud breeding 85–91
Coat composition 123
Coat density 133
Coital crouch 13
Colourpoint 148–149
Continuous variation 61–68
Cornish rex 124–128
Coupling 55
Cousin mating 87, 98–99

Cream   139–140
Crossingover   55
Cryptorchidism   165–166
Cymric   150

Deafness   167
Developmental threshold   67–68
Devon rex   124–128
Diploid   20
Domestication of the cat   5
Dominance   31
Dominant black   111
Dominant white   120–121
Down hairs   123
Dwarfism   163, 167

Early domestication   5
Egg   15
Egyptians   5–6, 8
Elimination of anomalies   156–161
Epistasis   46
Expressivity   52
Extra sex chromosomes   24–25
Eye colour   122

F_1, F_2 29
"Factors"   26
Family selection   77–79
Felis bengalensis   21
Felis bubastis   6
Felis catus   4, 21
Felis caudata   8
Felis chaus   6, 8
Felis concolor   21
Felis domesticus   4
Felis geoffroyi   21
Felis leo   21
Felis lybica   4–10
Felis nigripes   21
Felis pardalus   21
Felis serval   21
Felis sylvestris   4–10, 105
Felis temmincki   21
Felis tigrina   8, 21
Felis tigris   21
Felis torquata   4

Felis viverrina   21
Felis wiedii   21
Felis yagouaroundi   21
Fishing cat   21
Folded ears   167
Foreign White   146
"Four ears"   168
Frost Siamese   141

Gametes   31
Gene   27, 62
Gene segregation   28–29
Gene symbols   29, 130
Genetic ratios   28–51
Genotype   31
Genotypes of breeds   131–152
Geoffrey's cat   21
Germ-cell lineage   15–17
Germ-cells   15
German rex   125–127, 129
Gestation period   15
Ghost tabby   46
Golden Siamese   142
Gonads   16–17
Grading up   79–80, 91–92
Group selection   78
Guard hairs   123

Hairless   168–169
Half-sister mating   84
Haploid   20–22
Hare-lip   169
Havana   137
Heterosis   162
Heterozygosis   83
Heterozygote   31
Homozygosis   82
Homozygote   31
Hybrid vigour   97
Hybrids   4–10
Hydrocephalus   169–170

Impenetrance   53
Inbreeding depression   96
Incomplete dominance   40–41

Independent culling levels   73
Italian rex   129

Jaguar   21
Jaguarondi   21

"Kangaroo" cat   170

Lavender   137
Leopard   21
Leopard cat   21
Lethal genes   154
Lilac   137
Lilac Siamese   141
Limits to selection   94–96
Linkage   55–60
Lion   21
Litter size   14–15
Little Spotted cat   9
Locus   27
Long hair   127, 133
Long-haired breeds   146–149
Longevity   14–15
Lynx rufus   8, 21
Lynx Siamese   141

Mackerel tabby   106, 134
Major genes   62
Manx   132, 150, 154, 170–171
Margay   21
Masking of genes   47–49
Maternal impressions   10
Mating like to like   93
Meiosis   19–20
Mendelism   2
Mexican hairless cat   168
Mimic genes   49–51
Mitosis   18
"Monsters"   154
Multiple allelism   41–45
Mutant genes   130

Non-agouti   107

Normal overlaps   53
Nuclei   19

Ocelot   21
Oestrus   13–15
Ohio rex   129
Oncilla   8
Orange   112–117
Orange-eyed White   145
Oregon rex   124–127, 129
Osteodystrophy   171–172

Panthera onca   21
Panthera pardus   21
Pairing segment   60
Penetrance   53
Persian   146
Phenotype   31
Piebald   118–120
Pink-eyed dilution   111
Platignum Burmese   142
Pleiotropism   54
Polydactyly   172–173
Polygenes   62–68
Polygenic characters   62–68
Porphyria   173
Prepotency   92
Progeny testing   77–79
Puberty   13, 15
Puma   21

Ratios   28–51
Recessive   31
Red Abyssinian   139
Red self   147
Red Siamese   141
Red Silver   144
Red Tabby   138–139
Repulsion   55
Retina degeneration   174
Rex   124–130, 149–150
Rufism   121
Russian Blue   137

Sacred cat of Burma 149
Seal Siamese 141
Selection 69–82
Self colours 135–138
Segregation 31
Selection index 73–77
Selection intensity 71–72
Serval 21
Sex chromosomess 21–23, 59–60
Sex determination 22–23
Sex-limited expression 60–61
Sex-linkage 56–60
Sex ratio 14–15
Shaded Cameo 148
Shaded Silver 148
Shell Cameo 148
Short tail 163
Siamese 43, 108, 140–142
Siamese allele 42, 108–109
Sib mating 83, 87, 89
Silver 43, 108–109, 143, 147
Silver Abyssinian 143
Smoke 43, 109, 147
Soma 16–17
Sorrel Abyssinian 139
Species hybrids 4–10
Sperms 15
Split-foot 174
Spotted tabby 106–107, 137
Squint 174
Strain 102–103
Systems of mating 69, 82–100

Tabby alleles 45, 105–106
Tabby Siamese 141

Tabby striping 28, 105–107, 134–135
Tail kinks 163–164
Taillessness 170–171
Tandem selection 73
Telegony 10
Temmincks' golden cat 21
Testes 16–17
Threshold character 67–68
Tiger 21
Tiger cat 21
Tonkanese 142
Tortoiseshell 113–117, 136–140
Tortoiseshell males 24–25, 114–117
Total score 73–77
Type 131–132

Umbilical hernia 175–176
Urolithiasis 176

Van 149

White 120–121, 145
White spotting 118–120
Wire-hair 130

X chromosome 22, 59

Y chromosome 22, 59

Zygote 31

OTHER TITLES IN THE ZOOLOGY DIVISION

General Editor: G. A. KERKUT

Vol. 1. RAVEN – *An Outline of Developmental Physiology*
Vol. 2. RAVEN – *Morphogenesis: The Analysis of Molluscan Development*
Vol. 3. SAVORY – *Instinctive Living*
Vol. 4. KERKUT – *Implications of Evolution*
Vol. 5. TARTAR – *The Biology of Stentor*
Vol. 6. JENKIN – *Animal Hormones – A Comparative Survey*
Vol. 7. CORLISS – *The Ciliated Protozoa*
Vol. 8. GEORGE – *The Brain as a Computer*
Vol. 9. ARTHUR – *Ticks and Disease*
Vol. 10. RAVEN – *Oogenesis*
Vol. 11. MANN – *Leeches (Hirudinea)*
Vol. 12. SLEIGH – *The Biology of Cilia and Flagella*
Vol. 13. PITELKA – *Electron-microscopic Structure of Protozoa*
Vol. 14. FINGERMAN – *The Control of Chromatophores*
Vol. 15. LAVERACK – *The Physiology of Earthworms*
Vol. 16. HADZI – *The Evolution of the Metazoa*
Vol. 17. CLEMENTS – *The Physiology of Mosquitoes*
Vol. 18. RAYMONT – *Plankton and Productivity in the Oceans*
Vol. 19. POTTS AND PARRY – *Osmotic and Ionic Regulation in Animals*
Vol. 20. GLASGOW – *The Distribution and Abundance of Tsetse*
Vol. 21. PANTELOURIS – *The Common Liver Fluke*
Vol. 22. VANDEL – *Biospeleology – The Biology of Cavernicolous Animals*
Vol. 23. MUNDAY – *Studies in Comparative Biochemistry*
Vol. 24. ROBINSON – *Genetics of the Norway Rat*
Vol. 25. NEEDHAM – *The Uniqueness of Biological Materials*
Vol. 26. BACCI – *Sex Determination*
Vol. 27. JØRGENSEN – *Biology of Suspension Feeding*
Vol. 28. GABE – *Neurosecretion*
Vol. 29. APTER – *Cybernetics and Development*
Vol. 30. SHAROV – *Basic Arthropodan Stock*
Vol. 31. BENNETT – *The Aetiology of Compressed Air Intoxication and Inert Gas Narcosis*
Vol. 32. PANTELOURIS – *Introduction to Animal Physiology and Physiological Genetics*
Vol. 33. HAHN and KOLDOVSKÝ – *Utilization of Nutrients during Postnatal Development*
Vol. 34. TROSHIN – *The Cell and Environmental Temperature*
Vol. 35. DUNCAN – *The Molecular Properties and Evolution of Excitable Cells*
Vol. 36. JOHNSTON and ROOTS – *Nerve Membranes*
Vol. 37. THREADGOLD – *The Ultrastructure of the Animal Cell*
Vol. 38. GRIFFITHS – *Echidnas*
Vol. 39. RYBAK – *Principles of Zoophysiology – Vol. 1*
Vol. 40. PURCHON – *The Biology of the Mollusca*
Vol. 41. MAUPIN – *Blood Platelets in Man and Animals*
Vol. 42. BRØNDSTED – *Planarian Regeneration*
Vol. 43. PHILLIS – *The Pharmacology of tynapres*
Vol. 44. ENGELMANN – *The Physiology of Insect Reproduction*

OTHER DIVISIONS IN THE SERIES IN
PURE AND APPLIED BIOLOGY

BIOCHEMISTRY

BOTANY

MODERN TRENDS
IN PHYSIOLOGICAL SCIENCES

PLANT PHYSIOLOGY

sistasis - masking effect - Not the same as dominance - effect of one gene able to cancel presence of genes at other loci

The W and T genes act this way

Mimic genes

r	camin rex
rc	devon rex

Sex linked genes -

O · · orange   entire yellow instead of mixture of yel/tabby and black) tabbies

(cream, yellow, red)

carried by X chromosome

OO - yellow   female
Oo - tortoise   female
o - non yellow   male
OY - male

gene O masks expression of A and a -

O is epistatic gene

polygenes - responsible for size & shape

group

1) affecting intensity of yellow → rufous

2) modifying depth of blue pigment → dilution

3) " depth of chocolate pigment

4) controlling amt of Agouti ticking in tabby areas of coat.